CW00801221
UNFORGETTABLE
IN
COUNTRY LIFE

an incidental memoir

ROBIN DALTON

an incidental memoir

VIKING

Viking
Penguin Books Australia Ltd
487 Maroondah Highway, PO Box 257
Ringwood, Victoria 3134, Australia
Penguin Books Ltd
Harmondsworth, Middlesex, England
Penguin Putnam Inc.
375 Hudson Street, New York, New York 10014, USA
Penguin Books Canada Limited
10 Alcorn Avenue, Toronto, Ontario, Canada M4V 3B2
Penguin Books (N.Z.) Ltd
Cnr Rosedale and Airborne Roads, Albany, Auckland, New Zealand
Penguin Books (South Africa) (Pty) Ltd
4 Pallinghurst Road, Parktown 2193, South Africa

First published by Penguin Books Australia Ltd 1998

1 3 5 7 9 10 8 6 4 2

Designed by Ellie Exarchos, Penguin Design Studio
Typeset in 11/14 pt Savoy by Post Pre-press Group, Brisbane, Queensland
Printed and bound in Australia by Australian Print Group, Maryborough, Victoria

National Library of Australia
Cataloguing-in-Publication data:

Dalton, Robin.
An incidental memoir.

ISBN 0 670 88187 2.

1 Dalton, Robin. 2. Literary agents - Biography.
2. Motion picture producers and directors - Biography.
I. Title.

920.72

Captions for endpapers appear on page 368

For Lyndall, Emmet Rory,
Carrick and Becan

acknowledgements

I wish to thank all those people who have enriched my life, my tireless editors at Penguin, and mostly Richard Cobden and Jeanette and Gordon King, in whose houses I sheltered whilst trying to cobble this together.

Thanks to Jack Porter for kind permission to reproduce an extract from a short story by Hal Porter, 'The Two Baronesses', from the collection *Mr Butterfry* (Angus & Robertson, 1971).

prologue

> *'These writings of mine are no more than the ravings of a man who has never done anything more than taste the outer crust of knowledge – even that during his childhood – and who has retained only an ill-formed generic notion of it: a little about everything and nothing about anything . . .'*
> Montaigne[1]

Jack of all trades, master of none, is what I, too, have been, lacking any ambition beyond the wish to complete the immediate task well, and an urge to savour the outer crust, to move on – to travel. This is simply an account of that journey.

Years ago I sat at a table in a tower in Italy and wrote a sentence. It was the key which unlocked memory – memory linked with manipulation, and in three weeks it grew into a little book written with no thought of an eventual reader beyond my children when they grew up. It was written with love and on impulse, about my family, laughter, other people, one's roots.

I was born a Sagittarian, a double grand trine Sagittarian. Although I am not at all certain that I know what that means, I see that the label 'double grand trine' enormously impresses people who know about such things. It means, I am told, that I possess the attributes of a Sagittarian 'in spades' – to excess.

I am not at all proud of them, whilst recognising their validity: a brutal frankness, a bull-in-the-china-shop frankness (surely denoting insensitivity?); an obsessive love of change and escape (surely responsible for the fragmented pattern of my life?); and a sort of cliffhanging luck (never to win the lottery or seldom to be in the right place at the right time, but saved by many bells at the last moment before disaster). A survivor, I suppose.

What I have survived has been enormous fun. My parents, grandparents, and great-aunts were the first providers of that fun, and I wrote about them in *Aunts Up the Cross*. Now, if the recollections are to be rounded, I must enter the arena of my own life as a major player rather than as a camera. There comes the uncomfortable suspicion that by tossing up bits of a life, snatches of memory, anecdotes of little significance other than the threads of one's own existence, that existence could appear tawdry or trivial (or, worse, boring) unless I can bring to life those characters who enriched and shared the mosaic of my life with me – the fact that in it, they formed part of a mosaic rather than a solid terrazzo 'mea culpa'. The solid terrazzo was there, in *Aunts Up the Cross*. There you would have met my grandmother, Nana, and her cast of constant literary companions, who were my shadowy siblings, from the pages of Dickens; my Great-Aunt Juliet, whose largesse was the fount which fed my mother's bottomless pit of extravagance; the other great-aunts and uncles, who, being the butt of family humour and target of antipathy, I never met; my much-loved grandfather, Sammie, the saintly male role model of my childhood – and my father, who spoke only to him and, except for my mother, to none of the other females whose house he shared. If you have not met them in that former memoir, try to imagine their rich, abundant personalities as you read any reference to them in the pages which follow.

Imagine that World War II has just ended and I, spoilt child, have left them behind.

There are gaps, inconsistencies, contractions – the jerkiness perhaps explained by the jostle of life and the fact that the fragments were written in some cases years apart – now retrieved by someone removed by later experience from the person who wrote them. 'To jerk', according to *Roget's Thesaurus*, has among its many meanings listed two I recognise: 'Be the sport of the winds and the waves', and 'Reel to and fro like a drunken man'.

My original title for these memories was *No Hard Shoulder* – a motorway sign denoting that there is no lay-by in which to pull in, but I am told that motorway signs, like life, change too frequently and therefore date. But I hope the journey may be of some interest: for anyone old enough, perhaps provoking nostalgic memories: and for those too young, providing a glimpse into a past which may amuse, and that some shape may emerge from the 'winds and the waves', and some order from amongst the incidents of my life; which order, I must confess, has frequently eluded me.

chapter one

It's actually quite easy to forget an entire marriage. That is probably why I never wrote about my first one in *Aunts Up the Cross*. In my adolescence and in the tight little circle into which I was born, marriage was simply the natural progression from school – possibly, what was termed in those days 'finishing school', rarely university. One fell in love, became engaged, seldom had affairs, unless as a prelude to marriage, but part of the incentive must have been the ceremonial adornments of the wedding. After the excitement of courtship, the natural next step was wondering what we would choose as an engagement ring, swiftly followed by dreams of the trousseau. I didn't marry my first serious love, partly because my parents thought we were both too young, and certainly too young to do what they rightly suspected we were doing; and, indeed, although I dented his young heart by marrying someone else, he never asked me. We are still friends and I remember him with affection, whilst, on the other hand, I find it difficult to remember my first marriage.

It lasted only five months before its dramatic final scene rounded it off, but the dramas, both during and after those five months, should have left me quivering with apprehension for life. Instead, I have forgotten it almost entirely and can only summon up the memory of its highlights - or lowlights - because in the early years following the events I recounted them so often. To family, friends, lawyers, judges, doctors; and, as time went on and they had taken on the aspect of a recorded chronicle, to prospective suitors with some embarrassment and consciousness of the need to get in first before some ill-meaning acquaintance regaled them with the official version.

By official, I mean the story as told by the avid Sydney newspapers. At the time, I was packed off (still only nineteen years old) by parents to Melbourne to stay with kind friends, thereby avoiding the trauma of seeing my own life in the headlines and never since having read the full story. My poor parents were left behind, and theirs was the trauma. I now regret that I've not even a faded clipping, or one of the startling posters from the newspaper sellers' boards in which I knocked the then eventful war news off the front page and the boards with only two words: SOCIETY DIVORCE.

I was eighteen when I met John Spencer, and World War II was three months old. He was thirty-one and just returned from some years in Europe, thereby already invested with glamour. He sent my mother flowers every day until I accepted his proposal of marriage made on the night of our first meeting. During seven months of our engagement I, too, was swamped with flowers and old-world courtesy. In the eighth month he started drinking and, alarming as this change was, it was not sufficiently so as to induce me to cancel the trousseau, the bridesmaids' dresses, the lily-of-the-valley dyed pink for the cake, in its turn dyed pink to match the pink tulle wedding dress; the pink and white daisies ordered with which to tether the bridesmaids' wrists in a daisy chain - a fancy which struck me as so stunningly original that I could not bear to forego its execution. It was far too late to stop the nuns in some distant Belgian convent who had been industriously stitching and hemstitching sheets, napkins, tablecloths and never to be used traycloths, for months - each one ostentatiously emblazoned with my soon to be brand new initials; or to take back the cream hide suitcases in ever diminishing sizes, the hatboxes and shoeboxes embossed in gold with those same initials; the shower teas - indeed, the church. Nor did I know enough of the world to recognise that what I had chosen was a true, classic, one hundred per cent genuine alcoholic. And nasty with it.

At the church I met my bridegroom with some trepidation, not having been able to contact him for some twenty-four hours previously. His best man, Bill McMahon, had assisted me in this search, but when I left for the church with my father, my most recent memory of my imminent husband had been a blazing row. In the car, my father suggested we cancel the whole affair.

'But you must promise me one thing, kid,' he said, 'if you don't marry him you'll never see him again.'

I still don't know if it was this thought or the monogrammed sheets that decided me on my march up the aisle to meet a glowering groom.

Having cut the cake, thrown the bouquet, and left the reception for our hotel bridal suite, I was locked in without food (or, I seem to remember with deeper regret, the chance to dress up for dinner in my new clothes) whilst my bridegroom disappeared - to a brothel, as I later discovered. I imagined, for years, that I had caught crabs on my honeymoon from hotel sheets. I had no idea what they were: aliens from another planet of experience. I don't remember much else about this honeymoon except events quite unconnected to romance, love, or even sex. Braces had been removed from my teeth in time for the wedding, but I was supposed to wear a 'plate' at night - a nasty red plastic affair supporting a strong gold rod in place across my teeth as I slept. John, quite naturally, threw this barbaric contraption out the window onto the beach, swearing that he did not intend to be married to a bloody schoolgirl. My teeth have survived the deprivation.

The hotel was the first to be built at what was to become Surfers Paradise, Queensland, then nothing but bleak and unpopulated acres of sand. Coming from a daily surf at Bondi Beach in Sydney, this did not present either a novelty or a paradise. I remember only a small zoo adjacent to the hotel, a monkey who reached through the bars and grabbed a handful of my hair, and losing the trailer containing all the precious rationed petrol for our trip down a cliff; in the background, a surly husband and days spent mostly in silence and tears.

After the honeymoon, I tackled the mysterious business of cooking and housekeeping in our rented apartment. He came home from army camp at weekends; I spent the week on the telephone to my mother's cook. I remember the first dinner I ever cooked, largely because he threw it at me. The potatoes stuck in my hair and the gravy ran down my face. Luckily, it was tepid, as I had been waiting two hours for his arrival - that is why he threw it at me. Monday breakfasts were worse because they had to be served by 4 a.m. so that he could be back in camp by six. He had first to be wakened from a drunken stupor, for which service I usually received a belligerent thump, and I then had to fry two eggs without breaking them. In all the cooking years since, nothing has ever made me nervous except for trying not to break a fried egg. Those, too, were frequently thrown at me. Worse than potatoes and gravy.

I was told repeatedly that I was spoilt and, like a young horse, must be broken in. That process revolved largely around the laundry. Sheets and towels, as well as shirts and socks, must be washed at home. I was too bemused to tell my mother this, and as I did not feel her cook would be much help I used to throw sheets and towels into the bath and spend the day stamping on them like some mad vintner. John liked this to take place on Saturdays so that he could watch. I was given half an hour to get the sodden mass out of the bath, myself into it, then into clothes, and on to Romano's - the most fashionable restaurant of those years - where John would play the bounteous host to a party of eight or ten; orchids or small favours at each woman's place; frequently some similar token for the men. About twenty-four hours allowed him to sleep off the night's excesses and then back to Monday's fried eggs.

My marriage consisted of five months of these weekends and five months of innocent pleasure snatched during the week. Most of the men and boys one knew were already away fighting, or in training camps, but there were a few visitors to Sydney with whom to have an occasional meeting or meal. Three such unfortunates became, much to their surprise and my embarrassment, the co-respondents named in my divorce suit.

One of them, a young American officer on a US liner briefly in port, Robert Greene, could indeed have been a genuine candidate had we had more time together, for I fancied him tremendously and we had long romantic sessions leading up to what I dare say would have developed into adultery had he been more than three days in port; had either of us had been a year or two older, or the year later than 1941; or had I not had what one still called the 'curse' and thought of in those days as a total sexual taboo. Instead we planned an idealistic post-war future in which John Spencer did not exist and we had three children whose names we solemnly chose and I dutifully recorded in a diary. A diary not kept under lock and key and a great bonus to John, for it made good reading in court and in the headlines. Needless to say, I never saw Robert Greene again and have no idea what became of him or if he ever knew of his brief notoriety, for despite the purple prose of the diary he was dropped from the final case for lack of evidence.

The second, also to be dropped for similar lack after the initial hearing, was a Hungarian portrait painter, Dinny Holesch, whom I had met at tea at Admiralty House, our Vice-Regal dwelling, whilst visiting Lady Gowrie. With an eye to prospective sitters he had asked if he might paint me, and subsequently came to tea with me to discuss our sittings. I think we had only one meeting - at most, two. John's detectives, however, were outside clocking up our matinée session; and his shock matched my chagrin. My father, feeling somewhat responsible for having taken me to tea with Lady Gowrie in the first place, sent for poor Mr Holesch to try and explain this strange Australian misfortune which had befallen him. His English was minimal and the papers served on him a total bewilderment.

'Well, Holesch,' my father eventually tried, 'do you or do you not know what adultery means?'

'I do not,' from a furious Holesch, 'but I can guess.'

I like to think that he suffered little from the experience but as his livelihood depended on painting paintable young women and most, if not all, of their husbands were at war, I feel his commissions may have dropped off.

Not long ago I learnt that his subsequent marriage may have suffered, for it seems that this murky piece of his past lived on to haunt those marital tiffs in which old bullets are dragged out with which to load the current gun. The daughter of this marriage is Laura Hampton, playwright Christopher Hampton's wife. We discovered this glorious coincidence when dining together one night in London: I was the notorious phantom of her mother's retrospective accusations - the femme fatale constantly pricking at the seams of her parents' marriage.

To the third candidate, Harry Belyea, I owe my freedom and eternal gratitude, and I feel guilt that I have not bothered to find out what happened to him.

Being Canadian he probably went home to Canada and I don't remember why he was in Australia; only that he lived in Melbourne where he had a fiancée, and was visiting Sydney briefly. My mother introduced us over dinner at a restaurant. After being driven home, one goodnight kiss on the doorstep caused me to invite him in for a cup of coffee, and whilst sipping our coffee - I on the floor with my shoes off and he in an armchair with his jacket and tie off - my divorce case proper took off.

It took off with scenes of pure farce in which I was too deeply a participant to find funny at the time. The two detectives who burst in with John both had their hats on - bit players in a B movie. Whilst they took down Harry's name and address I was more concerned in finding a shoe which had rolled under the sofa. Everyone talked at once - the detectives threateningly to Harry, Harry politely to the detectives - I beseechingly to John, whilst simultaneously trying to apologise to Harry. My overwhelming emotion was embarrassment, both at the turn my hospitality had taken and my inability to find my shoe.

It also did not occur to me to leave with Harry, even if fully shod. My one thought was to allow him to make as dignified an exit as possible. He and the detectives left together. John's priority was to rape me. We scuttled around the small flat until, trapped beside the bed, I fell over onto it and John ripped my nice new dress from neck to hem with one splendid lunge.

Absolutely on cue the telephone rang. He picked it up: I yelled 'Help' in its direction, kicked off the remaining shoe and ran for the bathroom - a room with a key. It was a small bathroom, and so, whilst John got off the telephone, grabbed his army revolver and threatened to shoot the lock off the door and then me, I crouched in the bath hopefully out of range and wondered what my chances were of surviving a leap from the second floor window.

One of the reasons I am so grateful to Harry Belyea is that he didn't go back to his hotel after an exceedingly odd dinner date with a comparative stranger; but, having had a good look at John Spencer, went looking for my mother who was still at the restaurant where we had dined. It had been my mother on the telephone. Within minutes she was at the door and behind her the burliest taxidriver she could find in the street, sleeves up and ready for a fight. I grabbed a coat; John grabbed my jewellery, including wedding ring, with which I was still incongruously bedecked – and we made our escape. Not before he delivered a parting speech worthy of Elinor Glyn[2]: 'I know you've never been unfaithful to me but by the time I'm finished with you no one else will ever believe it, and if I can't have you I'll make sure no one else will ever want you.'

When my divorce case was first announced – THREE CO-RESPONDENTS NAMED was a fair sensation, and my father's comforting comment was, 'Never mind, kid; it's not every girl who can rustle up three co-respondents during a war' – we heard again from the taxidriver. He arrived at my father's door offering to give evidence, as his one brief encounter with the contestants had filled him with righteous rage and the basic constant Australian wish to 'have a go'. By this time, however, my family had learnt that the decision to contest the case would mean collapse of case for lack of evidence and the continuance of my status as Mrs John Spencer. I seem to remember that you couldn't divorce a serving officer in 1941: my only grounds would have been cruelty under the then antiquated divorce laws, and that had to be for five years' duration. In five months I had only lost the nerve in a front tooth and gained some memorable bruises, but John was clearly warming up and it certainly wasn't a risk worth contemplating. Also, Kenneth Street, then the Chief Justice, and a close family friend, advised my parents not to submit me to the ordeal of a defended divorce suit.

So, all depended on Harry Belyea, the one co-respondent on whom even a shred of evidence existed – alone in my apartment at 10.30 p.m. without jacket or tie and a slight lipstick smear from our one chaste kiss. Would he agree not to defend on his own account? He did: lost a fiancée in the doing; and I hope found a happier life with a more trusting wife.

I never saw John Spencer again, but I did see my jewellery. Many years later his second wife called on me in London. On the telephone she explained that she wanted to meet me but couldn't come to tea to which I invited her that day as she wanted to look her best when we met and that would involve a visit to the hairdresser. The date was set for two days hence.

'I've always longed to meet you,' she said. 'I was so jealous of you when I married John and I said to him, "What was Robin really like?" and he said, "She was a dear, sweet, little girl with the most beautiful legs in the world." And –' with this she reached out and patted one of the legs – 'you have!' On the outstretched arm I spotted my wedding ring, my engagement ring, my wedding present ring, my birthday diamond and pearl bracelet, and, looking upwards, my Christmas diamond and pearl earrings. I wondered if the rings had had to be altered.

She seemed a very nice woman and certainly eager for a chat. 'John was so proud of you, you know,' came next. 'He had albums of photographs of you that he used to pore over; you were like his little daughter he had produced and launched on the world himself.'

I murmured, as I poured the tea, that he had had a very strange way of showing his affection.

'Oh well,' came another pat of the hand, 'you hurt his pride, you know. You were very immature.'

A sip of tea and a sigh, and then, 'I'd say two things about John as a husband, wouldn't you? He's both ghastly and wonderful – with the accent on the ghastly!'

John Spencer finally died, of drink one assumes, and I only hope she continued to have some wonderful moments and also managed to hang onto my jewellery. Sadly, he didn't die soon enough to make me a widow in the eyes of the Catholic Church. So one subsequent Catholic fiancée, Torbert Macdonald, failed to put love before a hysterical mother and the priests; and my own dear husband, Emmet, suffered excommunication, a registry office wedding, and death without solace of religious rites.

By the time my decree became absolute I was twenty-one, in a world at war, and in a part of the world where we experienced all the excitement of a front-line recreation base and few of the dangers. For my twenty-first birthday my father gave me a divorce and a typewriter. The first had cost him a lot of money, and with the second he hoped I might make a little of my own.

chapter two

My English friends tell me that, compared to our contemporaries in England, our war was a picnic. And so it was for the females, but the heightened excitement was the same. The Americans arrived in Australia. We were not in imminent danger of being bombed, our main excitement being shelled from the harbour by midget Japanese submarines; the only casualty a German in Newcastle. But the men with whom we spent our time were, for the most part, on a few days' leave from the jungles and beaches of our northern bases and we never knew when they left if they would be alive to return. What would seem like shocking promiscuity - not only physical but emotional - in peacetime, was felt as a beneficence of the heart. The fact that it was also rarely that one was caught out in one's perfidious spread of affection blinded one to the dangers. The pleasures were freshly minted each week, as the turnover in admirers was brisk. If possible, our affections were limited to one per squadron, or P.T. boat, or Marine battalion, and the chief dread was that their leaves would overlap. They seldom did. We did not consider ourselves promiscuous. We were in love.

My father's gift, the typewriter, gave me the idea that I might actually work for these young gods. In three weeks I managed to complete a two-year secretarial course - two to three hours' sleep per night and endless cups of black coffee supplied by my mother - who never slept anyway, if something else, however trivial, was going on - got me through. But it can only have been lack of competition that won me the post of secretary to the Commanding Officer of the Ordnance Department of the Southwest Pacific Area. I typed out the orders. Very soon my boss left it all to me. This came to a halt when one hundred igloos - large enough to accommodate an aircraft each - and two jackets arrived, instead of the other way round.

My boss wrote me a glowing reference which can only reflect more on his niceness than on my suitability for office life. We were propping up the war, along with our eyelids. They were years of no sleep - of nights when we went straight from the dance floor, the arms of our escorts, or a dawn swim, to home, breakfast and work. We had our quota of rationing - food, clothing, petrol. Food rationing was simply a challenge to my mother; and during clothes rationing we went to the Strand Arcade where we could have our legs painted to look like stockings (unobtainable) for two shillings and sixpence - one shilling extra for seams.

As for petrol, for a while we had gas balloons on top of our cars. When the US pilots came on leave I sometimes managed to borrow my father's car and he never knew where the petrol came from: sucked through a tube direct from a parked B-17 at the airfield. When one of these pilots' leave was up, a friend and I stood on the Harbour Bridge at dawn as he saluted us by flying under it - a court martial offence if identified, but he was up and away to the war before the authorities were awake. Another 'buzzed' me in Newcastle where I was staying and flew so low he stopped the Town Hall clock.

Apart from the Australian casualty lists, war for us meant nylon stockings and Almond Roca from the PX (one look at the pink tin and I am transported back to the war); gargantuan meals at the US Officers' Club, the Bernly in Springfield Avenue, particularly our introduction to pumpkin pie at Thanksgiving; glasses of milk for dinner in the mess on board the occasional US battleship in port; and, as the Americans left, tearful farewells and gradually dwindling love letters.

The two fiancés I had gathered (not concurrently) had both gone home. I hardly noticed the departure of the first one, Josh, and had for years assumed he had been killed on a bombing mission. I cried quite a lot, however, when Torbert was brainwashed by the priests in Boston in the midst of our efforts to get me across the Pacific for the wedding, but my tears had dried by the time the British Navy arrived.

I fell, this time madly, in love again, with one of the naval officers, the young David, Marquis of Milford Haven, and my divorce was also the main reason we never married. We were never officially engaged, but hoped to marry, and because David was young, penniless and accustomed to parental approval and support, we imagined ourselves in the old-fashioned mould of needing family approval. In those days, any direct descendant of Queen Victoria needed to ask the reigning monarch's permission to marry and, as he was a ridiculously distant member of the Royal Family, and indeed a direct descendant, and the Duke of Gloucester was at that time Governor-General of Australia, he started off by a tentative approach to him, and got a fairly gruff rebuff. I was a divorcee. We put it 'on hold'.

By the time he left, I had a determination to get out and experience that other faraway world I had glimpsed; and David and I hoped that things would look rosier for us in England.

chapter three

I managed to get out of Australia with the help of a friend of my father's who was Managing Director of Qantas, Hudson Fysh. My father didn't approve of David as a prospective husband for me, any more than David's mother was to approve of me as a prospective wife, and so our plans were, I am ashamed to recall, clandestine. More on my side than on his, for I was at least produced when I eventually reached London, in the hope that his mother and I would love each other – as, at first, we did. As I was dependent on my parents for the money to get me out and the influence to get me a passage, I had to come up with a better reason for going than love with a dodgy future.

His name was Johnny Mackay and he was not only beautiful to look at, sterling in character, enchanting in personality, but suitable in every way in my parents' eyes. He was far, far too nice and decent a young man to have been treated as I treated him – as my passport to England; a future husband approved of by my father.

Johnny was a paratrooper in the 27th Lancers, waiting to be dropped into Japanese-held territory when the atom bomb was dropped instead and the Pacific war came to its abrupt end. Instead, he was shipped back to England, closely followed by my 'trousseau'. Every cabin trunk ever amassed in her travels by my Great-Aunt Juliet was brought into service, as well as the splendid honeymoon suitcases left over from my marriage. My mother acquired dress racks from the department stores on which to hang the dresses being made by teams of little women before being packed in the trunks. My grandmother's silver and china cupboards were raided, and the contents carefully packed into tea-chests; the lot sent off to Johnny's mother in Glasgow by British Army transport.

Although officially engaged to Johnny, and unofficially to David, it never occurred to me to change the habits of the war years. Our nightly haunts, Romano's and Prince's, were still there and although the influx of US and British troops had dried to a trickle, there was still ample opportunity to meet, dance with, and flirt with a constantly changing team of admirers. That is such a lovely old-fashioned word, and one whose meaning and usage has disappeared. I do believe that in the 1940s we actually had 'admirers', whether or not we possessed qualities worth admiring hardly considered. Unconsummated passion was acceptable: you were not expected to go to bed with a man before profession of love on either side, although this declaration sometimes opened the door.

And so, whilst I hung around waiting for Mr Fysh to get me out of Australia to join Johnny, David, and the trunks en route to Glasgow, I busied myself with just such an admirer. His name was George Silk, originally from New Zealand but now one of the star war photographers of *Time-Life*. He was about to be posted by his magazine to Shanghai, and in fact left days before I did: not before, however, I had tentatively promised to marry him, too. Looking back, I think Shanghai was the main attraction, and I am not sure I don't regret at least a trial trip there, the last chance to have seen it in its great days in 1946.

Hudson Fysh's instructions were to keep myself in a state

of constant readiness as without any sort of permit to travel outside Australia I would have to be loaded onto the first aircraft with a light cargo load. Permits carried various priorities, of five grades, and as far as I can recall, women did not rate any of them. However, he sold me a ticket and warned my father that the ticket was only for the service on the actual flight: it was up to me to get onto continuing aircraft after each stopover. The first leg would get me as far as Kandy, where my chances were reasonably good. Bottlenecks were Karachi and Cairo and I must be prepared to be stuck there for an indefinite period. I was young enough and eager enough to be undaunted by the prospect. I am now, an overprotective and anxious parent myself, grateful to my parents for not showing any sign of the reluctance or apprehension they must have felt. For a week my bags were packed, and we all went to bed alert to a telephone call which Mr Fysh advised us would come about midnight when all mail and cargo had been weighed for the early morning flight.

The call, when it came, gave me four hours' notice. Four hours in which to say goodbye to my father and my country for many years – to my mother forever. All I remember is the excitement, the dawn boarding of the Lancaster bomber, and the surprise at my arrival of the other five passengers, all fairly senior and eminent gentlemen in either the Armed Forces, the Government, or the Diplomatic Corps. I sat between two of them in bucket seats in a row facing sideways along the aircraft and they took it in turns to hold the paper bag in which I was very sick indeed. We landed at Perth, and then on to the Cocos Islands and somewhere over the Indian Ocean makeshift bunks were slung above our seats so we could lie down: or perhaps it was only I who lay down?

The flight to the Islands must have taken many hours. We stumbled off the plane through the thick, humid night to a cluster of tin huts bordering a dark beach, and, clutching a lantern, I was guided to a shower along the beach. I shared the shower with a family of giant crabs the size of footballs in circumference who came lumbering on spindly legs across the sand to stare at me; and I raced thankfully back to the plane. On to Kandy, and a hot three-course meal in the open - oxtail soup, curry, and spotted dick and custard in a temperature well into the hundreds.

We landed at Karachi at night. It was April 1946. We were told to run from the plane to the airport building as serious rioting had broken out and the authorities wanted to get us refuelled and out of the country as soon as possible. At the desk a jostling, yelling crowd were pushing their permits and tickets at the harassed and sweating officials. This was my first bottleneck. There had been little competition at Perth, or Kandy, and only two passengers had been exchanged for our original six. Now I was asked to show my nonexistent priority permit. It was very clear that Karachi was to be my base for the immediate future.

One of our intake at Kandy had been a Russian Israeli bound for Jedda. Mr Skolnic, standing behind me as I pleaded with the officials, rounded on our fellow passengers and the ticket controller alike.

'How can we leave a young girl stranded here alone?' he asked. 'You are not gentlemen if you allow such a thing to happen.'

Embarrassed silence from the gentlemen prompted further chivalry from Mr Skolnic.

'Very well. *I* am gentleman. I give up my priority to her. I take next plane.'

It was explained to him that his priority was not interchangeable - that I would still have to stay, and that if he did not use it himself he would have to join the end of the queue.

'Very well. I stay to look after her,' he announced, and in a flash his ticket was snatched from him, permit removed from it, and we stared together into the hot, black night. Out of the blackness a truck appeared, disgorging some packages. We shrieked at it: our suitcases were thrown into the open back and we scrambled in after them, lying flat on the boards as we shot across the tarmac, out the gates and onto a rutted road, bullets popping around us.

I remember the hard wooden boards of the truck, the shouting faces by the roadside, the bumpy ride, the bursts of gunfire in the sky, and the hotel when we eventually arrived. Of this, the image I retain is of long green corridors lined with patient faces of all colours sitting on bundles of belongings – all, our driver explained, waiting for tickets out, and because of the shooting in the streets allowed to shelter in the hotel corridors. I remember the bliss of a bed, the surprise of no door to my room except for slatted swing shutters opening onto a wide verandah, the shouting and the shooting a few yards away, and nice Mr Skolnic escorting me next morning to the British Control Centre. I remember a charming young British lieutenant, Bill Jones, whose job it was to allocate permits and who was bored with all the British girls who were stationed there. He took me to dine and dance in the Mess; he took me by carriage to look at the local sight – Whale's Teeth, failing the Taj Mahal, by moonlight. Walking in the local bazaars, ducking the bullets, and, risking his superior's wrath, he gave me, after three days, a permit. Mr Skolnic, whom I eventually heard of again, was there for six weeks, reflecting, no doubt, on the thankless condition of being a gentleman.

My benefactor on the next leg was Russell Currie. He was, I believe, a senior official with the Bank of England, and he and the other passengers adopted me as their 'mascot'. Cairo was two nights on a houseboat on the Nile, dinner at Shepheard's, and a determination on all their parts that I should remain on board for our next leg, Augusta in Sicily. Another night there; a sack of oranges and lemons to take to England,

and on in a Sunderland Flying Boat to Poole Harbour - my first sight of England.

We went by train into London, and then I was taken by Qantas to a hotel they had provided - Bailey's in South Kensington. I didn't check in: I hauled my bags into the nearest telephone booth and telephoned, on Johnny's instructions, friends of his in London, Jerry and Nan Hochschild. He, a consultant anaesthetist, she, an ex-actress, lived at 48 Portland Place.

'Where are you?' said Nan and when I told her I was at Bailey's she instructed me to stay exactly where I was in the foyer until she arrived to fetch me. And so my first home in London was in a delightful maisonette in Portland Place; my first friends the warm and welcoming Hochschilds, and my new life begun in the first post-war spring.

chapter four

For the undamaged survivors the 1940s were a magical period. Danger, dread and uncertainty all behind us, the future seemed only sparkling and full of promise. The feeling of being alive was positive. We complained about rationing and the difficulty of foreign travel, but coming out of Australia and out of the war these appeared as yet another two small adventures. It seemed to me a time of plenty, a time of wonder and excitement. If London and Londoners were tired, I was not; and I shudder to think of my Australian energy, brashness, enthusiasm, delight in the smallest fresh encounter - for they were all fresh and untainted by past experience and expectations - ploughing my way through English sensibilities. I made friends easily and quickly and discarded two of my suitors equally quickly, and brutally. I was not, in this respect, nice, kind, or even honest.

On Nan's instructions, I opened an account at Fortnum & Mason's and each week they delivered my rations in a sturdy little cardboard box: the one egg cushioned between two carefully wrapped rashers of bacon and the minuscule portions of butter and cheese. These I turned over to Nan's cook; not that I remember a single meal at home in Portland Place other than breakfast. I fear I was a spoilt and ungracious guest, as ungenerous in my grabbing at pleasure as in the breaking of ties.

I had telephoned both Johnny and David from the Bailey's callbox whilst waiting for Nan: both of them on duty - one with his regiment in Scotland and the other at the Naval Signals Base at St Merryn in Cornwall. I made plans for a quick visit to Glasgow before returning to London to meet David the following week.

Just as London had filled me with excitement, Glasgow filled me with dread. Johnny was as enchanting as ever; his mother gracious and welcoming, with not the slightest hint of a tight or disapproving lip as she handed me the handwritten telegram of inordinate length she had taken down from the telephone operator. From George in Shanghai, leaving no doubt as to our relationship. No distant uncle, he. I did not attempt explanation; we both studiously ignored its contents.

My memory of Glasgow then - now one of the most culturally exciting cities in Europe - is of greyness, dark stone, windswept nondescript streets, even the places of recreation and amusement heavy with institutional pallor. The dance hall we went to amongst the elite of Glasgow seemed to me a mixture of a regimental drill hall and the Masonic Hall where I had, as an adolescent, solemnly learnt the waltz and the foxtrot. I did, however, have my first taste of fresh salmon - in those days it only came from Scotland. Canadian or Tasmanian salmon - to say nothing of the deep freeze - lay in the future. I cannot blame Glasgow for my treatment of Johnny and his no doubt supremely thankful mother, but it added desperation to my determination to cut loose as soon as I could decently claim my luggage. Allowing for my quick return to London to meet David for a joyous weekend, this took a total of three weeks: two more weeks in Glasgow and then I was free.

It remained to explain my changed status to my father. No

longer 'engaged', I was once more his liability, and an allowance was arranged to keep me in England. It was £30 per month, which would, amazingly when one considers today's rates, have been sufficient for my basic needs, but was in fact secretly augmented by my mother and grandmother to Lucullan proportions.

My grandmother was bullied by my mother into selling shares, silver, anything in fact not actually bolted down or which had not already been transported to Glasgow. My mother recklessly squandered even more housekeeping money on her passion, the horses, and between them and bursts of generosity from Great-Aunt Juliet I managed to live in a rarefied world of Paris haute couture and whatever frivolities London had to offer.

They were numerous and easily grasped. David and I started a weekly pattern, which was to continue for two years, until he left the Navy. I met him on the platform at Paddington Station as he got off the sleeper from Par. We rushed home to one of the variety of apartments and houses into which I moved, for breakfast and rapturous embraces before he left for the Admiralty and his regular Friday meetings. It had the same feeling as the blissful Fridays at boarding school when I was able to take the train to Sydney to have the braces on my teeth adjusted and managed to cram in two whole cinema double bills before going back to school. Every Saturday night we went to the theatre, dined at Ciro's in Orange Street and wandered at midnight across Leicester Square to the '400'. Leicester Square was a gentle moonlit place in which to wander. All London seemed gentle, and benign. There will never be another nightclub like the '400', with its soft dreamy music, its enveloping quiet intimacy – the bandleader, Tim Clayton, once famous and one's friend because he played 'your tune' as you got up to dance; Rossi, the headwaiter equally famous who tried to give us our same table on each visit; our precious marked bottles of rationed liquor with our names on the label, safely stored for us; the serene knowledge that we were young, and favoured, and alive. The room was always full of friends, glimpsed in the dark through a happy haze. One friend swears that she married her husband because on their first evening there he managed to bone her kipper in the gloom.

My first London visit to a theatre was the best possible introduction to a world in which I was later to be involved – John Gielgud's production of *Lady Windermere's Fan* at the Haymarket. Apart from the production, I had not associated a theatre with such exquisite opulence or sense of occasion. After that, we saw almost every West End production of the 1940s, but I am glad that the lovely Haymarket was the first and I am aghast that I never kept the programmes. The restaurants we went to on our Friday nights, now vanished, were the Belle Meunière in Charlotte Street, all red plush banquettes and fringed candle shades where we ate what we fondly imagined were black-market steaks – in reality, remembering the flavour, I now recognise as horsemeat; the Bon Viveur, our favourite, in Shepherd's Market where one gazed at a gaudy mural of an imaginary Mediterranean paradise while a three-piece string orchestra played romantic tunes on a tiny balcony; Edmundo Ross playing at the Bagatelle in Mayfair Place, grander and more formal, for evenings when we dressed up; round the corner the Milroy in Stratton Street, a nightclub larger and brighter than the '400', less intimate but thrilling to me because you walked down a plank over a bomb crater underneath a tarpaulin to reach it, and inside there was the joint owner, Harry Roy himself[3], on the bandstand and occasionally leaving it to whirl you round the dance floor: its sister restaurant opposite, Les Ambassadeurs, both started by John Mills, the Polish resistance fighter who lived to become a key figure in post-war London's restaurant and gambling world; sometimes to dance to Carroll Gibbons at the Savoy; and, of course, always the Savoy Grill, and always for lunch the Berkeley Buttery. There was a variety of little lunchtime bars, too, which came and went and enjoyed their brief favour, but with Londoners. Tourists in the 1940s did not exist as they do now. The English were the happy tourists in their own capital. The Mermaiden Bar, running through from Dover to Albemarle Street, was a particular favourite. It was part of a now vanished establishment called Manetta's. The bar at the Mayfair Hotel was also a favourite meeting place, and the Gay Nineties run by Eric Maschwitz, who wrote 'A Nightingale Sang in Berkeley Square' – in fact, in Bruton Street, just around the corner from the Square.

My first years in London were spent in moving house, unencumbered by possessions. Nana and Great-Aunt Juliet's treasures, having been shipped down from Glasgow, had no roof to house them. A Sydney acquaintance, David Stewart-Dawson, had a warehouse – some relic of a family business – in the city. He gave me space, trestle tables laid out and bulging with the silver, china, glass. I took no interest in who came to divest me of these trappings of another life. Some token payment may have been made, but I don't remember any. I saw no need in my life for one dozen Limoges oyster plates; twenty Royal Worcester gold and white teacups; a Queen Anne silver tea service, and the like. I sometimes look wistfully in antiquarians' windows or through salesroom catalogues, wondering if I might catch a glimpse, or a hint of who may have been sipping tea or eating oysters from my dowry.

My priorities were far more frivolous in the 1940s.

The black market was a game everyone played. My black-market butcher was in Shepherd's Market: the shop, I see, still there, although I expect our benefactor is long gone. Clothes rationing operated on a system of barter: everyone had their own pet supplier of once-worn models and we were then thin enough to wear them. Black-market restaurants were given an added fillip with the introduction of the Stafford Cripps five shilling meal[4]. We were meant to be sustained by austerity, which proved a spur to invention. I remember a sparse establishment in South Kensington bordering the tube station, improbably called the Imperial, whose owners may have sometimes wondered later what happened to the *jeunesse dorée* who had flocked to their doors when word got around that one could stretch the five shillings to satisfying levels. My mother's food parcels from Australia were much sought after – Toheroa soup from New Zealand, and passionfruit, the acme of luxury. How lucky most of us are to still have serviceable livers when I recall, too, the afternoon drinking clubs, chief among them the Tree Trunk in Albemarle Street, where we arrived at three o'clock when licensing hours shut us out of the restaurants and stayed, drinking lethal gins, until six o'clock when the pubs opened. There was always a pianist, and although it seemed to me that nobody worked, or thought of work, I suppose we were gathering our resolve to start up again in a more sane world. Most of our friends were 'on leave' or still waiting to be demobbed, and, imperceptibly, they became the members of professions permanently at leisure, should they wish it, in the afternoons – writers, actors, painters, and a fair smattering of the simply rich. What protected us, I wonder, from becoming alcoholics or drug addicts? Perhaps it was the frivolity itself. The future did not appear a threat: only an anticipated adventure. Goethe's 'divine frivolity' was our antidote to any possible depression. I don't think we had ever heard of such a condition; certainly never of 'stress'.

In June of that year, David being established there for the foreseeable future, I visited Cornwall for the first time. I had both his dog and his car in London, and we would set off those weekends when David was on duty, sometimes in leisurely fashion along the country roads – motorways an undreamt of German-sounding phenomenon – staying the night halfway. Or take the night sleeper from Paddington and tip the guard to allow Simon, a golden cocker spaniel, the most neurotic dog I have ever known, into my bunk for the night. Through these beginnings Cornwall has come to mean for me the 'home' I think of when I think, away from her, of England; just as the streets of Sydney are, in my heart, my other home. All else, even though tethered by affection, is temporary.

I realise now that, thanks to Johnny, David and some parental indulgence, I saw England from a viewpoint of some privilege. Of the social conditions of those years I only saw the bright side. Social consciousness were two words whose meaning I had never even contemplated. This did not mean that I was unaware of how the majority lived. I had in my childhood seen a great deal of this but only through contact with my family and always cushioned by, if not love, then certainly compassion, our numerous servants cushioned by my mother's and my grandmother's and perhaps the ever-present laughter in our house providing an antidote to what may have been the bleakness of their lives. And my doctor father's patients from the worst slums of the city, always dependent on and sure of his care and concern. I expect I thought, if I thought at all, that such a comfort blanket existed in the life of everyone.

Unlike the majority of young Australians who travelled to Europe I did not belong to a group, nor mix with other expatriates. I never ventured as far west as Earl's Court nor bought Australian newspapers. I don't believe I thought I would ever see Australia again, so enticing was life in London and I didn't miss my family. My mother and grandmother both wrote to me two or three times a week. Life was a prolonged holiday which I did not envisage ever ending.

Through David, I made one half of the friends who for the last fifty years have anchored my life, and got to know, in varying degrees of intimacy, an astonishing number of interesting, famous, or infamous people: astonishing only in that I neither recognised this at the time, or, if I had done, did not care. They drifted into our lives in numberless parties, cities, and circumstances; their acquaintance enjoyed, their brief friendships embraced, but not by me cultivated.

The other half of my base of friendships sprang from a telephone call made to a friend of a friend of my mother's my first week in London - and later the two strands leading from her and from David mingled and interwove themselves into the only background an exile will ever know; a background begun arbitrarily at the moment of separation from roots.

This friend was a woman of great individuality, Violet Eaton, some twenty years older than myself, but for whom age meant little. I had telephoned her from the flat in Portland Place my first week in London, having written in advance to announce my arrival. Vi, a passionate devotee of the dance floor, had, after receiving my letter, waited especially in London for my call anticipating a night at the '400', as she shared this passion with my mother's friend and could not imagine why any young man would be foisted on her unless he were a good dancer, and unattached. Her voice, when she realised that 'Robin' was female, registered shock, but gallantly garnering what benefit she could from this Antipodean package, she suggested an afternoon at her bridge club (her other passion). This, she thought, must be the reason for Audrey's unwanted visitor. The shock that I did not play bridge - scarcely discernible in her voice - registered in full when we met, coffee at Gunter's[5] having finally been proffered by Vi in desperation. I wasn't a man. I didn't play bridge. I was all of twenty-four. We got on wonderfully well over coffee. Vi discovered I was to spend the weekend with David's mother in a neighbouring village. David and I were invited to drinks and there I re-met an early childhood friend, Margaret Vyner[6], now married to the actor Hugh (Tam) Williams[7]. So Maggy and Tam, Vi and their other friends, became overnight my new family – my links with childhood, my refuge at Christmas, my gateway to the other fifty per cent of English friends made through them.

David's mother, Nada, was a woman of immense charm and personality and, bearing in mind her own background of the much publicised scandal of the Gloria Vanderbilt custody case in which she was found in bed with Little Gloria's mother, was unlikely to have disapproved of my own very minor 'scandal', although I had not hidden under a cloak of seeming respectability and had chosen to opt for divorce. I was taken to meet her first at lunch at the Berkeley, shortly after my arrival, and found her delightful, amusing, and immediately friendly. She told David at once that she liked me very much and I was invited to their country house near Maidenhead the following weekend.

On the way down in the car, David gave me two casual warnings. At lunch would be his uncle who had been 'let out' for the weekend and David hoped his behaviour wouldn't be too strange. Usually, or at least periodically, I learnt, he was 'locked up'. The periods coincided with manifestations of various forms of mania, once or twice involving the use of a carving knife. Even in the raffish surroundings of Sydney's Kings Cross in which I had grown up I'd not encountered this. In my own family, Great-Uncle Harry's undoubted oddity had seemed harmless enough. He had only been 'dropped on his head'.

That wasn't all. His sister, Tatiana, had a 'keeper', an elderly female gnome whose task was not to let Tatiana out of her sight.

It was a particularly enjoyable lunch. David's uncle sat with a small square white handkerchief on his head imitating Queen Victoria, and subsequently rolling on the lawn. His mother retired to her room for a rest whilst David and I went for a walk and Tatiana leapt from behind bushes pushing our heads together and entreating us to kiss before being dragged away by the custodian. We had started off great friends.

chapter five

That first summer of 1946, the first peacetime summer, David had two weeks' leave and we decided to visit the Mediterranean, for me only imagined through staring at the picture postcard wall at the Bon Viveur. We went by train, via Paris. The trains were decrepit, held together by rattling bolts and pieces of wire, it seemed - best not to look out the window. There were no restaurant cars, no sleepers, very few seats not occupied by troops still being moved around Europe. We shambled, if a train can be said to shamble, through the shell-scarred towns and villages, hot and tired and happy, David sitting on his suitcase in the corridor and I on the lap of an obliging soldier. Deep red rocks against deep blue sea - the first glimpses of the sea in the Var region are still for me the instantly summoned memory of that year.

The Hôtel La Réserve at Beaulieu reopened after the war the week we arrived. We were the first guests, our Room Number 22 the prettiest, and the manager, M. Potfer, welcomed us as the first sign of returning normality, and forever afterwards called me his good-luck mascot. I am glad that I would not want to go to La Réserve now, ruinously expensive - different people, different atmosphere, different world. Its first impressions, though, stay with me as fresh as ever. I had never had melon for breakfast before, never had champagne in the bath, never seen a woman lie bare-breasted in the sun, never known that in France, as part of a couple, you could register in a hotel with your correct name and not a falsely assumed marital one - something not done, if not illegal, in England and unheard of in Australia.

At the end of two weeks David had to report back for duty and we braved the rattling old train again. This time it let us down. Twenty-four hours after embarking it panted slowly into the Gare St Lazare, barely half an hour before our boat-train was due to leave the Gare du Nord. The taxi which sped us across Paris arrived as the barriers clanged shut. The train stood tantalisingly on the platform. We pleaded in vain to be allowed to run for it. Finally, David shouted, '*Mais je suis l'officier du Navy Britannique et je serai A.O.L.*' The guard lifted the barrier just enough for him to squeeze through, saying grudgingly: '*Alors - allez - mais Madame et le bagage doivent rester ici.*'

Like Linda in Nancy Mitford's *The Pursuit of Love*, hot, hungry, tired and dirty, I sat on our pile of suitcases and wept. I was rescued, not by a dashing French Duke but by a kindly porter who deposited me with a mercifully honest taxidriver. Luckily I had my own passport and just enough money for the taxi ride. He took me to a passably comfortable and totally respectable hotel in the rue Boissy d'Anglas. I booked a room and rang the only telephone number I had in Paris, that of the parents of Nicki d'Ivangin, the young Russian dancer who had been dear to me and my family all through the war in Australia and who had recently died.

Nicki's brother answered the phone, delighted that I was in Paris, thrilled to meet me at last - and fortuitously able to collect me in half an hour. I had time for a hurried wash and, starving, desperate for some coffee, I waited on the pavement outside the hotel.

Nicki's brother, when he arrived, was resplendent in the outfit of a Thomas Cook tour operator. He was in the company of some thirty-odd American tourists, and he escorted me proudly to the front of the bus, en route to Versailles for the day. I was too young and too tired to protest, and so, in a state of consciousness heightened by hunger and exhaustion, I learnt all about Marie Antoinette.

In the four days I remained in Paris I learnt, too, much about the Paris of the Russian émigrés. We went, *en famille*, to visit Nicki's grave, in the Russian cemetery at St Geneviève des Bois, on the very day a close colleague of Rasputin's assassin, Prince Yusopov, was being buried. I met many of the mourners, some of them relations of David's, and through the d'Ivangins I met many more Russians - Princesses who were head vendeuses at the haute couture establishments; noblemen who were secretaries at the grand men's clubs; waiters and taxi-drivers who were not all Princes but who, for the most part, behaved like them. And I was reunited with Wolfgang, last seen in Australia, Nicki's dearest friend.

I owe a large slice of my life to Wolfgang Cardamatis - half-Greek, half-German painter - since his teens brought up, protestingly, in Australia. He dropped the 'Wolfgang' some years after he shed his German passport, and adopted one of his seven other names - in reality Johannes, but now simply 'Janni' and therefore more Greek. I owe him years filled not only with gaiety and hilarity, but with depth and abandon. I learnt from him almost all I know and from which I derive pleasure of great painting; of minor art; of the conscious use of observation; of the stones of Venice as felt and seen by an inhabitant of that magic city. He taught me how to see with joy. I owe him, too, my one brief Venetian love affair, without which I believe one must feel cheated; for he lent me for the occasion - indeed orchestrated its happening - the beautiful young man with whom he was then living. Wolf was not possessive in his affections. He wanted everyone he loved to love each other.

I owe my best times in Paris as well as in Venice to Wolf. After Nicki's death, he lived there in a series of attics, by his wits and his charm and unashamedly off his friends for years. When David and I arrived he was always waiting at our hotel for a drink, a meal, a bath, and to entertain us and to show us a Paris we would not otherwise have known. If we drank too much a great deal of the time, as I fear we did, we were drunk, too, with youth and excitement. I owe to Wolf my one encounter with Picasso, just as I owe to my youth the fact that I failed to benefit from it.

One summer, Wolf was living in Antibes, and his newest friend, Mario Ruspoli[8], was living next door. We three became firm summer friends, whilst up in the hills Picasso was organising his first show of pottery and the beginnings of his gallery. We helped him hang his canvases and display his plates and it never occurred to me to ask for so much as an autograph.

Wolf lived for a while in a garret in Paris with a ginger kitten called Cleopatra, who ate only fillet of sole, or the occasional breast of chicken. Cleo's upkeep eventually became too taxing, so Wolf rose one dawn and deposited Cleo warm and secure in her lidded basket on Colette's doorstep - secure himself in the knowledge that she would be taken in. Many, many years later I had occasion to visit Maurice Goudeket, Colette's widower, and I longed to ask him if he remembered the arrival of Cleo, but our conversation was for the purpose of establishing some copyright in Colette's work: Cleo seemed too frivolous an intrusion.

Wolf and Nicki and I had been a firm threesome in Australia; Wolf and I now became like brother and sister in Paris and London. Paris in the 1940s was somewhere David and I went whenever he had leave and often I stayed behind with Wolf for a few days. Paris in the 1940s was perhaps more than anywhere in the world the embodiment of the feel, smell, sound of that vibrant decade. I know, now, from other people's histories what a demoralised and tired decade it was, but for me it was vibrant.

I didn't, of course, realise that in spending my nights at the Vieux Colombier, at Madame Arthur's, at Scheherazade, at Jimmy's Bar and in listening to, drinking with, laughing with, dancing to Juliette Greco, Jacques Becker, Claude Luter, Charlie Parker, Stephane Grappelli, Sidney Bechet, I was at the centre of something special, short-lived but resounding. It was special to me, but I saw no significance, outside the moment. I do remember how wonderful Juliette Greco was in her ordinary black dress and her extraordinary long nose before Darryl Zanuck, haute couture and fashion diluted her originality. I do remember the gaiety and urgency of Claude Luter's music, and I do remember the sad, doggy little face (because I have it with me in a photograph) of Eartha Kitt, coming on to the transvestite *boîte*, Madame Arthur's, after her own performance as one of Katherine Dunham's troupe. At Madame Arthur's, the audience frequently ran out by the back entrance as the police stormed in by the front. I remember the violins playing at one's table at Scheherazade, and the fact that caviar was for the general. I remember going to Jimmy's Bar with Jimmy Donohue[9]; La Grenouille in Montmartre - the usually drunken proprietor, Roger; and Patachou, who cut off all the men's ties at her bar across the way. I remember Suzy Solidor asking me to tea, where I neglected to go.

Days shopping at the Marché aux Puces are recollected by the random purchases made before I had any dwelling of my own, now much treasured and providential possessions. The canary still sings in its gilded cage; the painted tin watering can, though battered, has a distinguished air to it; the glass bottle in the shape of a gun is, I expect, a collector's item, for there are people who collect bottles. Before the Rue Jacob was as fashionable or as expensive as it is now I bought frivolously and copiously: frivolous because I had no permanent home and the nature of my purchases - an inlaid chess table, massive brass firedogs, an Empire *causeuse*, a green woollen carpet with bright upstanding wired white and yellow daisies - was hardly suitable for a nomadic girl who didn't play chess. I sold, eventually, the chess table for a regretted pittance. The carpet, before I had realised its rare and singular charm, was plucked bare of its woollen daisies by careless youths and eaten bald of its grass by energetic moths. The *causeuse* found two subsequent and suitable L-shaped rooms, and in between adaptable accommodation goes back to my daughter's attic. Only the dogs have survived in constant use.

With my monthly allowance, and egged on by Wolf, I shopped at Jean Dessès for dresses, at Jeanette Colombier and d'albouy for hats, at Guerlain for scent. One night at a restaurant a waiter brought a note to my table: 'Thank you for wearing my dress so beautifully', it said, and was signed 'Jean Dessès'. I smiled at M. Dessès, then threw away the note - and shortly thereafter gave away the dress. All the couture houses were eager for custom and the excitement was heightened by the fact that they had been in hibernation throughout the war. I chose the house of Jean Dessès as my particular pet because early on I had met their head vendeuse, a charming and elegant lady called Jacqueline Harrari, and we were fortuitously the same size. I dressed in the height of fashion on every penny of my allowance from Australia, either through clothes brought over to England on Jacqui's back and thereby free of both Customs and rationing or through trips to Paris, long hours of fittings and almost as long snippings on my part of all the grand labels, which, if left intact and of course if I had retained any of the clothes, would now garner me a small fortune. These beautiful creations were thereby shorn of their identity - I didn't even keep the labels. My loyalty to Jean

Dessès suffered a brief lapse when Christian Dior burst upon the fashion world with his New Look. I bought two of his first creations, discarding the labels before braving Customs.

On those frequent trips to Paris, usually with David, and sometimes left behind with Wolfgang and therefore into trouble, I also shopped madly for hats. Hats *were* mad in those days, as they recently have become again, but they were exquisite things and somewhere in the back of a cupboard I have one solitary example which has survived - a little brown felt beret miraculously still with the label d'ALBOUY. There was a wonderful confection by Jeanette Colombier - black tulle and jet and soaring plumes and eye veils which also survived in a cupboard for some years, until discovered by Wolfgang and made into quite another creation.

In Australia there had been a Viennese refugee sculptor who made his name locally, Arthur Fleischman. A year or so after I had arrived in London, Dr Fleischman followed and tracked me down, asking for introductions. Prince Philip (then plain Lieutenant Mountbatten just prior to his marriage) was dug up by me, and David's Uncle Dickie (Mountbatten); and Fleischman went to work. In no time, he was under Royal patronage and busy, rich and famous. He telephoned to say he wished to show his appreciation to me for having 'launched' him and was about to offer me a token of this appreciation. I thought of furs, diamonds - several Jean Dessès dresses, perhaps. The good doctor wished, however, to sculpt me. It was an excessively hot summer. Afternoon after afternoon, David drove me to his baking studio where I posed under the glaring summer light. When finished, it looked pretty, far too pretty for me, and in any event I had nowhere in my life to put it. Its pouting terracotta face remained in shadows, under stairs and in cupboards for some years. One day Wolfgang - visiting me in London with his current friend, another painter called Timothy Hennessy - dug her out of the cupboard and by night she was transformed into a person. The terracotta face was covered in Max Factor pancake make-up, rouge, false eyelashes and my very expensive (and fashionable) chignon. Nana's jewellery and Great Aunt Juliet's lorgnettes hung around her neck; crowning it all was the black jet and net Jeanette Colombier. Looking back, she was a beauty, but she lived on, as a joke, unappreciated, on my bookcase for months: a figure of fun and a conversation piece. When tired of this, she went back, scrubbed, into a cupboard; the hat was, I expect, discarded in a dustbin and the chignon given over to the moths . . .

She had a third life, some years later. My doctor husband found her, fell somewhat in love with her and put her on the top of his desk. (We never could get all the Max Factor out of the cracks: she has an interesting and unusual complexion for a terracotta lady.) Tommy Steele, the singer/actor, came as a patient. 'Is that your wife?' he asked Emmet. 'Cor, isn't she lovely - just like Vera Lynn.' The thing is, I can see it - I *am*, I suppose, a bit like Vera Lynn, I mean, not lovely, and so Dr Fleischman had caught some genetic pattern and fixed us both into it. Now, she is in my bookcase, soberly adorned with just one necklace, and people ask who she is: no reflection on Dr Fleischman, only on me. I looked like her once.

It was a time when we three - David, Wolf and I - took three of the iron chairs from the grass verge then bordering the Champs Elysées, and sat in the middle of the Avenue, forcing the cars to drive around us. It was still the time when cars were hoisted onto the cross-Channel ferry by cranes. There is much more opulence now, in our materialistic western world, no recent memories of hardship, death and danger, less excuse for abundance taken recklessly, certainly little style. I savoured the experiences; I liked my new acquaintances; I was enchanted with my possessions; it was all enormous fun, but I did not appreciate the singularity of my luck - singular because that particular brief era of excellence will not come again in my lifetime, and probably not that of my children.

At the end of my first year in London, George Silk had followed me from Shanghai. I was still living in the tiny one room flat in Kensington Close found for me by Nan. I could not believe that I had ever seriously - or even fleetingly - contemplated marriage to George, nice and attractive as he was, but felt very responsible for his presence. He, on the other hand, having come all this way, was determined to resolve the matter one way or the other. It was the week before Christmas. George became impatient with my prevaricating, my obvious lying on the nights when David was in London and I didn't want to see him, and my chronic inability to say a definite 'no'.

He hit upon the idea of flushing me out of my flat and into his life in a final spectacular gesture. Every day, in the week's run up to Christmas, a huge Christmas tree was delivered. One just fitted into the flat, although it meant pine needles down the neck when squeezing into the bathroom. The other six or seven trees were lined up by the porters in the narrow hall. George gave up as Boxing Day dawned, and I am sure he has sometimes since reflected on his lucky escape.

chapter six

With David I got to know quite a few Kings, ex-Kings, and almost Kings. This family network of Royalty was a useful thread running through Europe and I learnt from my encounters the advantages of being close to Royalty, now a fast vanishing breed. In their houses, one tends to eat superior meals; in their company one meets amusing and talented people (who have gathered, perhaps, for the food and the company); and, from being with them, one becomes immune ever after to the influence of those trying to impress socially. On the whole, real Royals don't try to impress.

But one of them whom I met with David late in 1946 was to influence my life from the moment of our meeting. On one Cornish weekend the officers of the Naval Station at St Merryn held a dinner dance, and there I was introduced to His Royal Highness, Prince Chula of Thailand, and his English wife, Lisba. They had met David the previous week and had asked to meet me when next I came down. I was invited to dinner the following night before catching the midnight train back to London, a night in the winter of 1947 – the famous winter of frozen trains, lost passengers, stranded farmhouses and wintry legend. We set off for dinner and I was snowed in for five days in the course of which a lasting friendship was formed.

Apart from Chula and Lisba, their Cornish ménage consisted of Bira, a then famous motor-racing driver, and Chula's first cousin once removed: removed by one generation upwards, but because of the complicated incidence of several wives in various stages of child-bearing, younger by a few years. Bira was not quite so Royal, being descended not from a King and Queen, as was Chula, but from a 'small' wife - as, indeed, is the present King of Thailand. He was also more purely Thai, as Chula's mother had been Russian, thereby, along with Lisba, losing him the throne, his rightful heritage: a heritage he was subsequently to be offered by the Government after the death of an uncle but wisely refused unless a referendum was held. He had no wish to be a puppet King and feared unrest from within. There was Ceril, Bira's English first wife, many dogs, and many devoted courtiers and retainers, secretaries and old friends - Russian, English and Thai. Through the years of constant and close friendship and involvement in the household I came to have a sympathy and affection for the Thai people I met there.

Bira was a leading member of the international motor-racing community, and I, who now loathe fast cars and noise, became an honorary member of his White House racing stable. David and I went with Chula, and Lisba, Bira and his wife Ceril, to most of the Grands Prix of Europe, helping to wave the flags, log the laps, climb into the back of parked cars at the back of the pits for snatched moments of sleep, celebrating the races at all the gala balls - Bern, Monte Carlo, Belfast, Jersey, Rapallo, Reims, San Remo - sometimes in Bira's private plane.

In those days, unlike today, I was not even frightened of flying (indeed, of anything). Bira's twin-engined Gemini was kept in a field near the house, so a taxi to take off involved careful avoidance of startled wandering sheep. I was prone to travel sickness. On one occasion, when Bira came to London to collect both me and David's dog, Simon, I viewed the gusting winds with apprehension. Bira gave me two large pills. I slept happily in the rear seat of the plane. Simon sat happily untethered in the front seat. Later I discovered the vet had given Bira the pills to sedate Simon.

Chula was one of the few very rich men I have known who enjoyed his wealth to the full. He spent copiously, wisely and well, and took care to see that his friends enjoyed it too. There were none of the apparent stirrings of guilt at spending or apprehension of losing it with which money curses some of the rich; nor was he dubious of the motives of those less fortunate than himself in professing friendship and affection. He and Lisba travelled constantly and in enormous style and comfort, but never alone, and they derived equal pleasure from the enjoyment of their guests. These treats were short jaunts such as David and I had to a week of lavish entertainment at the Edinburgh Festival in 1947, then sparkling new and exciting in concept - or longer trips on the *Queen Mary* or *Queen Elizabeth* to America, always with a guest or two. Shorter ones to various European countries, or even longer ones to Thailand (and even - once, many years later - to visit me for three days in Australia), were meticulously planned and lovingly bestowed. At Tredethy, their Cornish house, equerries and secretaries saw to it that this ugly Edwardian house was still run on Royal lines.

A typed itinerary of the weekend's events lay on one's dressing table, the manner of dress and hour of one's required presence, a short biography of other guests provided and punctuality demanded. Many of Chula's little quirks of behaviour strike me still as eminently sensible and thought out so as to give him the maximum enjoyment. He owned several cars but did not drive himself so that his attention was never distracted from his surroundings or company. He always sat at the head of his own table with his wife by his side, saying that as he had married her and as they seldom had the chance to dine *à deux* it was reasonable to suppose that he would prefer her company to anyone else's.

Both he and Lisba were intensely musical, his preference being for chamber music, and so, four times a year, leading chamber trios and quartets were brought to Tredethy and about one hundred guests were invited, not for the intimacy of their acquaintance or the necessity of proffering hospitality, but for their enthusiasm for the musical programme.

There was a vast library; music, fun, games, and fascinating conversation and unusual incidental amusements. One of these was the dressing up in what had been the Thai crown jewels, these having been left directly to Chula by his grandmother, being the widow of an Absolute Monarch and thus able to dispose of her possessions as she chose. 'Granny's Belt' was a particular, and rather hideous, favourite: a solid wide corselet affair made of gold links and diamonds clasped by a huge buckle of yet more solid diamonds. The jewels were only removed from the safe for State, or similarly grand, occasions requiring that medals should be worn and, before they vanished back to the safe, we would spread them around us on the drawing room floor and prance about in Granny's Belt. Children's dressing-up games, really.

There were other privileges to be gained from intimacy with Chula. We were escorted privately around Scotland Yard's Black Museum by the Commissioner for Police. I didn't look at the grisly bits.

I don't expect I would ever have had, or wished for, such an extensive and intimate tour of Cambridge if Chula had not arranged it one glorious summer's day, proud as he was of his own years there. I would not have had wonderful and concrete memories of the historical events of those years and of the people who shaped them if I did not now have copies of the home movies, called Tredethy News, which were religiously recorded by Shura Rahm, Chula's Swiss-Russian major-domo, friend and secretary. These would not qualify for film festivals but they are of abiding interest, being a week to week record of Chula's life - not only on home 'Tredethy' ground - but of many political and social events of the times. I was living through history - we all live it, we are it - but I seem to have been lucky enough to have been often close to key moments of it, and stupid enough never to have appreciated it.

I owe to Chula my most enriching and abiding friendship: my nearest to family in my heart now left to me in the world, excepting children. One weekend at Tredethy a fellow guest was Chula's old time friend and one time youthful Oxford Don, Steven Runciman[10]. Steven performed his party piece - the reading of palms - on all the other guests but steadfastly refused mine. His gift is genuine, and now, I suspect, frightens him. Then, when we were younger, it was the centre of entertainment.

On the last night of our long weekend, Chula cornered Steven and forced him into a room with me. He was not to be bullied. He took my hand in a peremptory fashion, gave it a glance and dismissed it with the chilling phrase, and a chuckle: 'I can see nothing ahead of you except long years of frustration and misery.'

A few years later, when again all other house guests had had their fortunes told by Steven and I was left out, I tried bullying him once more. This time he dismissed me with: 'You have a very good mind. I wonder why it is you never use it?'

More years were to go by until he foretold in all seriousness my husband's palm and I think I understood then why he was reluctant to look into a tragedy awaiting me.

At Tredethy, perhaps the only slight sign of displeasure creased the Royal countenance if the guest showed a disinclination to strip. All guests were required to participate in the nude sunbathing in the fenced-in bathing enclosure. There was nothing prurient about these gatherings, although I am sure the good locals of Bodmin viewed them with suspicion. And they speeded up easy comradeship. When one is introduced to a stranger, be they local vet or Cabinet Minister, totally naked, it somehow aids the consciousness to discount social defences. Acquaintances become friends more quickly – the phrase 'down to bare essentials' takes on a fresh meaning.

I first met Henry Maxwell – Chula's oldest and dearest friend, harking back to Harrow and Cambridge – when we were both naked, although Henry, playing ping-pong at the time, wore shoes and socks. He was Chula's most favoured and most frequent travelling companion and became a dear friend to me. Henry's stories of trips with Chula added to the store of Chula's own. He once visited Queen Juliana and Prince Bernhardt in their vast palace in Holland as just such a companion. On being shown to his room on arrival, told the hour for dinner, having changed into the appropriate dress, he sat and waited for someone to escort him back to a gathering point. Dinner time drew near – so near that Henry was obliged to venture forth into the maze of corridors in the hopes of finding a friendly face. Eventually he fell among familiars and found himself seated at dinner next to a distinguished-looking man of around his own age. Conversation was in French. Henry kicked off by asking his neighbour his occupation. '*Moi?*' replied the astonished man, '*Mais moi – je suis l'ami de la famille Royale.*'[11] This label afforded Henry endless pleasure: from now on, on all his jaunts with Chula, he was able to identify himself by this appropriated, and appropriate, title.

Chula was a rich fund of Royal stories, many from his two uncles who in turn had been Kings of Thailand, both of them childless, or one boasting only a daughter. When the first, Vajiravudh, was King and the Athlones came to Bangkok on a State visit, the Monarch met their yacht in full military regalia accompanied by his younger brother, splendidly bedecked and beribboned as Admiral-in-Chief of the Royal Fleet. As the Athlones stepped ashore and the band struck up a ceremonial march, the King indicated his bowing brother with a flourish: 'May I have the honour to present – my sister!'

He was proud of his English, but there is no word in the Thai language to denote the sex of a younger or older sibling. They are identified by age.

This brother, who in turn inherited the throne, was the last Absolute Ruler of Thailand. In 1932, democratic ambitions were beginning to stir in the country. King Prajadhipok's advisors pleaded with him to leave the country on a grand world tour, in the hopes that the dissidents and protesters would lose heart and that, when he returned, any threats to his person or his position would have been removed. He took this opportunity to visit, not only fellow monarchs around the world, but leaders of state in those countries who had managed to dispose of said monarchs. In particular, Mussolini.

They spoke in French. Over dinner, Mussolini inquired into the domestic situation in his guest's country. King Prajadhipok demurred at first, explaining that it was a complicated story - would take long in the telling - but adding that if his host was truly interested, he would attempt to explain, and would sincerely welcome Mussolini's advice from the benefit of his vast experience, he himself being quite unaccustomed to dissent in any form.

They settled over coffee. Prajadhipok outlined, at some length, the problems facing him on his return. He looked hopefully at his mentor for comment. After a long pause, in a sad voice pregnant with thought, came Mussolini's reply.

'Majesté, c'est mauvais . . .'

Since hearing this tale, I have always nurtured a rather soft spot for Mussolini.

His response must have struck a fatalistic chord in his guest, for Prajadhipok promptly returned, to be welcomed by the first of the country's many bloodless coups d'état and became, as a result, the first democratically deposed King and the last Absolute one.

The most charming King - or ex-King - of my acquaintance

I met with Chula was Umberto of Italy, of whom I don't remember much except an amusing dinner at Claridge's. Although all David's cousins, however distant, were past or present Royalty, charm did not rate high on the agenda, but they must have been interesting if only because they meet a lot of interesting people and therefore have lives rich in anecdote, as was Chula's. But I only remember most of them because of what *we* were doing at the time. King Leopold of the Belgians meant a summer spent on the Italian coast in 1947 – or was it 1948? – water-skiing from his boat. Prince Bertil of Sweden lived just along the coast in France from where I spent a long, hot summer on Bira's yacht, and we dropped anchor often on his foreshore, and swam ashore clamouring to be fed. I helped pull the needles of a sea urchin from the foot of Prince Alexandro Torlonia, whilst his wife (David's cousin), the Infanta Beatrice of Spain, held his hand. I would bet he remembers only the sea urchin, whilst I remember him yelping. I had never heard a grown man make so much fuss. I never bothered to keep in touch or follow up the proffered invitations, although I did strike up, and keep up until her death, a desultory friendship with his amusing sister, Marina. Marina had been married to the US tennis player, Frank Shields, who later was to achieve more fame as the grandfather of the actress Brooke Shields. Once we dined in Paris with the young ex-King Peter of Yugoslavia and his wife who, on that occasion, threw her powder compact at him. I cannot remember the provocation, but I can remember the restaurant, the early great days of San Francisco and what we had to eat – crêpes stuffed with seafood. Great restaurants were beginning to emerge from the austerity of the war; every new taste similar to the adventure of a child's first post-war banana or orange.

I met the Windsors only twice. The first time was in Monte Carlo at a Gala at the Casino in the late 1940s, where David and I had joined them. They were gay then, in the old meaning of that word: her eyes electric blue and sparkling, he smiling and genial. The second time, thirty years later, was in Paris at a private party in semi-darkness in an apartment on the Rive Gauche. I was taken on after a dinner with the Alain Berheims so cannot remember the name of our host, if ever I caught it. Flamenco dancers performed for the fifteen or so of us gathered in the salon. The Duchess's eyes no longer seemed blue or sparkling; they were darker and sharper – her voice snappier and querulous. He was a shambling, pathetic figure. Two sleek young men danced attendance, to one of whom Wallis Windsor exclaimed loudly as the dancing began, 'Take David home!' and, turning to the Duke, as to one of her pet pugs, 'Go home, David, go home!' He was led meekly out.

Some of my first theatre friendships, too, were made with David. With him I first met Bea Lillie[12] in 1947. I seldom drive down Park Lane on a misty autumn evening without remembering a pea soup fog – David at the wheel of our car, Bea, pissed and weaving in front with one hand on the radiator and the other waving a white flag. It was Bea who took us both to a party at Noël Coward's in Gerald Road. Years later, another life later, Noël and I were to become friends, but on that night I only remember him taking me and David up to his galleried bedroom to see his paintings on the walls.

On that night, too, I was to meet one of the people who graced my later life with her abiding friendship – the beautiful and buoyant and endearingly funny Dorothy Hammerstein, that night at Noël's with her husband, Oscar, and her daughter, Susan Blanchard. Later, Dorothy came to mean New York to me. Her exquisite houses became my New York base, where I visited her once a year as she grew older. Older but never less funny nor less beautiful.

That first night was simply one of a thousand nights: of names plopping in and out of my life – now, I fear, onto this page but I hope not with too strong a thud – of no significance unless the brief memories throw a chink of light onto the players. A chill thought – who remembers the players?

If David was indirectly responsible for me knowing so many Kings, chance and upbringing had been responsible for having met a fair smattering of Heads of State. Australian Prime Ministers came naturally into our orbit, given the restricted circle of Sydney society. Robert Menzies was an acquaintance of my parents: I met him whilst growing up. The gaps in our prime ministerial acquaintance were the Labor PMs – no one but a member of the Liberal Party, Australia's conservative representatives and about as far from liberal ethos as is possible to achieve without right-wing extremism, ever swam into our little pond. One heard about them actually having private lives, but these lives did not intertwine with ours. But Liberal Prime Minister Harold Holt was a friend. Drowned whilst surfing, his body never recovered nor even partly washed up inside a sick shark, he was the subject of many subsequent rumours about espionage, CIA activities and various cloak and dagger explanations. Personally I always found him far too jolly a chap to ever suspect any cause other than an imprudent swim. Two other Heads of State, however, convinced me long before the media began to inform the world that there need be no connection between a responsible position in world affairs and a relaxed and uninhibited private life – Bill McMahon and Jack Kennedy – both of them in my life as my bridegroom's best friend and best man at two of my weddings: one achieved and the other aborted.

Billy had been a romantic 'escort' in my teenage years. No more than bruised and swollen lips and late nights between us but enough for me to think of him forever after as simply a good dancer, an entertaining companion – certainly not a future Prime Minister. When it transpired that he was also John Spencer's best friend, I added 'best man' to his tags in my memory.

For the planned second marriage, until the priests and the family managed to extricate Torbert from his proposed mortal sin, Jack was to be our witness and ally. Jack and Torbert had been room-mates at Harvard - inseparable for years; in P.T. Boats together in the Pacific, although Jack was shipped home before I was to meet Torbert, on leave in Sydney. Our engagement lasted only long enough for Jack to be appointed best man for the wedding which was to take place as soon as I could be got out of wartime Australia to the US - but the Church got there first. So I did not actually meet Jack until some four years later.

In 1948 David and I were in France - he staying with his mother at her house in the hills above Cannes, I at the Hôtel du Cap at Eden Roc. At the bar by the sea on my first day I ran into Torbert. He was on holiday with the entire Kennedy clan and we joyfully joined forces. He was by now married but protested - naturally, as is usually the case with errant husbands alone on holiday, unwillingly and unhappily. I was not married to David; but smarting under the indignity of his mother's growing disapproval, and remembering the fervour and fun of my time with Torbert, it took little more than enthusiasm on his part to resume our relationship. Some nights, when David was not with his mother, I spent with him, but the rest of my time was spent with Torbert, Jack, and those Kennedy sisters and brothers who were there. Individually I only remember Bobby, in his teens I think, and the baby, Teddy, and the noise they all made in the pool.

The night after we met, Jack took Torbert and me to a memorable party. Memorable for many reasons. The host was Argentinian Alberto Dodero, said to be the power and the money behind Juan Peron. By his side, acting as hostess, was a cute blonde young American of about nineteen, now the rather grand widow of a Spanish nobleman.

The locale was a magnificent house by the beach at Cap

d'Antibes, gardens and terraces going down to the sea, which Dodero was said to use only for parties. He and his guests slept in an equally magnificent house up the road. Fountains played champagne. Two dance bands played different rhythms in different parts of the gardens. At each guest's place was a small token - small in size but not in value. At our table I have always believed that I watched the first meeting between Rita Hayworth and Aly Khan. Elsa Maxwell was beaming beside them and it has been reported many times that they had met earlier with her, but it seems in my memory that they met that night. Jack drank too much and fell into one of the fountains. I lost my temper with him and demanded to be taken home.

He had hired for the holiday a tiny Deux Cheveux - the baby Citroën whose headlamps were so close together that we had christened it 'Stewart Granger'. (Many years later Jimmy Granger became a friend; he was very beautiful but his eyes were rather close together.) I waited, fuming, in the huge circular hall, Torbert sulking beside me, whilst Jack went to fetch the car. A footman in knee britches waited behind every one of the six marble pillars soaring to the domed ceiling. With horn blaring and headlights full on, up the shallow marble steps came a bouncing 'Stewart Granger'. The footmen chased Jack round the pillars as he weaved between them: Torbert and I jumped in and we bumped down the steps into the night, tempers and sulks forgotten.

The night never was. I read subsequently in a newspaper diary that Jack's son, aged twenty-four, pedalled up the steps of a hotel and into the foyer on his bicycle, so perhaps Jack remembered it, too, and had told the story.

We spent the next two weeks together. Jack and Torbert were sharing a suite at the Hôtel du Cap. I had a cupboard in the *combles*, normally one of the servants' rooms. So most days, for an hour or two, I sat at the desk in Jack's sitting room writing, at his dictation, to the potential voters back in the States who he hoped would get him re-elected to Congress.

'Dear Mrs Blank,' I wrote on one of the postcards with which he supplied me each day, 'I want to thank you for all your support. I'm enjoying a much needed vacation and I do hope your husband's back trouble has cleared up/daughter's baby has arrived/mother's angina is better. Kind regards, Sincerely, John F. Kennedy.'

I often wonder if the recipients kept the cards, now have them framed, or have tried to sell them, only to be told they are forgeries.

I threw away all Jack's subsequent letters to me – a few casual enough notes to London announcing his arrival, messages from Torbert, amicable details of I do not remember what, but certainly not forged. The night he became President I could hardly believe it. The night he was assassinated it seemed to be happening to someone quite other than my youthful friend. And the myths now building up around him have that same quality of unreality.

I saw no evidence then of the sexual appetite and obsession now emerging from accounts. I don't even remember any female companion. He was Torbert's friend and we were a companionable threesome. The sexual encounters, if happening in those early days, were kept hidden from me – prostitutes perhaps when I was not around?

His letters to me were real enough and could since have been put to good commercial use. If I could be born again and granted one material wish it would be to live and die in the house in which I was born, a house boasting a vast attic, stored with relics and memories from the past, present and into the future. In those attics would be the concrete reminders of my ancestors' lives, the mysteries surrounding my parents' emotions, my own changing person and, above all, the letters. I need not have destroyed Jack's – nor T. S. Eliot's, infinitely more interesting (all but one thrown away). I had crossed paths with Eliot briefly during my stint as the London representative of Swedish impresario Lars Schmidt. This was a sinecure, rather than an arduous job, dreamt up by Lars as a means of contact, and it was through the performance of Eliot's plays in Scandinavia that we corresponded. I wish I had his letters, Jack's letters, the couture clothes I bought on our Paris trips, the lost or given away family treasures, the proffered and never accepted presents.

One letter I have kept which gave me pleasure and a frisson of pride was from Noël on reading *Aunts Up the Cross*. It is so typical of him that I find that sufficient excuse to quote it here: I feel, too, that the 'aunts' may have been tickled had they known that Noël Coward 'dearly loved' them.

Les Avants sur Montreux

My dear Robin,

*How sweet of you to remember to send me 'The Aunts'. I dearly love them and enjoyed every word. I was fascinated by the school being called 'Doone' because Mr R. J. Blackmore was a close friend of my mother's and was very nearly my Godfather: I forget why he wasn't actually, but I think it was because he died while I was 'on the way'. (A jolly valid reason.) It is so gaily written (*your *book not* Lorna Doone *which was on the turgid side). It also makes a vivid period picture of my favourite Australian city. I'm jolly glad Bill insisted on your sending it.*

My love and thanks to you both

Noël

My worst recollected carelessness was the occasion on which, in 1947, I was taken to tea in his cottage in Cookham with the painter Stanley Spencer, who on that and on a subsequent visit offered me any of the paintings stacked on the floor, in the sink, in the bath. We sat on packing cases while he boiled a kettle, uncapped milk bottle at our feet. He was a strange little man, and I politely looked at the paintings, and just as politely declined. If I had taken some of the paintings I might have been able to afford the house in which to store everything discarded.

Perhaps the worst missed - or thrown away - opportunity was my failure to celebrate VJ night with Winston Churchill on the roof of the Admiralty. David's uncle, Louis Mountbatten, had invited David and me to join the party of VIPs gathering there. We dined first at Ciro's, and set off much too late on foot towards Whitehall, struggling against the crowd through Leicester Square and into Trafalgar Square. My subsequent horror of crowds had not manifested itself and so we joined the jostling throng, the mounted police, the fainting revellers swaying under the fireworks with great good humour. Halfway there, we decided it was just too much trouble, turned back, and collapsed thankfully into the doorway of the '400'. I never met Churchill.

chapter seven

In the autumn of 1947 I was temporarily homeless and invited to stay with a friend in her pretty little house in Elizabeth Street. Whether or not it was strictly her house became increasingly doubtful during the delightfully *mouvementé* weeks of that autumn. We were still festooned with the tattered but deliciously gaudy remnants of wartime standards of behaviour: standards which were partly born out of a desire to please the poor boys on leave as well as a recognition that never before or again would we enjoy ourselves quite so much. My friend, also from Australia, had married the last of her wartime lovers and now back in England, with her husband stationed in Germany, had not had much time to adjust to a more stable emotional climate. Also, a serving officer's pay did not compare with the fortune of her peacetime suitor. Sporting a huge engagement ring where her wedding ring should have been, husband hidden in Germany, she moved into the Elizabeth Street house, all expenses paid by her 'fiancé', and managed to steal a weekend free from time to time in order to visit her husband. However, a third contender appeared – a young Italian nobleman with whom Henrietta (for such shall I call her) announced herself enamoured on return from a trip to Capri. The Italian, Pino (for such shall I call him), very soon followed her to London. The appointed weekend presented little problem to one of Henrietta's inventiveness: she would have one of her 'headaches' (I suspect we had both read far too many bad novels). Her benefactor, Hugo (for such shall I call him), was told she must rest in a darkened room all weekend and that he must entertain himself.

Pino, when he arrived, was all she had promised - charming, good-looking, and incredibly soigné with that ironed silk neatness of the Italian upper classes. As we very rarely left the pink flounced satin bower of Henrietta's bedroom anyway, we three lay chatting on the vast bed, sipping champagne prior to their evening *à deux* at Ciro's and the '400'. The doorbell rang. No one being expected and apprehension stirring, I was dispatched downstairs to see who it was.

On the doorstep was a fresh-faced youth, pink and polite, with shining shoes and a shining smile and a small suitcase.

'I'm Gary,' he explained. 'I've come for the weekend to stay with Mrs –. Arranged by my mother. From Norfolk.'

I raced upstairs.

'Oh, my God! I forgot. His mother is a friend of mine. I said I would show him round London. Bring him up.'

Gary's introduction to London will have, I hope, stood him in good stead over the intervening fifty years. His first taste was of champagne on a bed, and a discussion as to how we would all adjust to the changed circumstances. Gary would have my bedroom at the top of the house; I would stay the weekend with a friend nearby; we would all four spend the evening at Ciro's.

The evening went well. We arranged to meet at lunchtime the next day and lunch together. I awoke to a telephone call from an actress friend, Elspeth March, who had tracked me down and who was currently appearing on stage in *Medea* with Eileen Herlie and Ralph Michael. Ralph Michael was about to have a screen test in which he had to play an Australian. He had never met one. Would I spare him an hour in which to chat? I thought I could do better. 'Tell him to come to lunch today with the girl I am living with and he can meet two of us' – time and address given, I dressed and went round to Elizabeth Street.

In 1947, along with many other restrictions and their attendant black-market loopholes, it was virtually impossible to find anyone to do private house repairs without a permit, unless in their spare time. Henrietta had found a small firm of decorators, father and son, who were to spend every weekend painting the house. They had started that morning in the tiny hall which was totally filled by their platform ladder and pots of paint. When I arrived, Mr Perkins, *père*, opened the door but father and son were in some state of spluttering agitation, eyes rolling upwards. I raced upstairs to find Henrietta, prostrate on her bed and nursing her hand.

'I think he's broken my thumb,' she said.

'Who?'

'Hugo, of course. He's just been here and he has behaved shockingly. I think he's mad. Poor Mr Perkins let him in – not his fault – and he's made the most frightful scene and my thumb is swelling already. It hurts dreadfully.'

Hugo had had a telephone call that morning from a kind friend who had also been at Ciro's the night before. He was therefore curious about Henrietta's headache and had come to Elizabeth Street to investigate, demanding entry from Mr Perkins, creating sufficient noise to alert Henrietta just in time to push Pino out of bed and naked and protesting into a clothes cupboard. Full, as it turned out, of my long evening dresses and high-heeled sandals – spiky ones, in 1947.

Back on the bed, black eyeshade in place, Henrietta rounded on Hugo for his suspicions, his bad manners and his disruption of her peace. Frustrated and furious, he clutched at the only reliable (to date) straw in his slippery, shifting world of relations with Henrietta.

'I don't believe you,' he shouted, 'but I'll believe Robin. She'll tell me the truth!' And he stormed up the stairs to my bedroom.

Gary had had a lovely night - much of the glitter and glamour of London of which he'd dreamed in Norfolk had come true - and he was still happily dreaming on when Hugo burst in. His brief moment of consciousness ended when Hugo, not waiting for the answer to his question, 'Who are you?', waited only long enough for pyjama-clad Gary to struggle to his feet before knocking him down again. In falling he struck his head on the windowsill and lapsed back into dreamland.

On the way down Hugo paused long enough to break Henrietta's thumb - in a struggle, she told me, to snatch off her throat the pearl necklace he had recently given her; in which attempt he failed. I had arrived on his heels before Mr Perkins had had time to get back on his ladder or Henrietta to assess her injuries.

However, broken thumb or not (possibly just *strained*? I asked her), should we not go upstairs and see how Gary had taken the sudden intrusion? We found Gary still blissfully smiling but unconscious, but soon revived and helped downstairs to the communal bed. The bump on his head took precedence over Henrietta's swelling thumb, but not over Henrietta's protestations of horror and apology.

'That,' she explained, 'was my trustee. Gary, whatever must you think? I am so sorry. He is quite mad. Daddy should never have made him my trustee. He bullies me dreadfully and watches over me like a little girl. Oh, dear! Whatever will your mother say? Robin, I think what we all need is a cup of tea. Would you be an angel as you are the only one who is dressed and, indeed, not injured.'

As I made the tea I could hear Henrietta continuing to explain to Gary the necessity, financially, for Daddy to have appointed a trustee for her, and the insane zeal with which the wretched man overstepped his duties. Gary was bemused, and perhaps just a little dazed. We thankfully sipped the tea. Through the indignant monologue from Henrietta I became aware of another sound - a muffled, gasping sound from the other side of the room.

'Henrietta,' I interrupted, 'I think there's some animal in the cupboard.'

'Oh, my God! Pino!'

We raced to the cupboard. He was crouched painfully on the upturned heels of my carelessly discarded sandals, naked except for a trail of satin ribbons and the odd feather and in a worse shape than Gary. Another cup was fetched, soothing noises made all round and preparations made for going out to lunch.

'Mr Perkins,' said Henrietta imperiously, as we left the house, 'you are not to let that man in again. If anyone tries to force their way in you have my permission to throw paint over them.'

We had a restful and enjoyable lunch and strolled back through the autumn sunshine. Mr Perkins was still painting diligently. 'All well?' asked Henrietta.

'Well,' said Mr Perkins, 'someone did try to get in and most insistent he was. When I refused to open the door he stuck his head in the letterbox to look in. He had a big red beard so I sprayed that full of white paint for luck.'

Ralph Michael! I never met him. I wonder if he ever met an Australian. I wonder if he remembers. Elspeth told me it took them a very long time to get the paint out of his beard for the next performance.

chapter eight

In the summer of 1947 before the episode of Pino, Henrietta had managed to convince Hugo that she needed a healthy holiday with a friend. The friend chosen was, sadly, even then somewhat eccentric and has, in fact, since been committed to a mental home. However, in 1947 she was able to serve Henrietta's purpose by supposedly joining her on a 'walking tour'. Weighed down with Hugo's banknotes but nothing more athletic than a few flimsy nightgowns, Henrietta and Pammie embarked on the cross-Channel ferry, blowing kisses to Hugo, and were met at Calais by Henrietta's husband, with car, on leave from Germany. Pammie was sent back on the next boat.

David and I contrived a holiday on the Côte d'Azur every summer, in addition to our Paris weekends and our racing trips with Bira and Chula, so we drove down and we all four met up at our old stamping ground, La Réserve. We had all been friends in Sydney during the war. (David had told me he *thought* he'd been to bed with Henrietta before we had met. He was not sure, having, it seemed, had quite a bit to drink, but he did remember a Chinese takeaway dinner in her apartment, and Henrietta disappearing to reappear in a black lace nightgown. The black nightgown had made such an impression that he was unable to concentrate on the remainder of the evening with similar clarity.)

Tam and Maggy Williams had rented a house down the coast; friends Eliza and Tommy were at another one; and we all set about the business of procuring enough French francs for our holiday, it being the years of the £25 travel allowance. Only Henrietta had smuggled enough in. The rest of us were condemned to the nightly prowl at the Carlton Bar. Cedric Keogh was the leader of the pack of English law-breaking currency traders. He had direct access to one, Max Intrator, who was to figure largely in the press headlines later that year. I had wangled an introduction to a Frenchman, Roger Peronnier, who came often to London, so Maggy and Tam and I acquired our francs from him. We were too late to save Eliza. She was the only one of us to actually write out a cheque direct to 'Max Intrator' - handed to Cedric under the table and later published on the front page of the *Daily Mail* when Max Intrator was caught.

DUKE'S DAUGHTER IN CURRENCY SCANDAL blazed the headlines, and Eliza was reported as having changed £3000. In 1947, £3000 was a fortune. Eliza had changed £300, and was fined accordingly. She successfully sued the *Mail*; damages were awarded her. She claimed only £300 and came out square: the *Daily Mail*, no doubt, could not believe their luck.

Tam was not so lucky. Living through the war had accustomed us all to living on the brink - of danger; of luxury; of penury. My new friends fitted perfectly into the framework of my upbringing. Few of us earned a regular wage; none of us had saved a penny; all of us dined nightly at the Ivy, the Caprice, the Savoy Grill, and drank champagne for breakfast. We took off across the Channel to sunshine and more champagne and the Parisian shops with not much thought of the future bills to settle. Roger Peronnier helped to push these horrid thoughts further into the background as he seldom came to England more than twice a year. Settling up was in the tradition of Great Aunt Juliet's account with Sydney department stores – '*mañana*'.

However, one day he arrived, unannounced, and it fell to me to telephone Tam with the request for a rendezvous. Tam had had a particularly bad day at the races and so the required £400 was a bitter pill to digest after an almost forgotten summer idyll. The francs with which he had furnished us had been well and truly spent. The Monte Carlo casino was still the haunt of international gamblers like the famed Dolly Sisters, but they were equally welcoming to '*les jeunes Anglais*' as long as bills were paid. On the night that David, Tam and Tommy had all gone 'Banco' at the tables we were cleaned out. Offers to wash up were ignored, so all our passports were impounded, rescued the next day by Roger's francs. Somehow Tam managed to scrape the sterling equivalent together; we all met for a forced welcoming drink for Roger in the Savoy Bar. Roger pocketed Tam's envelope, bade us all a courteous farewell and went up to his room and shot himself.

We were unable to find out if the £400 was still, neatly folded, in his pocket and could only, miserably, read the news headlines about his body. He had done us proud and we felt guilty that we had not given him a jollier send-off . . .

I had my unpredictable but adequate allowance from home. David had his naval pay and the allowance of £5 per week given to him, and also to his cousin, the then Prince Philip of Greece, by their uncle, Lord Mountbatten. We decided that between us we could afford to rent a furnished flat of our own. Through friends we found a charming two bedroomed flat in the Kings Road for £8 per week, of which we solemnly paid half each.

As David was able to be in London only at weekends, I had ample opportunity to make many new friends, but of these, one was to become central to my life. This was the photographer Baron, then the first of the eminent photographers to be socially 'acceptable', barring Cecil Beaton. He owed this partly to his unique and lovable personality, partly to his connections, and not a great deal to his talent. In youth, he and the then young Dickie Mountbatten had both been in love with a fascinating Frenchwoman, Yola Letellier, and had met at her feet in Paris. They had remained friends; in time, Uncle Dickie had introduced Baron to his nephew, Philip, and in turn Philip introduced him to David and me.

Baron became one of my dearest friends; we spoke every day on the telephone until his death. Through him I met and mixed with many of the London characters of the 1940s, a third world to add to the Royals and the theatre people – nights at the Pheasantry with Augustus John, who literally chased me around the table of the proprietor's back room; at his studio with painter Felix Topolski, where I experienced my first and last lesbian approach. Such was one's Australian inexperience in those years that I didn't fully realise its meaning.

(It was not at all unusual in 1947 for innocence to go hand in hand with a certain amount of experience. Vi Eaton, who, for years, lived a peaceful and workable *ménage à trois* with husband and lover, was nonetheless totally ignorant of some facets, rather than the basic facts, of worldly life. Two homosexual men friends were coming to stay: bedrooms to be allocated, the supply of single beds a problem.

'Let them share a double bed,' said her husband, 'that's what they would prefer.' Vi was astounded. 'I always thought they did it standing up!')

Baron told me later that I had sat gingerly on the edge of a sofa acting like a Lady Mayoress of Kensington whilst a drunken Barbara Skelton attempted to pull down my pants. She sat on the floor at the feet of a tall, dark glamorous girl, another Barbara, whose second name I don't remember but who was an habituée of our 'circle' because she was the girlfriend of a genial American living in London, Fred Tupper, then the PR representative of Pan American Airlines. The two Barbaras were enjoying themselves in what appeared to me a most curious fashion, indulgently watched over by Felix and Baron, before Barbara Skelton turned her attentions to me. Baron took pity on my prim lips, murmured protestations and firmly crossed legs and took me home. I don't remember seeing Barbara again and now, having read her books of reminiscences, regret not having known her better, although perhaps not in the guise first offered to me. She went on to marry writer Cyril Connolly (twice) and publisher George Weidenfeld, and I never got into close sexual proximity with a female again.

Baron was, in due course, to give me away at my wedding and become godfather to my daughter, but he was reputed to be at the centre of a very disreputable world indeed. One heard lurid tales of orgies. With me he was a loving and gentle friend. We met when David had gone skiing for two weeks and asked Baron to look after me. Introductions to Baron's friends opened up avenues of enjoyment: painters, writers, photographers – skimming the surface, I now realise, of a murkier world underneath of which I remained largely innocent.

His best friend, the painter Vasco Lazzolo, discovered a magic pill which was supposed to make us all madly sexy. You put it underneath your pillow and at the crucial moment of intercourse you were supposed to pop it and inhale. David and I tried it once, but as we were madly sexy anyway it didn't appear to do more than slow up proceedings. We were always losing them under the pillow. I think they were yellow and I expect they were the first primitive precursors of amyl nitrite: known, I believe, as 'poppers'.

After the first year and the first flush of enthusiasm shown to me by David's mother, an icy curtain had descended over her initial warmth. I never discovered the exact reason but have since been told that I was considered 'fast' and a bad influence on David, and indeed was the subject of a flurry of worried correspondence between his two aunts, Lady Zia Wernher and Queen Louise of Sweden.

I think the true reason for the cooling was that I had no fortune, or prospect of one, with which to augment his frugal naval pay. The bad influence was pretty farcical. Apart from Torbert, the fleeting Americans and the horrid experience of John Spencer, I certainly had known little else of the great world of sex. I was an innocent abroad and it was David who introduced me to a world I had not dreamed existed: louche photographers, popping pills, and new experiences.

I also tried, in a fashion necessarily desultory because of the frequent attraction of taking off on trips, to settle down. My parents never suggested, nor even hinted, that I should work, but the allowance needed to be augmented if the trips were to continue and the couture houses not given up. I looked around for work which did not entail regular hours, or even days, and which would allow me to come and go as I pleased. Needless to say, this led to a startling turnover in jobs.

A newspaper column seemed the ideal. I had written a precocious one for a time in Sydney, with copious and amateurish illustrations; this was little more than a weekly diary of my doings. I had no difficulty in persuading the same editor, Eric Baume of *Truth* newspaper, that I could provide them with a fascinating résumé of the week's events in London. Delivery was on Wednesdays. Baron took the portraits which headed my column. I rose at 6 a.m. on Wednesday mornings and dashed off my few hundred words, culled mostly from my engagement book (a life crammed into tiny pages – Christian names only – sometimes luncheon or dinner on several consecutive days with a Mark, an Otto, or a Douglas. Who were they, one wonders, and where are they now? And how do they remember the forties? Perhaps, like me, they have difficulty remembering them at all).

These working stints could never be considered taxing. The England of the '400' and Ciro's, Ascot and Henley co-existed alongside the London of the Pheasantry, the marvellous institution in the King's Road, and the Gargoyle in Soho - a more bohemian, intellectual watering hole - and into this world I was introduced by Baron, by the Tangyes and the friends made through them: another new experience. One of these was Mark Culme-Seymour. He was spectacularly good-looking, hopelessly charming, and tended to marry the oddest people - elderly princesses whom he erroneously thought were rich, or waif-like creatures, even more adrift than himself. The marriages did not last long. Mark and I spent many nights in the Gargoyle. Some of those nights drinking with Guy Burgess and occasionally Donald Maclean, now I recall little of them except their drunken arguments.

The column continued for about a year. I tired of it before they did, probably because more intriguing opportunities opened up which did not necessitate the early Wednesday mornings. More rewarding was a monthly travel piece I wrote for Sydney Ure Smith's prestigious little magazine *Art In Australia*. This allowed me to push guilt to the back of my mind as I whirled off to Oslo with Lars Schmidt, Belfast with David, Dublin with George, and had fun writing about it on my return.

Not surprisingly, David, too, had his rare lapses from fidelity, but his, always confessed, were usually one night affairs propelled by alcohol and devoid of romance. Emotionally, he never wavered in his loyalty to me. This did not mean I was not furiously jealous. As two of them were with Hollywood actresses after some celebrity party to which I had not been invited, I never met them, but the third was an eighteen-year-old bouncy blonde, introduced into our circle by Baron and generally considered anybody's. At the subsequent party after David's confession, I glared at her with hatred and contempt – both melting into liking on hearing her talking to Baron, Vasco and some friends. Painter Vasco had criticised Baron's photographic skills. Sunny leapt to his defence.

'How can you say that? He's a *famous* photographer!'

'Well,' said Vasco, 'that's not saying much. I'm a famous painter but I'm not a very good painter.'

Sunny thought for a moment. 'Oh, I see what you mean . . . I'm really not a very good fuck.'

chapter nine

Not connected with my own journalistic attempts, but through two friendships, with Johnny Hannay and Jeannie Nichol, I had entered another world of intimacies - the inhabitants of London's Fleet Street. Johnny was a regular fixture of the Williams household. During my first year he had become my weekday escort when David was on duty in Cornwall, and I incited Tam's irritation when I refused his tentative, but nonetheless serious, proposal of marriage. 'Why can't you marry him? I'm sick to death of him being in love with Margaret.'

Tam was responsible for my second serious marriage proposal about this time. Another constant member of our group, a customary fellow guest at the Williams' Christmas gatherings, was actor Guy Middleton. Guy was attractive, amusing and not known for his hospitality. He was inclined to go to the loo when his turn came for a round of drinks. One day, Guy rang and asked me to dine at L'Ecu de France in Jermyn Street, one of the better restaurants of the 1940s. A chauffeur-driven limousine was sent to fetch me; a rug was tenderly laid across my knees. Something afoot, I thought. Not far into our meal, Guy made his proposal. He thought it high time he got married and, looking around, had alighted on me. After I dismissed this idea as absurd, Guy lapsed into snappish gloom and I was sent home in a taxi. The following morning Tam telephoned. 'Did you accept him?' he wanted to know. It seems Guy had asked his advice and Tam, thinking of our Christmas numbers and the wish to keep them in the family, had suggested me, which Guy had thought not a bad idea at all.

Johnny was working for the Savoy Group of hotels, and subsequently was made a director when, calling on his wartime experience in the Special Forces, and his wartime buddies, he was responsible for breaking the oil strike which, but for him, would have broken the back of the Savoy. It was an opportunity to get out - if not the tin hats - then a few old army revolvers and some khaki overalls, borrow some army trucks, and drive them through the night from the north of England with enough oil to keep the hotel going. We, his camp followers, watched from the hotel's upper windows and cheered as the lorries braved the pickets and crashed through.

The Savoy was 'my' hotel. Johnny, as director, provided a second home. A wardrobe (still in situ) from the Berkeley when furnishing my first apartment; a daily bath when the pipes froze in the winter of 1947; and my introduction to Jeannie. Jeannie has since become well known both in her life and since her death, through her own books, and the books of her husband, Derek Tangye, about their life at Dorminack at Land's End. But in 1946 she was still the Press Officer at the Savoy, Derek was still a working journalist and she was my best friend. Jeannie was everyone's friend, but special to me. We were of an age and a similar temperament. Her Savoy office was the centre of gaiety as well as information, and Fleet Street made it their base. Christiansen of the *Express*, Noel Barber, Frank Owen of the *Mail*, Don Iddon from New York, Bertie Gunn (father of the poet, Thom Gunn), Noel Monks, a fellow Australian, are some of the names I remember from our daily gatherings in the Savoy Bar. And, of course, all the celebrities of the 1940s who made the Savoy their base, and Jeannie's office the heart of that base.

Jeannie and I started a club – in competition with the Thursday Club. The Thursday Club was the brainchild of Baron: amongst its members his twin, Jack Nahum; the painter Vasco Lazzolo; Prince Philip; David; Pip Youngman-Carter, then editor of *Tatler*; Philip's private secretary Michael Parker; actor James Robertson Justice; and anyone else of interest (and male) who happened to be in town. They lunched at the original Wheeler's in Old Compton Street. Thursday night was a lost cause if you happened to be the wife or girlfriend of any of the members.

We were determined to wreak our revenge on at least one man per week, and so our club was born. We invited a man to lunch each Wednesday. In the morning, a red carnation was delivered to the man of our choice: he was to present himself at one o'clock at the Bon Viveur in Shepherd's Market: and before he was decanted at sundown he was to write a piece in our club book. A. P. Herbert (Sir Alan Herbert, MP and Knight) wrote our club rules, and we entertained many of the visiting journalists from America – A. J. Leibling, Sam Boal, Danny Kaye, and all our London friends and acquaintances. Alan's rules read:

RULES (if any)

1. *There shall be two original members, namely: Robin Spencer, Jean Nichol.*
2. *The original members shall, in no circumstances, pay any subscription – a privilege to be reserved for New Members.*
3. *At all Ordinary Meetings there shall be one guest only, a Man, who shall be alone, defenceless, and decanted with a Red Carnation.*
4. *There shall be an Annual Meeting, at which the refreshments shall be provided by the Guests.*

5. *The general tone of the Club shall be hostile to the use of alcohol.*

In addition to writing the club rules, Alan became both intrigued and incensed by the lurid story of my divorce, and the truth behind it. This was to become the driving force behind his campaign to have the unfair, antiquated divorce rules changed. He worked at it tirelessly and eventually with success, and it is gratifying to reflect that hordes of British women now owe their freedom from brutal husbands indirectly to my teenage bruises.

Somewhere amongst the itinerant Americans at the Savoy I met a Hollywood publicist over in London to promote the opening of the film *Duel in the Sun*. It seemed appropriate to him that I should give up my journalistic stints and become a Public Relations Consultant, except that I do not think they were graced with such grand appellations in those days. I was deeply entrenched in the newspaper world: contacts were no problem. All I needed were a few bright ideas.

I only had one, but a fairly spectacular one, if limited in audience rating. I needed Johnny's help and I got it. On the Embankment side of the Savoy, on the night of the opening, the requisite number of windows were lit in the hotel, and the intervening ones darkened, to spell out in lights across the river the words *Duel in the Sun*. Nobody questioned who might be watching from the gloom of the South Bank, or how the Savoy staff had managed to engineer the electrics. It was my one act as a publicist and I cannot remember what happened to my employer or the film.

But, London was beginning to attract tourists again – proper peacetime tourists who wanted proper places to live and guidance on where to shop. So *Contactus* was my next foray into work. Siegi Sessler, the Polish restaurateur who with his fellow Pole from the Polish Armed Forces, John Mills, had started Les Ambassadeurs, now formed his own immensely popular club, Siegi's. There was a suite of three rooms on top - empty - and a restaurant below, full nightly of people asking Siegi where they could shop, hire a car, rent a flat. I moved into the three rooms by day, we had cards printed with *Contactus* emblazoned on them, and I wrote some very peppy sales talk to go with it. David and I, and whoever else I was with, ate at Siegi's for nothing and I think we did some good business. The restaurant was in Charles Street; by this time I had moved into Mount Street nearby, and it was all very pleasant. We were the first of such agencies to start up in London, and had I had the staying power or the ambition to continue it might still be going strong.

In London, occasionally, a friend from Australia would arrive, but not until the 1950s did they appear in any numbers. They were my fleeting links with home, fleeting only but tethered by shared memories. During the war, at one of my mother's Sunday night gatherings, Peter Finch, the actor, had managed to find the bathroom but, in his haste, not the bathroom light. Nor the lavatory. Relieving himself in the bath and hearing a dull and muffled thud rather than a metallic tinkle, he groped for the light. My mother had stacked the bathtub with bowls of trifle. Those of us to whom Peter recounted the accident declined pudding.

Finchy was an endless source of stories. Before he left Australia for England and fame he became engaged to a friend of ours. The wedding was to be a fairly prominent social event: no veil but at least a bridesmaid, and society gossip columnists. Everyone turned up except Peter, who caught the train to Melbourne instead. When he married his lovely Russian ballerina wife, Tamara, it was from my family's house as my parents were the nearest he had to a family in Australia. He had been born in England, and was more or less abandoned in Australia by both parents.

I had been in England for three years and living in a pretty house in Trevor Square when the telephone rang one evening. Eight people were coming to dinner and I had just laid the table and squeezed the eight little gilt chairs around it. It was Peter. I had not heard from him for the intervening years but his excitement overcame any need for preamble.

'I've found my mother!' he shouted down the telephone. 'I've just met her. She's terrific. I want to bring her round to see you at once. Can we come now?'

Churlish to say no: just time to rush round the corner to Harrods for more food and forage for two more chairs from bedrooms, squeeze all of them closer together, lay more places, explain to other guests as the clock ticked on way beyond eating time that we were waiting for Peter. I waited two years before I ran into him again one night. He was not with his mother and so I never met her and neither was she or the dinner ever mentioned again.

A few other Australians contacted me – those who were, like me, to spend the better part of their lives in Europe and make their niche there in their chosen professions. Jocelyn Rickards brought one of the first of her famous (in her own books as well as in their own lives) lovers, Freddie Ayer, to see me; and went on to become a successful stage and film designer. Wolfgang brought the young Diane Cilento, en route to drama school, magnificent with her original Roman nose long before she married Sean Connery. Loudon Sainthill and Harry Tatlock-Miller arrived, Harry to open the Redfern Gallery, and Loudon to design some theatrical hits of the time. We each went on our separate ways, never to form a clique, thrusting out different tentacles. Only the young Michael Blakemore was to remain important, much later, in my life. Then he arrived on my doorstep, abandoning his comfortable Sydney background and working his way as a ship's steward, determined to become an actor. I had no idea what to do with this 21-year-old youth, although he now tells me I was very 'kind' to him, and he went on to become a consummate actor, a wonderful writer, and a top world-class theatre and film director before our lives were to mesh again.

I was busy in other areas.

chapter ten

Lars Schmidt was (and indeed is) a divinely attractive Swede. Then in his late twenties, we met at Sandown Races with a naval officer colleague of David's, Bertie Hardman. Bertie and I had known each other since Sydney; Lars had recently met him skiing. Lars and I both pretended enormous interest in horseflesh as we broke away from the rest of the party between each race on the pretext of visiting the Paddock and inspecting the horses. All through those irresponsible crazy years Lars was the only serious threat to David's position in my heart, but threat he certainly became and it did not occur to me to hide it. A certain pique had something to do with it. David had agreed in late 1947 to be best man at the wedding of his cousin, Prince Philip, to Princess Elizabeth, and from being an unknown young naval officer he was thrust into the forefront of media attentions and consequently those of socially ambitious mothers. The temptation to accept the subsequent invitations now showered on him, in which I was not always included, from various foreign ambassadresses with marriageable daughters and the like, was strong. I could not really blame him when I considered how I had spent my weeknights whilst he was in the Navy. What is worse, I had been largely responsible for his leaving the Navy, urging him to give up such a regimented life, take his seat in the House of Lords, and take a job. As always, fun and freedom seemed more enticing than permanence. I wasn't so happy with the occasions when freedom meant freedom from me, and fun meant having fun without me. Lars was my riposte, although I didn't see it that way and Lars was reason enough himself.

After our first meeting in London, we arranged that I should visit him in Göteborg as soon as possible. Unfortunately, he had a wife (years later he had another better known one, Ingrid Bergman). I flew to meet him in Oslo for our first weekend together. This later bore fruit as an article for *Art In Australia*, and growing bolder we decided we could meet closer to home, combining my next article with a summer week on the islands off the west coast, driving there from Copenhagen. The midnight sun never set: Lars and I arrived in Göteborg after a week lying in it, burnt black except for peeling noses – I supposedly direct from grey England as a friend of Bertie's on a brief trip to Göteborg and Lars supposedly after a business trip to Copenhagen.

Through Lars, I somehow slipped into another job. He was at the beginning of his subsequent distinguished career as a theatrical impresario, and starting in those days as Sweden's brightest young literary agent, the earliest champion of his friend Ingmar Bergman. I was to be his Girl Friday in London, on the lookout for likely plays and a contact with English authors. From this beginning came my friendship with Peter Ustinov, then a fledgling director set to direct Bergman's *Frenzy* in the theatre; and my association with T. S. Eliot through the Scandinavian production of *The Cocktail Party*.

My relationship with Eliot was conducted largely on the telephone and through the discarded letters.

Peter and I, however, shared some hilarious Swedish experiences. We went together to Göteborg to celebrate the most important Swedish festival, that of Midsummer Night's Eve. On this night, the first crayfish of the season are eaten. The week passed in a haze of 'Skol' and aquavit, crayfish and dill, lighted candles and everyone creeping round the house in long white gowns carrying them and wearing crowns of leaves. Dressed in these, the children and women of the house burst into bedrooms at dawn crying out guttural greetings. This was superb material for Peter's comic genius to parody.

At the end of our week, a dinner was given in our honour by Lars's parents at their beautiful estate outside Göteborg, awash with more aquavit, more crayfish, and white-gloved footmen behind every chair. We were toasted relentlessly by all the twenty or so guests: 'Skol' - a raised glass across the table; 'Skol' - we slurred back, and another glass drained, so as not to offend. At the end of dinner, one of the guests got to his feet and spoke at length, in Swedish; during which there was much nodding of heads, bowing and smiling in our direction, much more raising of glasses, much applause and twenty pairs of expectant eyes trained on us. It was obvious that this was an elaborate toast to us and that a reply was expected. Peter did not fail. He rose majestically to his feet and, at equal length, replied in faultless phonetic and incomprehensible sounds. Our kind hosts and fellow guests were too polite to show their bewilderment. They smiled, nodded, raised more glasses and dutifully applauded.

When we left Sweden, Peter confided to me that he had actually mastered only two words of Swedish, culled from the newspaper headlines reporting his frightening flight into Göteborg when the landing gear had failed to operate: *nervepreenderer minuten*.

The following Midsummer Night's Eve we were in London and Lars insisted on us having our midsummer's Swedish celebration in the Trevor Square house. The crayfish were to be shipped in that day. Peter and I were to race to the airport to collect them and the accompanying crate of aquavit. All I had to do was to provide the boiled potatoes, the dill, the glasses, and the guests. At midnight we were to raise our glasses to Lars and distant Swedish friends.

We expected our crayfish on ice, not actually in it. When located, they glared reproachfully at us, through their ice prison, four solid blocks of it, resembling some beautiful modern sculpture - or a hundred glass paperweights compressed into one.

We had time to borrow a pile of icepicks from the Savoy, some sacking on which we deposited the four blocks; and the party took on the appearance of a roomful of mad sculptors frenziedly attacking their prey. Icepick in one hand, a glass in the other, we hacked away far into the night, scattering headless crayfish and blood all over the floor.

When he could, Lars came to London. Sometimes David was in town - sometimes not. In the former case, introducing them seemed simpler than juggling. In those days, a small aeroplane could be hired at what cannot have been enormous cost, considering how frequently Lars did it. We hired one to go to the Grand National in 1948. It was a six-seater: David was in London and it seemed churlish not to ask him along. It was a very windy day: I was very sick indeed, and the plane was not equipped with sick bags. Lars retreated to the back seat with his form guide, as far away from me as he could manage. David took his place beside me and held out his hat, and my head, as I was sick into it. Through my miserable retching I was aware of a small inversion of values: no doubt as to which of the two of them could be relied upon *in extremis*.

It wasn't enough to tether me to earth. The next time we hired a plane to go to Paris for dinner (England was locked into the Stafford Cripps five shilling meal and horsemeat steaks at the Imperial couldn't compete with the Tour d'Argent) David was already there, visiting his mother, but I had told him I would be there for the night. On this occasion he turned up at our hotel and locked me in the ladies' lavatory in an attempt to stop me leaving for the airport for our return flight.

But the pattern was set, and enticing: never to be rejected. So, when Eric McIlree, an Australian car manufacturer - not a close friend of my youth, but an acquaintance of many years - turned up in London in quest of the insurance due him for an aeroplane he had had shot down from under him over Vietnam (the French troubles - not the later American ones), I was ready. The insurance money was to be collected in Paris; Eric had never been to Paris. He telephoned to know if David and I would go with him to show him around, in a plane he intended to hire for the trip. We were at a loose end (I can't remember many tied ends), and so within hours we were ready to go with Eric. We set him up with a girlfriend - a friend of mine living in Paris - his first night, and in eight days the four of us managed to spend the best part of the crashed plane.

It must have seemed worth it to Eric, for within months he reappeared in London, on the telephone again, leaving that day in yet another hired plane for another night in Paris. This time, Lars was in London; we had an hour in which to change our plans for the evening and meet Eric at the RAC Club where his chauffeur-driven limousine waited to drive us to Croydon. I had not had much time to explain to Lars exactly who Eric was; there wasn't much to explain. I had forgotten, if I had bothered to find out during our previous fairly bacchanalian week, how little we had in common: probably little more than an Australian passport. We found out much more on the drive to the airport. Eric sat between us. I had no chance to look at Lars. Eric regaled Lars with the account of our previous trip and the places we had been to, but was even more lyrical about the night ahead of us. He slapped my knee repeatedly in his excitement. This time he wanted to see all the sights - Les Folies-Bergères, the Lido, a trip on the Bateau Mouche - none of the *recherché* haunts David and I had led him to, enjoyable as they may have been. By the time we reached Croydon, we were worn out, and my knee was tender. Eric paid the driver, asked if he could wait with us in the car whilst he cleared airport papers for take-off, took his own bag into the Control Room with him, and left us staring dumbly after him.

'Can we stand it?' I asked Lars.

'Definitely not,' he said. Our bags were still in the car. We instructed the driver to turn round quickly and drive us straight back to London. I never saw Eric again, and I don't suppose he forgave us; nor can I see why he should have done.

Flying trips to Paris must have been our instinctive and most easily accessible response to the restraints still in force in post-war England. No one, in those days, thought of a quick trip to Amsterdam, Geneva, Brussels and certainly not the vast adventure of the Stratocruiser to the US. David occasionally went without me en route to visit his mother, now living in the south of France, and on these occasions I would try to meet him in Paris on his return trip. I had booked one such trip to coincide with Lars's return to Göteborg after he had been in London for a few days.

On the morning of Lars's departure, several dozen majestic red roses were delivered to me, with his loving note. I had time only to jam them into a bucket, still in their cellophane wrapping, before driving with Lars to the British Airways terminal at Victoria. Then, no one drove to the airport: passengers bussed to Northolt Airdrome from Victoria. We sat, holding hands and weeping, side by side in the departure hall, waiting for his flight to be called. Farewells being an emotional business, Lars tenderly told me to go home rather than endure painful moments of waiting. I went, thankfully, as I had not much time to pack and go back to the terminal in order to catch my own flight to Paris.

It seemed a shame to leave the roses. I had never had such a magnificent bouquet in my life. I grabbed them as I left the apartment, dried my tears, patched up my smudged mascara and caught a taxi to Victoria. There I was to meet a friend booked on the same flight and who had invited David and me to spend the night in her apartment in Paris.

Lars was sitting where I had left him. He saw the roses first, my transformed and happy face next. I returned to my seat beside him. His flight was finally cancelled, just as mine was called.

At the check-in desk, a frantic Frenchman was pleading with the ticket clerk to get him on to the fully booked Paris flight. In those days, I think there was only one a day. His wife was having a baby – now, that very minute. He had to be on that plane. I thrust my ticket into his hands, the roses into the arms of my puzzled friend, introduced them and asked her to explain to David when he met the flight that I had been unavoidably detained.

Some time the following year Lars got a divorce. I was told that, Swedish fashion, I was officially named as the reason. I gathered it was rather like a job application when asked for references – you filled in a form, paid your fee, and got your freedom – but I fear my lack of general seriousness did not recommend me for stable relationships. Ties were loosening between us; and simultaneously . . . four years of pressure from David's mother and the censure from some members of her side of the family were beginning to take their toll. I was considered not only a femme fatale but from Australia to boot. I never met my critics; his father's relations, the Mountbattens, remained charming and friendly, from the time I had first spent a weekend visit to them – a weekend notable for the fact that not a single fish was caught in one of the most famous stretches of trout river in southern England. I had been lent a rod – tried my hand at it for the first time – and frightened every fish for miles around.

In order to prepare for the Royal wedding it was thought advisable that David move in with his grandmother, the granddaughter of Queen Victoria, at Kensington Palace. So we gave up the lease of our Chelsea flat and crept as silently as possible, on our nights together, up the back stairs of her apartment to David's room in the servants' attic. A concern was how he was to afford an appropriate wedding present to the bride and groom - soon to go on display. One night at a large dinner party I sat next to a businessman (name forgotten) who proudly told me he was manufacturing what, in 1947, was a most up-to-date and expensive record player - a Deccola! Until then, we had had gramophones; records did not slip automatically, one on top of the other. By the end of dinner I had procured, free for David, the very first off the production line and the manufacturer had procured valuable publicity as it went on prominent display.

The fact that I could not accompany him to the Royal Enclosure at Ascot (even had I wished to) was but a tiny indication of the pinpricks suffered by David. We were not to know of the vast, ironic turntable awaiting those standards; but I was also having a wonderful time and, although in love, found the world full of amusement - a state I had found sadly lacking in marriage. But we had five happy years of love, fun, and friendship; a friendship which lasted until David's death. My first marriage was by now happily forgotten, its consequences lingering, but life has also been lived long enough and well enough to recognise the blessings that fate has bestowed. Saved, in all probability, by the Pope and the antiquated Royal approval laws, respectively, from missing the joys to come later with my second marriage. David, understandably and very suddenly, got married to someone else (through the mistaken idea that she was very rich), leaving me with his dog, his car and, just as we had parted in Australia years before, both of us in tears: he, sitting on my bed on the morning of his departure, having delivered both.

Shortly after drying mine I met Stanley Haynes. That liaison lasted for four years until I was to meet my husband, through him finally grow up, and look back with amazement at the creature of those years. Perhaps this is one of the things that growing up means. I cannot feel any shame or guilt at my behaviour, partly because I cannot believe that the creature was me. I am also incredibly glad that I felt none at the time, and was therefore able to enjoy life to the full without a thought to the future. I don't think I hurt anyone much and my chief regret is that I made nothing of any of the opportunities offered me to concentrate on a direction in life.

But as four years of that other life were spent with Stanley, some residue of enrichment must remain, however traumatic its termination. Stanley was a writer/film producer of self-taught erudition and culture and through him I regained something of the influences of my childhood with my grandmother. He taught me to listen to music – to need music. Before him, I had existed without it except for Chula's concerts and the occasional opera outing. He was one of the five men who had formed Cineguild, a unique grouping of complementary talents responsible for some of the better films of the 1940s in England – David Lean, Eric Ambler, Ronald Neame, Anthony Havelock-Allen, and Stanley – between them writing, directing or producing. Stanley wrote and produced with David, *Oliver Twist*, *Great Expectations*, *Madeleine*, *The Passionate Friends*. I was to become his fourth wife – something which horrified my grandmother but which my parents took in their stride – I suspect by this time relieved that I was about to settle down with someone – anyone – within reason. Over the four years, I hesitated, as I detected an inkling of why the last three marriages had not survived – largely to do with Stanley's moods, depressions and, in my case, jealousy. Admittedly, the last with just cause. David had discovered the error of his marriage quite rapidly and we had resumed our relationship on his visits to London from New York where he was now living.

Stanley was in Fiji making a film when I met the man I was to marry, at someone else's engagement party. The hostess, Rada Penfold-Hyland, an Australian friend of my youth, took my hand and drew me across the room to a young man standing on his own.

'I want you two to meet,' she said, 'because you are the two nicest people I know.'

I had certainly done nothing to deserve that but she was right about Emmet. We spent the next two hours talking together, and when the friends with whom I had arrived beckoned me away for dinner I knew I had met an exceptional soul and I also knew that we were in some way inextricably linked – by past lives, present life, or future lives I didn't know, but after our meeting, in brief fleeting flashes his image would come, unbidden.

Apart from the journalism, and the film PR, over the years I had continued to earn very small and spasmodic sums of money in a very desultory way: the incipient careers nipped in the bud either by the attractions of a man, or a journey – the two usually combined. Having exhausted the possibilities of Scandinavia, I had fallen upon the Rahvis sisters.

Rae and Dora Rahvis were larger-than-life sisters who cut a flamboyant swathe through London's fashion world. They operated from a large and elegant house in Upper Grosvenor Street. Rae lived on the top floor with workrooms below; mirrored and chandelier-decked salon on the grand first floor; and, as a new venture, a boutique ready-to-wear department on the ground floor.

I had a friend, Diana Strathcarron, who had been asked to manage this boutique. She enlisted me as her partner, neither of us knowing anything about salesmanship, the sewing on of a button or the shortening of a hem, but both in possession of a useful address book. We did well. Enjoyment was provided by frequent trips upstairs where we were privy to the spectacular rows between Dora, Rae, the seamstresses, and quite frequently the clients. It was great fun.

I was expecting Stanley to be in Fiji for several months but the thought of any other romantic attachment did not occur (except for a very brief encounter with the one-legged American cartoonist, Al Capp). Only those odd flashes of memory of the young man with whom I'd spent two hours. Sitting in the dentist's chair one day, mouth agape, my dentist, both Australian and a fund of gossip, said, 'You met that young Irish doctor of Rada's, Emmet Dalton? He has consulting rooms downstairs - such a splendid chap, and he's just discovered he has a potentially fatal heart condition - probably not long to live. He only found out when he went for a medical for National Service call-up.' Bruce went back to his drill and probe; my heart plummeted. As the tooth was filled, I discovered more: Emmet had a rare heart deformity - a subaortic stenosis; heart surgery was in its infancy. Perhaps it would improve in time to save him - perhaps not. I thought about him intermittently over the next six months, but short of an attack of toothache, there was no way I could monitor his progress.

At the end of six months, Rada asked me to her wedding party. Stanley was still in Fiji. I did not particularly want to go, but wondering if I might meet the doctor again, I went, arriving early, eyes constantly on the door. He wasn't there and my disappointment was intense. An old lover, Dick Austin, was and so, having agreed to dine with him, and said our goodbyes, we headed for the front door. As it opened for us, Emmet walked in. I learnt later that he had not wanted to come either but he hurried through his last patient and made the effort in case I should be there. Two minutes later and both our lives would have been different. I asked Dick to wait a few minutes: Emmet and I stood just inside the hallway - no time for preliminaries: he asked me to dine. No time to risk there being no second chance: I asked him to come to dinner with me the following night.

chapter eleven

I had settled into my first permanent home, no longer rented, but bought, decorated and furnished by myself – a lovely and romantic attic apartment in Mount Street looking down Berkeley Square: up ninety-two stairs. An added bonus was that Bill Gustav, the manager of the adjacent Connaught Hotel, kept a maid's attic bedroom permanently available for me on the nights (more than once) when I arrived home without a doorkey. The stairs could not have helped Emmet's heart condition but, if it seriously worried him, he hid this from me. He was quietly spoken, handsome and intelligent, but inexperienced in what till then had been 'my' world of travel, and parties, and international 'society'. I, although unaware of it, was inexperienced in the 'real' world. Not so much inexperienced as unthinking. I had certainly encountered cruelty and kindness, good and evil, life and death, strength and weakness, purpose and aimlessness, but I had not given them more than a passing nod of acquaintance as I had flitted through life, accepting opportunity. Here was a young man who not only recognised but lived with them all, choosing the positive side of life's coinage – he was kind, wise, full of purpose, and was not afraid to confront life or his probable early death. Above all he was good, and strong, and by some miracle chance – or

'The way we were' – the 1930s – with Snow Swift.

A lamb to the slaughter: wedding to John Spencer, 8 October 1940.

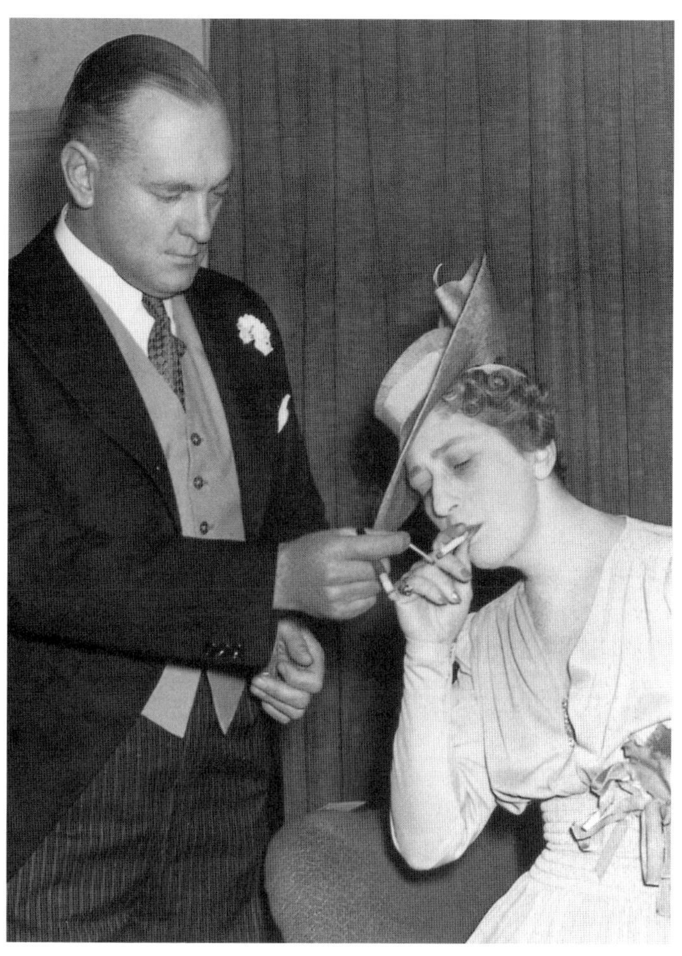

My mother and father, steeling themselves for the wedding, October 1940.

With David Milford Haven, Sydney in wartime, 1945.

George Silk has tracked me down in England, November 1946.

London, 1946 – sent home to Grandmother and Great Aunt to prove I had arrived!

With David at La Reserve at Beaulieu, 1946. Clothes rationing did not run to swimsuits – I am wearing brassiere and briefs!

'The way we were' – the 1940s – with David, Victoria and Richard Patrick, taken by Baron. What kept the hats on?

With Jean Nichol and Sir Alan Herbert at Sir Toby Milbanke's Thames River Party, 1947.

With Lars Schmidt and Peter Ustinov, London, 1947 – skol!

perhaps upbringing harking back to memories of a role model in my grandfather, Sammie - I recognised this. I discovered that it is possible to grow up suddenly - to burst into adulthood - if you meet a twin soul whose strength beckons you into maturity.

He came to dinner. He had never been asked to dine by a girl. He still lived with his parents. He was a devout Catholic and like many young Irishmen had considered the priesthood before medicine. He was twenty-eight years old. He was also, I was later to learn, a wonderful doctor.

That first night we talked for hours. There was never a doubt in his mind that somehow we were to marry but the struggle with his religious beliefs and his aghast parents was a fierce one. For my part, I was content to wake up in the mornings and, with a silly grin on my face, hug myself with incredulous joy, repeating aloud to the empty room, 'He's so *good*! He's so *good*!' If this makes Emmet sound dull, pious or precious, it is my paucity of words. He had tremendous humour and tremendous understanding and love for people.

He tried to convince his parents that he was doing what he believed to be the right thing as well as being what he wanted in life. He spent hours with the priest at Farm Street, with Monsignor Cashman, the Papal Nuncio in London, trying to find ways in which we could be married in his Church. I offered to become a Catholic but he would not hear of it. It did not occur to me to wish John Spencer, the obstacle to a church wedding, dead; and we both rejected as spurious the possibility of applying for an annulment of my brief marriage. We were both conscious of time passing; of the precariousness of Emmet's future; of the probable years it might take to procure such an annulment and of the falsity of what securing it would entail. I would have had to declare my intention never to have children with John Spencer, and perhaps even ask him to co-operate in such a declaration. Fat chance.

While Emmet was struggling with his priests and his parents, I busied myself with the practical consideration of where we would live. I hated leaving my chic apartment but it made sense, along with turning our backs on the stairs, to find a house where Emmet could also run his medical practice. We had just settled on an intriguing tall sliver of a house behind what is now the Hilton Hotel - the narrowest frontage in London of just enough width for the entrance on ground level and one window above the front door for each of the rooms above, widening to normal proportions at the rear mews - when chance dumped a package in our laps.

Diana and David Strathcarron were also looking for more space and had found an imposing end of terrace house in Albion Street, overlooking the north side of Hyde Park. The area had become the happy hunting ground of prostitutes during the war and the Church Commissioners, who were the freeholders, were looking for respectable tenants to bring the area back into its earlier repute. The houses, four storeys high, formed a perfect late Regency terrace and the recessed doorways and basement steps formed a perfect backdrop for vertical sex. Every morning almost every doorway was littered with discarded condoms. The interiors had not been architecturally tampered with. The Commissioners hoped to attract respectable tenants who would both redecorate the interiors and sweep the ladies off the doorsteps. Competition was high - rents were low - the priority of the landlords being desirability of lessees.

Diana had managed to get them top of the list, as a Lord would have been a great kick-off to set the tone for the rest of the street. Sadly, this particular Lord was having a temporary cash flow problem and so they reluctantly decided they couldn't afford the house but passed it on to us. No title but a solid professional occupation. I was on the Commissioners' doorstep before the doors opened the following morning and we won the twenty-six-year lease on the understanding that we would take on both the restoration of the house and the banishment of the ladies.

I said goodbye to the jolly Rahvis sisters and my jolly job and five months after our meeting at Rada's wedding Emmet and I were married. Religious prejudices overshadowed our wedding as they had overshadowed the wedding of my parents, and my husband left home and his weeping Catholic mother and unspeaking Catholic father at 9 a.m. one morning to meet his divorced Presbyterian future wife at Caxton Hall. Baron gave me away. An American friend, Blevins Davis, lent us his new Rolls-Royce for our wedding journey, along with his chauffeur fresh from the Queen's employment, and therefore a flourishing English feather for an American cap.

Chula and Lisba had asked us to spend our brief weekend honeymoon with them in Cornwall, and so we set off for three days in which two events occurred which were to influence the next five years of my life, as well as changing it forever. First, we were convinced our daughter Lisa was conceived in Cornwall on our wedding night. Then, the next day Chula put to Emmet a question which started me on the road to being, for want of a more exact terminology, a Thai spy. A pregnant Thai spy. 'Would you object to Robin having a job?' was the question.

Chula's request was occasioned by an approach to him from his own Government for advice. Public relations had never been a particular concern of the Thai Embassy and therefore there had never been the post of Press Attaché. But now some Thai newspapers were printing garbled versions of reports carried by responsible English newspapers which emphasised the poverty of the north-east province of Thailand. This poverty was actually relative, exaggerated, and localised; but the reports carried with them editorial comments stressing that the English, supposed friends and allies, wrote disparagingly of the poverty and primitive conditions of Thailand, and the inefficiency and corruption of the Thai Government. The inference was: 'Look! These are our friends and see what they print about us in their leading newspapers.'

Fodder for Communist propaganda, then a tiny stirring in Thailand and taken seriously only by a few, Chula amongst them. Champagne communists amid the western-educated upper-class intellectuals were a breed which in those days, in South-East Asia in the 1950s, seemed far-fetched indeed. The stories were gathered by reputable English journalists in the bars and at the cocktail parties of the grander hotels and embassies, and printed in good faith in the more serious English newspapers. Not one of these newspaper men in Bangkok spoke Thai to my knowledge, and very few of them had close Thai friends except amongst the old Oxbridge, Etonian, Harrovian Thais whom they met at the smart international gatherings. What was needed was someone to influence the British press Lords at a fairly high level, and so the Government came to Chula. Intensely practical, he saw that a Thai national would never understand the British press mentality sufficiently; that few English people both knew enough high-ranking British journalists or newspaper proprietors, or knew enough of the Thai nature; but, if such a person could be found who fulfilled these two qualifications and was not even English, so much the better.

There I was; it seemed to him an inspired chance. I was Australian: I was not tainted with preconceived prejudice. Or precious little knowledge. I had just married an Irishman, a national of a country who would understand the plight of another small country (this he told me later). Of course, I said 'yes' at once. At first I thought only of lovely tax-free wine and minor diplomatic privileges, with no intimation that this was the beginning of a five-year love affair with Thailand and the

Thai people, to end only with the death of my husband and the almost simultaneous defection of my immediate boss, General Phao, with £3 million of the country's money, to Geneva (where he eventually shot himself).

I was allowed to work from home, sharing Emmet's secretary and only occasionally going in to the Embassy in Ashburn Place. I already knew Prince Wongsa, the Ambassador, and his wife, aunt of the young Queen, who was later to open the first Thai restaurant in Bangkok. (I rather think this may have been the first in the world.)

To begin with I, carefully tutored by Chula, wrote earnest letters to the *Times* and the *Guardian*; met with south-east Asian experts on the *Economist* and the like in the cheery belief that I too seemed expert. I was assumed by them to be so, I imagine, or I must have seemed an odd choice to these learned chaps, especially as I became increasingly and obviously pregnant. But my borrowed view was an inside one, an infinitely wise one, a Royal one tinged with the history and culture of the Thai people, not gleaned in the bar of the Oriental Hotel by all the stringers of the papers who knew the political personages and were self-appointed experts.

With hindsight I wonder which was the true view, and how valid and objective such truths can ever be. I believed in the basic innocence of the people. Now, over forty years later, I learn from one of these bar-room specialists that my lovable General Phao, my genial boss, was chief of the entire opium trade, with a few minor businesses like prostitution on the side. This, though, still emerges from the memory of his benign despotism as a sort of innocence; or at least a naïveté, his as well as mine. Three million pounds and the *entire* opium trade can never be termed petty corruption, and it was this corruption which he loudly disclaimed on behalf of himself and the Cabinet, while pressing crisp hundred-dollar bills into my palm whenever we met.

He was a big man. Not only for a Thai, but by any standards; with a smiling face and shining white hair, and an outgoing manner. We first met in London when I had officially been Press Officer at the Thai Embassy in London for over a year. On that occasion, he came with Chula and Lisba to lunch, and invited me and Emmet to Thailand. Our daughter was eleven months old when we left, in separate aeroplanes, which caution I suspect was the seed of my ever-after fear of flying.

General Phao was not only Chief of Police - the most powerful post in the country - but Deputy Prime Minister, Chief of Intelligence and, rather conveniently, Finance Minister. In Bangkok, we were met both by emissaries of the Government and family retainers of Chula. We stayed in Chula's house - called a palace, but in reality a large, cool and comfortable villa by the river with a waterside pavilion. We slept under vast, tented mosquito nets and, before air-conditioning, were wafted off to sleep by the gentle whirr of the ceiling punkahs. In the mornings, the smiling servants wheeled in a trolley of exquisite exotic fruits to my bedside, followed by my personal contact, General Phao's aide-de-camp Lieutenant Thana, with a list of the day's appointments.

General Phao and I got on exceedingly well together. The Prime Minister, Pibul, in addition to not being my immediate boss, had a less sunny and outgoing personality. Whilst the pattern of my work brought me closer to Phao, protocol linked me with Pibul whenever he was in England or I was in Thailand and, in addition to the formal audiences over small cups of tea or coffee, there were official farewells on leave-taking. These were the occasions for a clasped handshake, after the traditional Thai greeting of palms pressed together in prayer-like salute. The handshakes were the opportunity for Pibul to pass over his own fistful of dollars, as distinct from Phao's. I never was able to count them until safely in private, and I never was able to thank him, as thanks are considered bad form by the Thais. The pleasure is, rightly, in the giving. In our case, there was considerable pleasure in the receiving, and puzzlement as to the exact nature of the gift. Was it a gift, or payment? I was paid, although not very much, by the London Embassy, and the amounts in cash were not only arbitrary in their varying size but spasmodic in occurrence. Once an ADC murmured, as I left Pibul, something about my expenses, and so, to my conscience, expenses they became. Payment would have made me uneasy in the face of the taxation authorities; a gift, unacknowledged, uneasy in the face of my western upbringing.

We saw Thailand under perfect conditions. It was the cool season. We lived in the most comfortable house in Bangkok. We ate the most delicious food imaginable. In those days, indigenous Thai restaurants were virtually unknown: Thai cooking was done by Thai servants in private houses. If you wished to go to a restaurant the cook was Chinese, undeniably good Chinese, but not authentic Thai. As we seldom went to a restaurant, our various hosts vied with each other in providing banquets, but the best cook of all was Chula's.

We spent a week at Chula's seaside residence at Hua-Hin – I terrified of the spiders and Emmet of the snakes. The spiders, the size of small crabs in fur coats, scuttled across the floor, burrowed their way under our mosquito net, and went into battle formation. We crouched on the bed trying to count their legs. Seven legs were relatively harmless – eight meant instant death. I may have forgotten the exact numbers but not the panic of trying to count. The snakes were chiefly in Emmet's imagination, nightmares, and occasioned by visits to the Snake Farm coupled with folk memory of Saint Patrick.

The Prime Minister, General Phao, and the Members of the Cabinet held a splendid dinner party in my honour in Manan Kasila House, the Thai equivalent of London's Lancaster House – Emmet and I the only outsiders present. In Thailand I felt like a large white slug amidst the fluttering, exquisite Thai women and my voice boomed loud and coarse in my ears, particularly as no one else spoke at dinner, not one of the seventeen other females. We arrived to a battery of arc lights and popping bulbs and an army of photographers, all of whom disappeared about halfway through dinner. At the end, we were ushered through a courtyard into a private theatre where the Royal Thai Ballet performed a ballet. The music was played on the ancient classical Thai instruments and the dancers posed and undulated in their superb costumes singing what were to me then incomprehensible sounds. Unmistakably, however, I heard 'Mrs Robin Da-a-a-al*tun*'. The beaming faces of my hosts confirmed it. The music and the song, like the ballet, had been composed for me: the words were presented to me on a printed sheet, and when translated read: 'Oh, Mrs Robin Dalton The Intelligent One, We salute you'. At that moment I knew that as soon as I could I must learn to speak Thai.

Interval and coffee, and the lights went out again, a screen came down, and I discovered where all the photographers had gone midway through dinner. They had gone to a darkroom and some few hours later I saw the film of our arrival at the dinner. The Prime Minister, General Pibul, asked if there was anything else I would like, so I asked if the song could be recorded for me. I had my record two days later and on the flip side Thai boxing music - a wonderfully stirring rhythm to which the contestants bash each other to bits, having first prayed that they may do just that. I have the record and the film - one scratched and the other battered - or I would not be believed, or myself believe, that these things had ever happened to me.

Although everything we saw was presented under the best possible conditions, this is not to say that they were false conditions. To visit the River Market or the Temple at Ayudhya up river, although the sights were the same, I had my own police launch to transport me. The temples were visited in the cool of the day with few other sightseers. When we visited the Self Help Settlements of which the Government was justly proud, our guide was the Director General of the Region, and a former Miss Thailand showed us round a northern jungle village. We had the best ringside seats at the Thai boxing match and we were helped onto the broad backs of the gentlest elephants. I asked if we might visit Chiengmai (then long before any tourists had heard of it), on the northern border of the Shan states, by train, so that we might see something of the country. I did not realise that this simple request would result in my own train, but by the next day I had my private train, searchlights mounted on the roof, with my very own guard of honour to farewell us and my personal bodyguard of thirty soldiers, armed with Tommy guns. I remember I gave the American Ambassador, Jack Pueri-foy, a lift - probably putting a curse on the poor man, who was killed in a road accident the following week. In Chiengmai we stayed in a newly built palatial villa owned by the richest Chinese merchant in the Province (opium, I expect), and my thirty soldiers paraded up and down outside my windows.

The Mayor was to give a dinner party in my honour on the night of our arrival. I arrived feeling distinctly ill; the doctor from the local hospital came and dysentery was diagnosed. After a week, I was well enough to get up but Emmet had to return to England, and our old friend Steven Runciman flew out to spend the remainder of the trip with me.

The Mayor's dinner party at which I had never appeared became a farewell luncheon instead. We were twelve at table, Steven and I being the only Europeans, and the place on my right was reserved for Dr Rabieb, who had looked after me so well during my week in bed. The Mayor explained that he was always very busy at his hospital and that we must excuse him if he was a little late. Soon, however, the doctor arrived and, smiling and bowing, we all exchanged greetings, heads turning politely and attentively to listen.

'And, Mrs Dalton, how are you?'

'Much better, thank you.'

'And your motions - how are *they*?'

'They are very well too.'

Many smiles and approving nods around the table . . . 'And your period - has it come yet?'

An almost audible sigh of satisfaction greeted my answer that it had indeed, with no mishap. I did not dare, however, glance at Steven.

We flew back to Bangkok in an aeroplane rattling with decrepitude and landed at Ayudhya in stifling heat to offload one passenger with a small briefcase and take on another two with many large cases and a dog in a crate. We stood panting under the wing as these two argued in increasing fury with the pilot. The shouts and curses and shaking fists eventually abated and the troupe climbed aboard amid shrugs from the crew.

'What was the problem?' I asked a neighbour as we settled for take-off.

'The pilot did not want to take them, as we are already very overweight,' I was told.

I flew back to England from Bangkok but not before General Phao had extracted from me a promise to return in six weeks in order to organise press and public relations for the first SEATO conference in 1955. Meticulously correct, he had already telephoned Emmet in London for his permission. So I had six weeks in which to be reunited with our baby daughter before flying out again.

Eden was then Prime Minister, representing Great Britain. Although most of my time was taken up with entertaining, on dance floors and bars, the foreign press, I had occasion to chat with the delegates and assess their degree of satisfaction with the arrangements, seating and sleeping. General Phao's attention to detail, passed on to his subordinates, equalled that of a great hostess or the most meticulously trained butler. A fresh toothbrush and a selection of toothpastes awaited each of his political guests, clean pyjamas were laid out in each room in case they had been forgotten, and, of course, a selection of beautiful gifts - boxed silver cufflinks, exquisite fans and, for the few women or the wives back home, a length or two of superb Thai silk without which no Thai visitor ever left. Eden did not appear to be a man ever to forget his toothbrush or his pyjamas and I did not dare voice more than a general query as to his comfort.

chapter twelve

All through the years of working for the Thai Government, and revelling in the experience of motherhood, I had the joy of seeing Emmet build a reputation for being the wonderful doctor he was and, not unlike my childhood experience with my father, share in some part of his professional life. We had had time to enjoy our beautiful house, clean the girls off the front steps, and engage the precursor of a series of servants whose eccentricities were to mimic, but never to surpass, those of my parents' household.

Diary never kept after the disastrous publication of my teenage romanticisms I nevertheless started, upon marriage, to keep a menu book – far more useful. Not only can I remember the guests but the food and the wine (a sharp pang of regret when I contemplate the wine). Still limited by rationing – clothing and petrol had slid off first. Eggs, butter and cream followed. Not until 1954 were we able to discard the black-market butcher and the horsemeat steaks in French restaurants. During clothes rationing, Great Aunt Juliet's heavy tasselled and fringed white linen guest towels had been blithely chopped up to provide nappies for Barbara and Alan Sharp's new baby, and I marked in the book the celebratory fillet steak on the night meat came off the ration.

We had celebrated our first week in the house by acquiring a married couple, Mr and Mrs Hawkins, as butler and cook, who we were to discover, almost immediately, fitted into the pattern of married couples as staff, recognised - but not soon enough by us - universally. A bad egg almost always shares a nest with a good egg.

On their first night in attendance, Mrs Hawkins cooked us an impressive dinner. Hawkins was impressive in every respect. Resplendent in white jacket and gloves, he held out my chair in the candlelit dining room, silver gleaming, fire softly glowing, napkins stiffly awaiting, wine impeccably poured. We left the house walking on air, preceded by Hawkins, car door opened with a bow and a flourish. On our arrival home, Hawkins, who must have had his nose pressed to the window, flew out the front door and, with another bow and another flourish, ushered us inside. What bliss to find curtains drawn, lights lit, bed turned down, night attire waisted and reposing invitingly on our bed.

The following night we went into dinner with happy anticipation. Candles were still lit. The wine splashed a little. The dinner was fine, Hawkins not quite so solicitous and something amiss with his tie. Halfway through the second course, a tieless and jacketless figure lurched through the door.

'Mrs H says,' it bellowed at us, somewhat belligerently, 'do you want any more veg?'

The next morning, as I dried Mrs H's tears and studiously ignored the snores coming from their bedroom, I learned we were not the first of their employers to have enjoyed such a brief period of euphoria. Mr H was the bad egg. They left that day, Mrs H in tears, Mr H shouting abuse, kicking aside the empty bottles - ours - cluttering their bedroom floor.

Shortly after this, by whatever telephonic grapevine I have forgotten, I managed to trace splendid, funny and fondly remembered Nancy - mad, Scottish Nancy - who in my parents' house had so memorably lightened my Australian youth and had given my father such magnificent excuses for tease. She was thrilled to hear from me - caught the train from Scotland at once (it did not occur to me to question the oddity of her, the perfect servant, being so immediately available) and re-entered my life. The house sparkled. I was cosseted. Emmet's suits were pressed and his shoes shone. Telephones were answered. Bliss again.

One day Nancy appeared blushing furiously and near to tears. She thrust a package into my hands. It had come through the post, addressed to her. Inside was a condom - used. We had just managed to clear most of them, along with the girls, off our front steps in the mornings, so it could not have been the first Nancy had ever seen, but this one had been directed, addressed, aimed at her. The nice Police Inspector who came at our request gently questioned Nancy in Emmet's surgery: was it possible that she had any local acquaintance who could have done such a dastardly deed? Nancy blushed more furiously and rushed from the room. I felt dreadfully for her and was about to follow and comfort when I saw the policeman and my husband exchange looks.

'Do you agree with me, doctor?'

''Fraid so,' said Emmet, 'but thank you very much for coming.'

Patiently, he explained to me that he and the police officer had come to the same conclusion: Nancy had posted it to herself, having first scooped it up with the early morning's cleaning.

Nancy's psychosis (for such it was) escalated with alarming rapidity, triggered by my first confinement. Whilst I was in hospital giving birth, Nancy sang around the house and took to wearing lipstick. On my return, she was as caring as ever, keeping me in bed for several days and pampering me with meals on trays. When I got up to dress for the first time, I discovered the shelf on which I kept my underwear empty.

'How sweet of Nancy,' I thought, 'and how unnecessary. She has washed *all* my underclothes.'

But no, Nancy's blank incomprehension mirrored the blank shelves. I had nothing to wear.

Emmet began to ask me what I had done with *his* underpants.

We had an old-fashioned coke boiler in our basement. Brassiere straps and scraps of linen were amongst the debris he discovered in the embers one morning. Mine. His, however, were discovered, unwashed, under Nancy's pillow.

We were driven to the lengths of bed-searching by a chance entry by Emmet into her bedroom. Lamps were disconnected and shoved under the bed. Looking glasses were pasted over with newspaper.

It was evident that Nancy thought evil rays were directed at her through lamp and mirror. A classic symptom, it seemed. But she was wonderful with the baby. And wonderful as always in every other way. A harmless lunacy seemed a small price to pay. Underwear was reasonably expendable.

Sadly, it came to an abrupt end the day she told our daily that I was trying to poison the baby. Next step, Emmet told me, would be that *she* would poison the baby. By that night, all of us in tears, Nancy was packed off to a nursing home, protesting and furious, but safe. All of us.

The Hawkins, and then Nancy, were to prove the first indication that I, like my mother, would attract eccentric servants. Nancy had never seemed unusual to me in the company of the servants of my childhood, all of them delightfully dotty.

My father, too, helped to make me feel nothing had changed since my childhood. During that year, when we lived each day to the full and Emmet grew tired more than he should have done, my father came over from Australia and stayed with us for five months, leaving shortly after my son's birth. He had never been to England before; it was lovely having him and to our delight, following trepidation, he got on splendidly with Emmet's family. Neither religion nor Ulster versus Eire were mentioned. He also managed to set fire to his bed, his curtains and therefore the house one memorable morning having tossed a lighted cigarette over his shoulder whilst in bed. I, heavily pregnant and alerted by the smell of smoke, found him in the basement, hands badly blistered from beating out the flames in the blackened room. 'Don't tell Emmet, kid,' he said, attempting to bandage his blistered palms.

All my old friends appreciated Emmet in their different ways: Steven with enormous, parent-like approval, having first met him at my bedside. Some friends were coming for drinks; I developed some infection; being bedridden didn't seem a valid reason to cancel. Steven telephoned the following morning: 'Robin, that was the most improbable party I have ever attended and *that* was the most improbable doctor.' Emmet became Steven's doctor almost immediately. Vi appreciated him a bit reluctantly at first because he didn't play cards, Wolf even more reluctantly because he had lost a part of my life, and my closest old homosexual friend, Arthur Jeffris, with envy[13]. Arthur, host extraordinary both in London and his Venice palazzo where I had spent a sybaritic summer or two, was aghast when he first met Emmet to realise he was lost to the feminine world. 'Oh, God,' said Arthur, 'if only I could dress him in a sailor suit and teach him to speak with a Cockney accent . . .'

chapter thirteen

My second pregnancy had coincided with stage two of the crash course in the Thai language bravely begun at the School of Oriental and African Studies at London University. The bravery was not on my part but on the part of the university, and above all, our teacher. Hardly anybody spoke Thai in London in those days and I think Stuart Symmonds was the only person who taught it. He had devised his method whilst in prison camp during the war, perfected it on his fellow prisoners, and was now facing his first five pupils at the university.

I was the only female in our ill-assorted group, and became glaringly more so as the weeks went by. My companions included Victor Sassoon, who wanted to learn Thai in order to live in Bangkok and teach English at the university there, and a Scottish missionary who was being sent by his Wesleyan ministry to the lovely hill villages of the beautiful Shan states borders to convert the happy peasants from their satisfying Buddhism to a dour Scots guilt. As no one in our class could understand what he was saying in English we were unable to gauge his progress in Thai. There was a car salesman from the Midlands who was being sent into the jungle to sell Land Rovers - presumably to replace elephants; and I have forgotten the fifth.

A small dusty room had been allocated to us in a narrow house in Torrington Square. After signing in at the main office of the university, we had no more contact with anyone except our group, locked together in our little world of *Ooos* and *Aeees* and squealing grunts. Once we had learnt to make the sounds to the symbols of the twenty-six consonants and the thirteen and a *half* (thirteen and a *half* will give an idea of the complexity) vowels, we left stage one. The system Stuart had devised was then, in 1956, a tremendous innovation. In order to teach us a totally new concept of language, in terms of alphabet and sounds, we had first to unlearn our own. We learnt phonetically, as children learn their first language, mouthing sounds to coincide with symbols on a blackboard. The sounds, coming from our assorted throats, were fairly horrid, but the symbols, written on the board and then into our notebooks, were beautiful. I loved the flowing symmetry of them. In the afternoons we listened to tapes and at night we did our homework and enlarged our vocabularies. My stomach grew in tandem with my stock of Thai words, and I am fairly sure that I was the only pregnant student at London University.

When the course finished and the other four dispersed to their various jobs, I continued with daily lessons at home from the wife of the First Secretary at the Embassy. My small red exercise book now looks both beautiful and bewildering to me – the Thai characters beautiful, their meaning obscure. I have written the English translation beneath each line and am fascinated by the strange phrases on which I concentrated: I expect the car salesman's efforts revolved around carburettors and spark plugs, miles per gallon and four-wheel drive, whilst I was laboriously searching for the tactful translation of 'coup d'état'.

ภายในปีหน้า ดังที่มลายู ต้องการ หรือเปล่า หากมลายู
Next year such as Malaya wants or not. If Malaya
เป็น เอกราชสมบูรณ์แล้วและ แม้ จะ สมัครใจ เป็น
is to be completely independent & if (she) will willingly be a
ประเทศสมาชิกของ สหภาพอังกฤษ ต่อไปก็ตาม
member nation of the British Commonwealth later.
อังกฤษก็จะต้อง มอบ อำนาจทุกสิ่งทุกอย่าง ที่
English must then give every kind of authority which
ประเทศเอกราช พึงมี ให้ แก่ มลายู หมด ทั้ง
independent countries should have to Malaya, namely ~~Also~~
การปกครอง และ รักษา ความสงบภายใน การเศรษฐกิจ
Government & protection of the peace internally; finance;
การศาล การทหาร และ การทูต แต่ ข่าวจาก
judiciary; military; & diplomacy. But news from ~~that~~
ลอนดอน มิได้บอกว่า อังกฤษ จะ ยก อำนาจที่
London does not state whether England will give all ~~these~~
กล่าว~~วนี้~~ให้มลายู หมดทุกอย่าง
mentioned powers this time to Malaya.

powers to Malaya ~~at the present time~~.

Some months after I had graduated from SOAS, given birth to two children, and was established as a recognised feature at the Embassy, I was invited by the editor of a London daily newspaper for drinks to meet his good friend from the Foreign Office. He had been, my friend explained, in the south-east Asian section and stationed in Bangkok, which he had loved and sorely missed. He wanted an opportunity to talk over old times, old faces, old places, and, having heard about me, would love to meet me for just such a chat. Emmet and I went to drinks where, in a room containing no more than a dozen people, the chap from the Foreign Office managed to avoid me entirely. I thought it odd, however, that he appeared to spend all of his time with my husband. On the way home Emmet told me that on departure he had said how disappointed he'd been not to have had a chance to talk to me, and had, in fact, made such an issue of this that Emmet had invited him for a drink with us the following week. He felt he had somehow been pushed into it and had the distinct impression that Mr 'O' wished to see me alone.

Emmet obliged. He was busy with a patient and I poured drinks for our guest and waited for the mutual nostalgia. There was, however, no nostalgia and no preamble. The ice had barely been put in his drink when he broke his own ice and made his approach.

The Foreign Office, he told me, had had their eye on me for some time. They were extremely impressed by the extent to which I had infiltrated the Thai Cabinet and by the trust and regard in which General Phao, in particular, seemed to hold me. They were well aware that I was the only *farang* (foreigner) ever to have become close to General Phao, and they, the FO, would dearly love to take advantage of this. They needed a favour from the Thai Government - a favour which could not be requested through the normal diplomatic channels. I seemed the perfect - indeed the only - route through which they could operate.

Mr 'O' barely gulped a sip from his drink before elaborating. I had not read many spy thrillers but I had seen a lot of movies and it seemed to me that this particular scenario was straight out of the rejected script department of a motion picture company. There languished in a Thai gaol a man who had fought on the wrong side in the war (as Thailand hadn't fought at all, this confused me somewhat). The Thais did not want him there - he was, in fact, an embarrassment - but they also did not want him at liberty in Thailand. There was no conventional political excuse for the British Government to request his release, as he was a Thai national, but the British Government badly wanted him out. The man wanted to come to Britain. Names were mentioned - Pridi, the Thai wartime leader, now in exile; Lord Mountbatten, who seemingly also wanted his release very badly. Mr 'O' stopped just short of saying they were at school together. A British submarine would rendezvous by night at an arranged part of the coast and take him aboard. The British Government would privately give an undertaking that he would never be seen in Thailand again. My task would be to propose this scheme to General Phao and to Pibul, thus relieving everyone of any possible embarrassment, and, if approved, I would finalise the arrangements.

The story came to an end as abruptly as it had begun. He stared at me. I stared back - mouth, I expect, if not open, distinctly ajar. I realised that I had been asked a question: would I, or wouldn't I?

'I'll have to ask my husband,' I said.

Poor Mr 'O', I now realise, could not have been prepared for what was to me then a perfectly normal response. They had not bargained for a spy who had to ask her husband what to do. He put a very brave face on it, made an appointment to telephone me the next day, and extracted from me the promise that - apart from my husband - I would tell no one else of our conversation, of the man in the Thai gaol, or the hovering submarine. I did wonder briefly what would happen to them both, but after giving him my refusal next day put the incident, if not out of mind, at least in a far back pocket marked 'secret'.

The decision to refuse was quickly reached. 'Don't be ridiculous,' said Emmet. 'You can't work for two masters and you have a perfectly straightforward and above-board job with the Thai Government, who are friendly to Britain, and you cannot possibly muddy that by working for someone else.'

The puzzle resolved itself slowly. When I no longer worked for them, I told Chula one day. 'You did right,' he said. 'If you had approached General Phao that would have been the end of your job. He never would have trusted you again.' About the man in gaol and the Foreign Office he voiced no opinion; he was interested only in the personal relationship between me and my employers which could so easily have been wrecked.

A year or two later I ran across two old friends in the space of a few months. One, Dick Austin, had been First Secretary at the Australian Embassy in Tokyo at the time and had been asked by his Government, on behalf of the British Government, what, if anything, he knew of me. As we had had an intense romantic attachment some years previously, discretion wrestled with quite a fund of knowledge but curiosity was uppermost in his mind as to what I could possibly have been up to. Nothing he could have told them had, however, put them off their approach. I imagine he made me sound like a girl who did not have to ask her husband.

The other friend, Fergus MacCaddie, was the then Commander-in-Chief of Australian Military Forces in South-East Asia, stationed in Malaysia. Both of them were given bulky dossiers on me and my movements since I had come to England and were asked to fill in on my youth. The information they gleaned from my dossier saved me years of filling them in on gossip when I finally met them, individually, again.

Then, some ten years later, with Chula, General Phao and Emmet all dead, I was at a dinner party in London and seated next to a man currently working in the south-east Asian section of the Foreign Office. He had known Mr 'O', then retired. As conversation was flagging and over ten years seemed long enough to keep a secret – and, in a sense, it was his secret I was giving back into his safekeeping – I told him the tale and my opinion that the Foreign Office was incredibly clumsy. I could, I said, so easily have given the whole thing away and blown, metaphorically, the submarine right out of the water - the man condemned to imprisonment for ever.

He gazed at me with amazement that someone so naïve could ever have been seriously considered for any undertaking, however trivial. He told me the facts of espionage life. There had quite obviously never been a man in gaol, a submarine, or any wish that I should approach the Thai Government on any pretext. I was simply being vetted as a candidate for recruitment by the British, and on my answer depended their decision as to whether to take their approach one step further. I had been proven a dud. I have occasionally regretted it.

The final elementary lesson I learnt over lunch not long ago with an ex-MI5 officer, now retired, once also a friend of Chula's. I had continued to puzzle over the circuitous route by which Mr 'O' talked to me. We had been together at a party at his instigation and he had ignored me. Why had he concentrated on my husband at that first meeting? My old friend patiently explained that my background, home life, personal relationships and general financial stability were important factors. I had probably been photographed at the party. My husband and house had been scrutinised. I had passed all the tests except the final ones: I believed everything I was told; and I did everything my husband told me.

chapter fourteen

I was four months pregnant when my husband first became seriously ill, the first indication being coughing up blood. For four weeks they didn't think it was his damaged heart, but lung cancer. Lung cancer at thirty-two didn't seem fair or right, not when we'd accepted the heart deformity. The tests would tell, and while waiting I had only to weather the sympathetic predictions of Irish Mary, my daily.

'How's Doctor?' she would say, and one day, when we'd been told to wait another twenty-four hours for results, I said, 'I'm afraid he's very ill, Mary.'

'Oh, dear,' she said, 'isn't it always the same, Mrs Dalton? It's always the nice quiet ones who go first.'

The tests were negative and we had another year and a half in which Emmet was able to see his son born before we discovered it was his heart after all, and Mary was able to have her laments in company.

Memory's own selector button operates at random. Now, when I think of my husband's last night with me, it is a vivid picture I receive each time of shaving his back before his operation. And going back twice, memories through memories, I remember that while shaving him, that smooth, muscular and broad back, I remembered back to the night we had first loved each other. The fire in my bedroom was alight and when he undressed and walked away from me across the room I was surprised and pleased and somehow proud to see that same back, not fully suspected in its perfect symmetry and strength under his clothes. I had loved him already, but this physical beauty of body was an unexpected gift he had brought me which I had not needed. Now, in shaving him, I hated to scrape off the few downy hairs and I thrust from my mind the vision of the scar which would soon mar it. A scythe cutting his body in two. We chatted a little about practical things – money, who would help financially with me and the children if he should die, as we had never saved money. He said, 'I don't worry about you. If you have been able to live through the last five years with this constant dread hanging over you in the way you have, you will be able to cope with whatever life has to offer in the future.'

I held his hand, his strong, gentle hand. There really wasn't anything to say. Goodnight, perhaps. A message to his father, who had never fully come to terms with our marriage: 'Tell him I don't hold his attitude against him. I understand. I know he loves me. He can't help it.' I don't remember. The things I remember are his back when I shaved it; his words which entered my very blood like a transfusion of strength; his hand as I took it, so like my son's now. And then, when he had said goodnight, his back again as he walked away from me down the hospital corridor to the bathroom in the new blue dressing-gown his father had given him in advance for his birthday. It was the first of December: his birthday – his thirty-fourth – was not for another ten days but there might not be need for a present by that time. I had already bought, too, our daughter's Christmas present, her first tricycle, so that he could share in the buying of it and by Christmas, if he should be dead, the present would not be such a lonely one. Our son, at fourteen months, would not be aware of Christmas yet.

His sister slept in the house that night so that I should not be alone during the long, long hours of the operation in the morning. But, in the morning, I could not stay in the house and thought for something to do, somewhere to go, which would match the effort he was making and would bring me close to him in our joint wish to live. His God, in whom I had never fully nor consciously believed, was perhaps just a refuge in a vast world of concept where I could call on his beliefs, and perhaps because I was a part of him they would come to help me. I chose St James' Church in Spanish Place - not Emmet's church, nor one to which, to my knowledge, he had ever been. Perhaps I wanted it to be my own choice or perhaps it was because I could buy food for lunch in the high street around the corner. I don't remember the idea of the food, only that the children and their nanny and my sister-in-law were in the house and I must, through all this time, have been buying food and cooking it. I would not have neglected this necessity.

The church was not empty. There were a few housewives like myself, an old woman or two, dusty pale sunlight mingling with the candles, and two cleaning women with straw brooms. I sat on the edge of a pew, an intruder, borrowing my place, and I could not presume on the God, the force, the whatever great strength in which I did not believe, to intervene and interrupt the flow of anything so basic as Emmet's life or death because of my own puny needs. Also, perhaps there was some superstition, a feeling that it was tempting the benevolence of this fate to ask for something not in its power to bestow. No: I must ask for something which required an equal effort from me and which I myself could provide if nothing and no one came to help me. He was called God, this force in whom Emmet believed, so: 'Please God,' I prayed, 'give me the strength to bear whatever is in store for us. Just let me bear it.'

I stayed until the time came when the doctors had said they could telephone and then I went home. His sister came to the door: she was smiling. 'It's all right - he's all right - it's all over.' *Then* I cried - oh, how I cried; and dried my eyes and she patted my shoulders and we went upstairs and the telephone started to ring.

The nice young house doctor rang and said I might come to see him in the afternoon, although he would be in great pain and would not be very aware of my presence. 'But it helps,' he said. 'It helps, just if you sit and hold his hand.' Oh, why was I frightened. Now, when I remember that I was frightened, the thought is a sharp pain that I did not give him as much help as I might have done. His sister offered to come with me and I needed her. I had been warned of the oxygen tent in which I would find him, and the blood drip on one side and the tubes from his wound draining on the other side, and I was afraid to face it alone. Nobody had warned me of his pain - of how his face would look black and grey with pain and drained of all blood and the usual tints of flesh. I held his hand but all he could say to me, if indeed he knew it was me, was, 'Take away the pain - oh, please take away the pain.' The pain was between us; it made a mockery of his strength and struck him down to the level of ordinary men. It jeered at the bond between us which in full consciousness would have restored the personality of my husband to that black and grey face on the pillow. Every two minutes they took his pulse. The doctors had told me that if his pulse rate remained stable he could leave the oxygen tent in twenty-four hours and we could begin to look forward rather than back. During each two-minute interval hung our lives.

Then for years there was a blank - a long gap in my memory. Only now, as I write this, over the years of that blank, do I remember that Tam and Maggy Williams bundled me off to a celebratory dinner at the Ivy. We laughed and cried and joked and I was swept along by their love and the shared enjoyment of our lives - theirs, mine, Emmet's. Champagne has never seemed so effervescent. At lunchtime the next day his old doctor came with more champagne. We drank and celebrated and I think I cried a little more. I remember the chimneypiece and resting my head on my hand on it and sobbing, 'Oh, George, I love him so much.'

'I know you do, old girl - I know you do.'

But was it that day or another day - a day when he was already dead and I cried, 'I loved him so much'? The tenses are mixed in the mind; the memory of the carvings on the chimneypiece is vivid - and the words and old George's sympathetic murmurings - but whether Emmet was dead or alive, *this* I do not remember.

That afternoon when I visited him the oxygen tent was gone. Emmet was still grey, with a stubble of unshaven whisker on his face which looked indecent, as if purposely left there to emphasise his pain and his helplessness. But he was better and in control once more of our lives and situations, as always. He was very proud of his pulse rate and made me feel it. He had never had a normal one before and was delighted at this novelty. He was able to tell me all the details of his operation and how very much worse his condition had been than they had suspected, and how marvellously the surgeon had displayed his skill.

'Are you happy?' he asked when he had finished. I could not say yes because I knew we had only won the first small victory.

'I feel as if I have just run a very long race,' was the best I could do.

'I love you,' he said. I didn't tell him I loved him too. I didn't say it. I don't know why. It seemed unnecessary to me, but for him to have used up his new little strength to say it to me may have meant that it was necessary to him, and in this I failed him. He asked for orange juice, and although there was a greengrocer across the street and I could have gone, it was late and foggy and past the children's bedtime and I needed to get home to them. 'I'll bring it with me later - around seven-thirty - will that be all right?'

I never told him that last time that I loved him and I never got him his orange juice, for by the time I got back to the hospital that night he had already started on the road to dying and the oranges lay forgotten forever on a waiting room table.

Then sharp into my memory springs the windowpane in that waiting room. It was solid, and there - an inescapable and tangible hard surface on which to concentrate as the ground beneath my feet became a void. It reflected me; and it was hard and cold and therefore a necessity to accept. I looked through it to the fog, and felt it and pressed my hands against it and talked to it. I told it he was dying, that this was what I had prepared for and it had come and I was standing up looking out a window into a fog with a white ceiling light reflected behind me and my husband was dying in the next room and that I must keep standing up like this in one place or another and clutch onto tangible realities to be faced - me and the sheet of glass and the unrelenting feel of it against my palms - and not expect or hope for anything more ever except the capacity to recognise reality. Reality had become me on one side of the glass and a foggy London night on the other; street lights outside and cars driving by and the necessity only of deciding what minute details of living to perform next.

They wouldn't let me go in to him. It had happened as I was coming up in the lift and when the lift stopped at his floor nurses and doctors were hurrying down the passage to his room. I sent messages: I asked the house doctor to tell him I was there outside but there was no time for messages, or place, or room around that crowded bed where they worked to restore rhythm to his heartbeat. I don't know what he felt, or thought, or said - if he asked for me - or was frightened -

or just again possessed by pain. I only know now that I should have forced my way in. It would have made no difference to his death, but perhaps to his dying. He did it alone, under the anaesthetic when they opened up his chest once more to massage that valiant heart. And I sat, surrounded this time, four hours later, by his family, but also alone and felt him die without me. I knew it - the moment of his death. A cold and shocking shiver took hold of me. Blankets were brought and brandy, but nothing took away the cold, and that, I am certain, was the moment of his dying. An hour later they came in and told me, and life without him began.

chapter fifteen

Maggy came and slept in the house that night. She read Lisa her bedtime story, telephoned the rest of Emmet's family, placed an announcement in the *Times*, and tucked me into bed with a hot-water bottle and sedatives.

My brother-in-law came the next morning to drive me to the hospital. I signed a piece of paper giving permission for an autopsy. The doctor told me it would help others. I held my hand over the words so that I could not read what I was signing. Driving through Hyde Park on the way to the hospital and back, the trees and the traffic signals, the dogs and their owners, the passing cars, the clouds in the sky, all seemed etched in bold outline, strong colours, larger and closer than remembered. I was seeing them for the first time as if through eyes peeled of a skin, gingerly, feeling my body wrapped in a protective but nevertheless fragile film. On the borderline of, but more intense than, consciousness. This sensation lasted for some days - days in which exterior life went on around me and a part of me entered into it but only a part. Drugged each night into sleep, the worst time was first awakening - the feeling of unnamed dread before eyes open - not fully conscious enough to identify the dread but clutched in its embrace.

For some days after Emmet's death, copious and carefully

chosen hampers were delivered from Johnny Hannay at the Savoy: delicious custards, puréed vegetables, cakes and ice-creams and fruit for the children; heartening soups and casseroles for the adults; champagne, foie gras and caviar to cheer away the evening tear - hampers collected the following day with strict instructions not to bother washing the dishes. Anonymous expressions of care and compassion were the most moving. I resolved to learn from this experience how heartwarming these can be. A beautiful coat for Lisa from the White House - a small fortune in couture prices for a three year old; on Christmas Eve a fat envelope stuffed full of five-pound notes pushed through my letterbox - no hint ever of the donors.

These heartening gestures were indications that all around me were people who worried about our practical future, not something I had ever dwelt on. Now I had two very good reasons to cultivate a more materialistic approach to life. They had to be fed, clothed, looked after, educated, and suddenly I became the protector rather than the protected. I could not take seriously what my grandmother considered a dirty word - money - but at least I had to give the lack of it some consideration. Not being trained for this, my random arrows at parsimony were launched in a certain spirit of adventure. It was a new preoccupation: the future had to be taken seriously.

Sadly my grandmother's largesse was not to have had a happy ending for me. Two weeks before she died, bedridden and alone except for a coterie of elderly harpies with their sights set on what remained of the cut glass and the silver menu-holders, and prone to the influence of the remaining sisters, she changed her will. Presumably secure in the belief that a liquid fortune gurgled happily away in some subterranean treasure chest she divided her estate, hitherto totally mine, into two portions - three-quarters to me and the remaining quarter to a variety of bizarre charities. One week later she added a codicil, reducing my three-quarters by a series of bequests to individuals; not least to her aged doctor, who was therefore disinclined to assist in a query of her mental stability. I would not ever suspect my splendid grandmother of becoming senile, even at ninety-four, but I expect her standards remained those of the champagne in the cellar. The charities chosen were bizarre only inasmuch as they touched little on her life, apart from substantial poetry grants to every school and university college attended by my uncle, but whence came her connection with the eminently worthy Royal Lifesaving Society, or the Home for Spastic Children? The silver, the china, the lace and the photographs simply disappeared. There was, of course, no cash. The house remained – a potential goldmine, but now divided into quarters and so forced into a sale; and into the hands of the long-suffering but now powerful estate agents who had been her tenants. My father had refused in the face of death to have anything more to do with her than he had in life, and so, distant as I was, both geographically in England and emotionally as a young mother, I had left the will in the hands of her new executors and became, overnight, a poor relation. I had not been well brought up to play the part. Only years later did I bother to reflect on my lost inheritance when I heard that the site of the house was no longer a sex arcade but the main Kings Cross Underground Station and at last reckoning had changed hands at very many millions, and now, for the first time, with the children relying on me, I felt the loss of them.

But, if my children lacked the Nana and Great Aunt Juliet of my youth, they had a fairy godmother and godfather. The night Emmet died I sent a telegram to Chula and Lisba, on their annual trip to Thailand. The answering cable, from Lisba, assumed the responsibility for Lisa's education from that day through university. I also telephoned our dear friend Steven Runciman on his island Eigg, off the coast of Scotland. Steven caught the sleeper to London and the next night, over dinner at my kitchen table, told me that he wished to educate his goddaughter, Lisa.

'Oh, Steven,' I said, 'how wonderful of you but Lisba has just offered.'

'Very well then - I'll take the boy.'

How incredibly blessed I was, with such friends.

I was prepared for trials and hardship and misery and the long drawn-out business of living for the children. It was a dramatic picture - visions of unlikely occupations filled my pondering hours. I saw myself in a flower shop, or as someone's housekeeper. The someone had no face but the flowers did and I have never been particularly good with flowers. People talked to me of courage and how one could possibly manage alone; of how we would survive, of the healing of time.

This last seemed to me an insult; I did not wish to be healed of my memories. Time, in any event, does not heal: it overtakes. You can't worry about bringing up children when they're growing up from under you. You can't pull in on the hard shoulder and watch the traffic go by. You can't worry about the overall business of being lonely when each fresh disaster has to be met head-on. Children's routines carried me along.

When Emmet died, England was waterlogged, grey, cold, and terrifying. I had bad bronchitis for the first and only time in my life: evidence of the link between mind, heart and body. I had little ready money and a large, expensive house which was suddenly transformed into a hungry monster, eating it up. Emmet's father and friends all urged me to move house. Bad advice, I would now tell the bereaved. Happy memories inhabit happy walls. I wish I had always stayed in the house in which we had lived: I wish I lived in it now. I wish I had not rushed to give away all Emmet's clothes. He is always in my mind, just behind the seeing eye, but how I wish there was a familiar room, a familiar chair, in which I could place him. We should not try to run away from pain; it has its place, sometimes a sweet place.

Sometimes, since, in bad times, that pain has given me strength: a sense of proportion. Then, I have wanted only to remember the blood - thick and smooth and red, red, red - as he spat it out. I have wanted to remember the hard things - I have wanted to be back there where I was living, living as he was dying and we were together. I have been part of him again, with him as we turned on the light so he could see where to spit the blood. No conflict, no decisions to be taken alone, the smooth feel of his strong, strong shoulders as I hugged them in the dark. He spat out the blood in the baby's blue pot. It had a yellow duck for him to cling to as he sat. When the blood came too thick and fast for the pot we measured it in his feeding bottle, and I emptied each full bottle down the lavatory after recording it for the doctor, so we knew each day how much he had lost.

Only blood he lost - neither heart, nor strength, nor love, nor humour. In the times between the pain and the coughing we slept rolled up together like two nuts, two peas, two birds entwined; I around him, holding onto his warmth and strength - not sapped by loss of blood, only touched by a tiny chill of fear, too weak to shake us in our cocoon.

It still envelops me - the cocoon - and, when needed, Emmet reaches out his hand to me.

chapter sixteen

I very much wish, of course, that I had not rushed to sell anything which I thought could raise money, my problem being the paucity of immediate cash and all those kind people advising me. I am sick to think of what I then recklessly sold, often to any crook who came to the door. Family silver had long since gone, but there was a fine hoard of wedding present substitutes, and jewellery. Alan Ladd's Georgian silver sugar coaster went for a few pounds and heavy Irish silver given to me on my mother-in-law's death: of great sentimental value now to my son. I had lost so much weight that clothes went, too - all the remaining Dior New Looks. I thought of our cellar, bursting with wine, and of the dinner parties I would never give again.

One of the more immediate and seductive delights of my Thai job had been the opportunity to acquire, at duty-free prices, an impressive cellar. I had long dabbled in a love of wine, unsupported by much knowledge although I liked to consider myself an expert, and boasted untruthfully of being a member of the august body of Tastevins. My bogus claim to this was not entirely without truthful foundation, but owed something to an alcoholic mist over the memory of my so-called training. On a trip through France sometime in the

1950s, Stanley Haynes and I had dallied in a village in the middle of the vineyards of Châteauneuf du Pape. We visited, as are all tourists encouraged to do, the local cellars, somehow made friends with *le Patron* and stayed a month, during which time I, euphemistically, helped. I remember hot, happy, damp and smelly afternoons spitting and swallowing, and tramping about in a haze of enthusiasm and alcohol. I did learn something, albeit under the aegis of a not particularly distinguished grape, and I remember that on taking our fond farewells some sort of embossed scroll was pressed into my hands. This, although long since lost, became, in my mind, my privileged entrée into the world of wine connoisseurs.

It did, nevertheless, stand me in good stead. I started to buy wine books and learn more. I realised how fortunate I had been in having a few startlingly clear early memories of imbibing. My grandmother's oft proffered glass of champagne had always been a good vintage from a *grande marque*. My first known experience of a great wine had also stuck in my mind because of its incongruous association. At seventeen or so, at a barbecue lunch at Palm Beach near Sydney, hot and sticky in swimsuits gathered round the sausages, dear rich and generous Arthur Browning had insisted on pouring a bottle of Château d'Yquem into a bowl of particularly nasty tinned cream of chicken soup. He had explained that this was how soup was served in Europe. Having no knowledge of that great glamorous, distant world, I decided that when and if I got there, I would steer clear of soup.

The next time I encountered Château d'Yquem was my first country weekend in England at luncheon with David's mother. With our pudding (at least I had learnt between the ages of seventeen and twenty-four that it did not go into the soup), she gave us a bottle remaining from the cellars of Imperial Russia. It was a rich, deep, golden brown. I can't remember the year but as her father, the Grand Duke Michael, had spirited it out of Russia with him before the Revolution in 1917, I imagine it may have been the late 1890s, and the date does ring some sort of a tinkle. But I do remember the taste, and the perfume. I understood for the first time the use of the word 'nectar'. So Château d'Yquem became for me a landmark in my lexicon of wines.

The second fortuitous circumstance was the fact that my husband drank hardly at all, and smoked seldom. He had had to give up the smoking early in our acquaintance on discovering his heart condition and had begun, with me, to drink wine for the first time in his life. As soon as my appointment to the Thai Embassy in London became official, I sent off for all the wine catalogues from the leading wine merchants and began to realise how cheaply I could stock what was miraculously a proper London wine cellar. There can be few left, but ours was stone-built, stone rack upon rack in arched soaring ranks, a solid thick door, and approached through a small courtyard rather than down a flight of rickety stairs. It was dry, cool and commodious and had been built for no other purpose.

The third astonishing happening was that it was quickly discovered that Emmet had what I was assured by some of our new wine merchant friends was that rarity, a perfect palate. As the crates of wine were delivered Emmet read all my wine books. Soon he could be blindfolded and identify immediately the wine, and often the vintage. He was invited by Berry Bros, Saccone and Speed and the like to luncheons in the city where he became a prize exhibit. I never equalled it; mine was book knowledge, and now I have even forgotten that. What is left is our first cellar book, and sad reading it makes. Bottle after priceless bottle of glorious liquid was squandered nightly on whoever happened to come to dine - few of them appreciative, I fear.

The cellar book, started in 1953, reads:

Ch. Margaux, 1953, ch.b. 22/6d.

Ch. Mouton-Rothschild, 1952, ch.b. 25/-.
Ch. Mouton-Rothschild, 1947, ch.b.
Ch. Margaux, 1945, 30/-.
Ch. Lafite, 1947, 1 magnum - no price listed.
Ch. Lafite, 1953, 22/6p.
Ch. Latour, 1953, 22/6p.
Ch. Calon-Ségur, 1937, 26/6d.
Ch. Haut-Brion, 1947, 21/6d.
Ch. Haut-Brion, 1953, 22/6d.
Ch. Cheval Blanc, 1952, 22/6d.
Vosne-Romanée, 1947, no price listed.
Richebourg, 1947, 19/6d.

And so on to lesser growths, like Léoville-Barton, Lynch-Bages, Palmer, Léoville-Las-Cases, dismissed in the shilling class. The great whites, the Puligny-Montrachets, and the Meursault Les Charmes, are not dignified by price either. Remorse prevents me from contemplating the guests, most of them quite unaware of what they were drinking. I am proud, however, of the food. I was learning to be a good cook. Removed from the telephone instructions of my mother's cook, I turned, as did most of England's post-war generation, to Elizabeth David.

As I moved house after Emmet's death, so the cellar - then and in subsequent moves - became a major problem; second only, if not equal, to what to do with the books. But at the time the wine could be said to be a financial asset as well as a storage liability. I had never met the wine writer Cyril Ray, but he had heard of my hoard and wrote to me. After some polite sentences of commiseration on the death of my husband, he came quickly to the point. He had heard I had one of the finest small private cellars in England. Would I consider selling part, if not all, of it? Lists of available wines went between us. He would take all, of course, but marked his preferences, accompanied by expressions of anticipated joy in the drinking, if I wished to retain some. The final list was drawn up, price agreed, and Cyril Ray no doubt had planned his first dinner party.

I had two brooches left: both should have had the sentimental value I now, too late, bestow on them. One, all diamonds, was my mother's; the other diamond and emerald, a present from David - both still in their Cartier boxes. I sold them at Sotheby's and kept the wine, explaining the switch to Cyril Ray, who wrote me a letter of congratulations.

'Despite my own disappointment, I salute the most civilised act I have ever seen performed by a woman.'

Sometimes now, along with contemplation of those unworthy gullets down which disappeared most of my wine, I see similar brooches to mine displayed in auction room catalogues, estimates well into the double if not triple thousands. I received £30 each from the Sotheby's sale.

But I began to regret the splendid hedonistic disregard for worldly goods with which I had been brought up, the lavish lifestyle of my mother and grandmother and great-aunt, in the following of which I had managed to be left stranded on an uncomfortably barren ledge.

chapter seventeen

One day came a letter from an acquaintance, a girl whom I had met once at a luncheon party, suggesting that I go and share her life in Italy. She was Swedish, divorced from a Russian; her baby son the same age as mine, and I had, from the chance luncheon encounter, inherited her Italian nanny.

'Come here,' she wrote, 'I am living in the most beautiful place imaginable, in a cottage in a heavenly park. Wild doves, peacocks, dogs, cats, chickens and horses everywhere - yesterday a horse walked into the dining room. The Contessa, whose estate this is, would let me a fifteenth-century tower, part of the main villa, for almost nothing - but it is too big for me. We could divide it in two, and we could share Brunella [our nanny]'. I don't know why I should have assumed, for the first time in my life, that it was desirable to have a horse in one's dining room, but I was carried away by her enthusiasm, by the vision she painted of sunshine, Italy and escape - and by the sudden idea of renting my demanding London house.

There were many more letters, always with the pattern of peacocks, peace, doves and solitude uppermost; but necessary mention of more realistic living arrangements. I was to have the upper two floors of the tower consisting of two bedrooms and a bathroom for myself, children and Brunella, and the attic where the doves lived. She was to sleep with her small son in one bedroom, with bath, on the ground floor adjoining our communal living room and kitchen. Somewhere among the increasingly jubilant flow of letters I discovered that my part of the tower was accessible only by an outside spiral staircase. Conditioned by nursery gates, barred windows and intercoms, I protested that I could not thus be cut off from the children after their bedtime.

'Don't worry,' she carolled back. 'All will work out - we will change if you wish. Anyway, there are many possibilities.' Quite obviously, from her first rough sketch of the tower, there were not; but with far more innocence and far less suspicion than I was later to view the relatively urban dwellings offered me by villa-renting establishments, I accepted her words and, at last, we left.

The tower was in a tiny village, Fino Mornasco, above Lake Como. I had not driven our car much during four and a half years of marriage and two pregnancies, but as it seemed essential for our future life, I decided to drive, via the Boulogne-Lyon car ferry. Only Brunella viewed the venture darkly. She didn't really want to go back to Italy and, most of all, she wanted nothing to do with her former employer. 'You will see, Signora,' she wailed. 'The Principessa [for such she was] is mad!'

I bought a brilliant collapsible drop-sided cot from Harrods, which was to serve Seamus as a bed in car, ship, train, and tower. Wedged inside it in the back of the car, he looked like some cherubic inhabitant of a human zoo, and he played and slept happily right across Europe. Nappy-changing was a bore, and often back-straining, trying not to dislodge the cot whilst dislodging the nappies. Putting the cot up in our three-berth sleeper meant that there was not an inch of space for undressing or even standing, so that Brunella, Lisa and I had to leap from door straight into bunk and wriggle out of our clothes once there. The Channel crossing was the roughest I have ever experienced. After one look at the choppy sea I had grabbed the last available private cabin, and so we were all four able to be sick in comparative luxury. A helpful young cabin boy walked up and down holding Seamus, who vomited periodically down his back. Brunella grabbed our bathroom before we left port and spent the crossing groaning and effectively blocking the lavatory with her head. I lay on one bunk being sick and trying to comfort my daughter who lay on the other, whimpering. By the time we reached France, the cabin boy had whisked down below, changed his clothing, and washed and dried Seamus's.

Just before arrival at Dover, Lisa had said: 'Mummy, what's that on Seamus's finger?'

'Where?' Half looking, too busy to show much interest, desperate to get to the ferry and out of the country, and with no time for trivialities, I glimpsed nonetheless, out of the corner of my eye, a shiny, angry, puce lump with a bright yellow centre engaging one-third of the total circumference of Seamus's middle finger. It did not appear to be a triviality. From Dover, I had had time to telephone my doctor in London and visit the local hospital. The hospital doctor had bandaged it, told me to put hot poultices on it all night, and to go to a doctor the moment we reached Lyon. 'If you notice red streaks travelling up his arm,' he said casually, 'that's the danger sign.' My own doctor thought perhaps I'd better start giving him oral penicillin right away. Being a doctor's daughter and widow I was full of half-knowledge, antibiotic prejudices and terror, so I decided against the penicillin, only to find there was no hot water on the train.

By Lyon, his tiny finger was all swelling - now with a greenish black centre - no red streaks. Lisa had been sick in her bunk in the night and had spent the remainder in mine. There was no restaurant car on the train. We tottered to a large hotel in Lyon, ordered breakfast, washed and demanded a doctor. The concierge directed me instead to the hospital, as I told him I was in a hurry to leave town. Sitting over breakfast coffee, I thought for the only time in my life that I was going to faint – fatigue, worry and travel nausea hit me with a wave, and if there had been a man anywhere in the world to whom I could have sent a plea, 'Come and get me', we would never have reached our tower. Instead we went to the hospital, where we were shunted into Casualty. There I spent four hours of horror in the centre of the Casualty Ward. The doctors and their assistants were brutal, dirty and blood-spattered. Cigarettes hung from the corners of their mouths and my tiny son was strapped, under a powerful light, to an operating table for nearly an hour before they operated on, without anaesthetic, his finger. It took four men to hold him down. I think local application of heat and a needle prick might have sufficed, but I was too cowed by terror of those red streaks to protest.

Perhaps by contrast, the remainder of our drive to the Italian border was calm and pleasant. The children fitted in with any timetable of eating or sleeping which suited us. As Brunella spoke no French, and was an island girl from Capri with no previous travel experience beyond her original trip to England with the Principessa, I was virtually in charge of three children; but I treasured the thought that once across the Italian border I could relax and leave much of the necessary arrangements to Brunella.

I was soon to discover that I could not rely on Brunella's Italian either; she spoke the Caprese dialect, and glared with resentment at the Northerners who attempted to communicate with her. We arrived in Milano in driving rain. Cots, pots, playpens and prams were tethered to the roof of our car by the most feminine of knots and I had omitted to cover anything with a tarpaulin; so most of our belongings were both precariously perched and drenched. Cars shot at us, horns blaring and tyres screeching, from out of torrents of rain, and I screamed at passers-by in pidgin Italian for directions. Brunella was determined on only one thing - that we must stop and buy the bare necessities for the children's evening meal before we left Milano. I thought it eccentric of her to imagine that my co-tenant would not be waiting with warm and well-stocked welcome, but to keep her happy I agreed. She scooted off through the rain and came back armed with packages, reiterating, 'You don't know the Principessa.'

Fino Mornasco proved to be a half-hour's drive from Milano. The rain had settled into a steady downpour when we arrived at the huge iron gates of the villa. The drive and the vast villa looked deserted and forbidding in the gathering darkness. Great trees banged against the windows of the car and wet leaves swept across the windscreen. There was no sign of dove, peacock, horse, or human. The children started to cry. The tower came into sight as we rounded the drive - romantic and beautiful, perhaps, but dark, dank and deserted certainly, and covered in copiously dripping creepers. Banging on doors finally produced a helpful house guest of the Contessa's, who in turn produced a toothless hag with a key - large, rusty and ancient. We drove on down the drive under an arch of dripping magnolias and let ourselves into the tower.

There was a letter from the Principessa to say she was spending the night in Milano - she hoped I would be comfortable. There was no fire, no hot water, no food of any kind. Brunella was right - the Principessa was not to be relied upon . . .

chapter eighteen

The tower wasn't a tower in the sense of its being part of another, larger, structure. It was simply one room on top of another - three in all - becoming increasingly smaller as it rose, so that we all managed to live, eat and cook on the ground floor in a large salon and antiquated kitchen, and the Principessa and son slept in the adjoining room. As she had warned me, my room shared with the children was above this, as was my tiny bathroom, finished all but for a gaping hole in the wall at the end of the bath. Through his hole an endless procession of lizards and spiders crawled to watch me bathe. Perched on top yet again was Brunella's room. The staircase was narrow and slippery - disastrously so in the rain - and wound precariously round the outside of the building.

A woman friend, Sheila Smart, came out from England to keep me company and was accommodated in a cottage in the stable block amongst the pregnant dogs, hens, pigs and peasant retainers. She was my only ally against the charming but totally unscrupulous Principessa, and we took it in turns to cook the meals and release the fieldmice each morning from the Italian traps set for them by the Principessa the previous night. The mouse traps were square houses, not so small as not to be palatial to a fieldmouse, well stocked with cheese;

and the grateful mice we set free on the tennis court each morning must have broadcast its comforts, and limited dangers, as the traps became ever more populous.

The cooking was a more hazardous affair. Whoever touched the oven door received a fairly hefty electric shock. We boiled or fried our food as much as possible.

The children thrived. Brunella was my rock. I did not miss my husband in the sense that I missed him later, and in cities. It was a time of peace and adjustment, embalmed in boredom and country events, enlivened only by the necessity to make minor decisions. Our days were spent lying in the spring and early summer sunshine by the concrete swimming pool. The pool had been a handsome legacy left by the occupying Germans who had commandeered the villa during the war.

Alas, the Contessa could not swim and, though happy for our sakes to have the pool, was determined that it should cause her no personal discomfort. Each day she would arrive in our midst in a splendidly frilled romper suit with parasol to match, with her shining black plaits of hair wound round her ears, followed by Michele. Michele was neither butler, nor gardener, nor bailiff, but something of all three, his duties ranging from mending a fuse to killing the poisonous frogs - deadly I was told - who frolicked in the pool and on our bathroom windowsills each morning. When the Contessa arrived we would exchange our morning pleasantries while Michele killed the frogs and occasionally a snake. Then, her parasol aloft to protect the gleaming black dye on her hair from the sun, she would wade into the two feet of water which were our daily ration and lie on the bottom - feet and bloomer frills floating gently on the surface. In these two murky feet my children gradually learnt to swim: we adults could do no more than duck.

Seamus began to talk - a hideous Caprese dialect being his first language - and my friend Sheila and I devised our rigid social life. At four o'clock each day the train to Milano passed through the village station and in the station waiting room were sold the best ice-creams in all Italy – and, so it follows, in all the world. At three o'clock Sheila and I dressed ourselves carefully, made up our faces and did our hair, and walked the mile or so to the station to watch the four o'clock train go by, eating our ice-cream of the day. The flavours were raspberry, strawberry, nougat, pistachio, lemon, peppermint, vanilla – the daily decision an agony. A few workmen played dominoes at one of the other tables; we exchanged daily nods.

Occasionally, we actually caught the four o'clock train to Milano and spent an evening at La Scala. Once we were late: the train was pulling out of the station as we came round the top of the hill and started to run, hampered horribly by our wooden clogs (a hangover from rationed shoes). The guard saw us, pulled out his whistle; the driver stopped the train and all the male passengers clapped and shouted in unison as we clattered down the hill: '*Due belle signore, due belle signore*' – and then hauled us aboard. Sometimes we went back to the villa and dressed up once more to drink an after-dinner coffee with the Contessa and her house guests. They were all of them old Generals, mouldering Russian Princesses, Austrian Barons escaping from a more vague boredom to our life of tiny and precise discipline. That is what it was: the discipline of doing nothing and yet occupying the mind and senses – a discipline since forgotten and sadly regretted.

We were given one tiny cup of strong black coffee each and one tiny, strong glass of Strega; and we sat gossiping under the light of the 25-watt chandelier in the gilded and brocaded splendour of the palazzo, peering at each other through the gloom. Sheila and I bought stronger lightbulbs for our own quarters but lived in fear of being caught using too much electricity, it being included in the rent. We also devised a much more satisfying drink for the nights we were not invited by the

Contessa. A bottle of the cheapest grappa, poured in the morning into two glasses of raisins, would swell by evening into a drink of rich and fiery delight.

As we settled into this routine I had no plans for the future. The house in London was let for two years; perhaps at some later date we would visit my father in Australia; and meanwhile there was wonderful, sturdy, cheerful, constant Brunella for me to lean on. One day Brunella seemed less cheerful; the next she sang not at all; on the third she said she did not feel well, and thought she should see a doctor. The local doctor had already been encountered over the affair of Seamus's finger, and so I took Brunella to see him. She emerged smiling. 'Is not serious,' she explained. 'Is making tests. For getting in Como in three days.' She sang again. I gave her not another thought beyond wondering how I could ever manage without her in my life again.

In three days, I was driving into Como and Brunella asked me if I would pick up the results of her tests. Still naïvely unsuspecting, I paid over the counter what seemed a disproportionately large sum of money - for what? For a slip of paper on which was written one word: '*positivo*'.

I spoke hardly any Italian: it was not necessary. All was clear. 'Brunella,' I said, 'is it possible you are going to have a baby?' ('Oh, God,' I thought, 'not *another* baby!') Brunella burst into tears; in between wailing about her mother in Capri she assured me it was not possible because she was virgin but that Forte was a very naughty man. Forte, she enlightened me, was her fiancé - very rich, very Greek, very naughty. Forte had made her do *something* on our last night in London, but she did not know what: she was virgin and so she did not understand.

Dimly, I remembered our last hectic night - scuffles on the stairs late at night, a dark, polite face encountered at the door on other nights asking for Brunella. Now, having divested herself of her problem to me, it became my problem - Mamma in Capri, the baby, Forte. All was up to me, with Brunella eagerly complying with all suggestions. The secure thought of Brunella in my life forever vanished: I would be left alone in what had suddenly become an abyss of the unknown and Brunella must be packed off to London and to her hitherto unsuspected and unsuspecting fiancé. First, the fiancé must be informed and Brunella had every intention that I should tell him. They had little language in common and none that both of them could write. Thus began the long history of my correspondence with Brunella's lovers; and, imperceptibly, I had gained a third child.

Forte, as a lover, was quickly disposed of. To my calm and indulgent letter, assuring him of my care for Brunella and asking only for details of her return journey, he replied: 'Dear Dalton - I know not of what you speak'. Further letters ended in abrupt and angry silence. Brunella wept a great deal and wailed louder about Mamma and how she would kill her. I foresaw once again the permanence of Brunella in my life, but with an added problem - her baby.

But she was determined not to have the baby, and in this I could not shake her. My Italian was barely a month old, not equal to the task of finding an obliging doctor in Milano. The local doctor was out of the question. I hung around the likeliest of the Austrian Baronesses one night after coffee, and in the smoothest conversational tone I could muster, asked her if she knew of a good abortionist nearby.

She was a duck, that Baroness. Hers is a name I shall never forget - Litzi Thun. A council of war was held next day over morning coffee in her room and distant acquaintances were dug up - each one further removed from Brunella. Names were provided who could supply other names and we had now only to do battle with the telephone.

I had no telephone. I had a contraption on the wall of the salon, in full range of the beady eye and eager ear of the

Principessa, which was a sort of one-way extension from the main telephone in the palazzo. The one-way was a capricious arrangement - sometimes I could hear the other party - sometimes they could hear me. About half the time some somnolent servant lurking in the dim corners of the main house actually answered the tinkle and connected me to the outside world. From then on, it was anyone's guess as to who was hearing whom. But a doctor was indeed located in Milano and, in a series of frustrating calls, it was established that he would see Brunella, would perform the operation, would keep her in his clinic overnight - and would charge eighty guineas.

I could not leave the children. Sheila was delegated to take Brunella and it was agreed that they should go separately and meet on the steps of the Duomo in time to go together to the doctor. The day was baking hot. Sheila left early for a day's sightseeing in Milano and I put Brunella on our four o'clock train. Sheila was a handsome and elegant woman, sympathetic and capable and not apt to be unduly disturbed by the ambience, whatever it should prove to be, of an abortionist's rooms, being of an age best described as 'past child-bearing'. However, the day having been exceedingly hot and tiring, she was in some despair when Brunella had not appeared well past the agreed time when they could still have met the appointment. Best to go to the doctor on her own and explain she had lost Brunella. The doctor was in an apartment building a bus ride away. Considerably more hot, tired and dusty, Sheila found the door only some ten minutes late and pressed the bell. In no time, she was let in, pounced on, surrounded, and nearly strapped down before she was able to convince the eager and aggressive nurse that it was not nerves which made her reluctant to undress and submit, but mistaken identity. But contact was made, and so was another appointment. Brunella was found, at the wrong end of Milano, and she lost her baby on another appointed day.

The summer drifted by. The Principessa left in a flurry of unpaid bills; the Contessa and I became fused in friendship by our joint ill treatment at her hands. Our involvement in the life of the villa was enlarged to include invitations to watch excruciating television programmes - all chosen by the Contessa's husband who, inexplicably, was never addressed as 'Count', but always, by all including his wife, as 'Ingegnere'. The Contessa had seemingly married beneath her in the social sphere but not in matters of influence. The tubby little Ingegnere had built some of the grander of Mussolini's roads and buildings and, having been suitably financially rewarded in Il Duce's day, and created his Finance Minister, was never thereafter allowed to forget it. If he fitted at all into a scheme of life at the villa, it was as an engineer and for want of a more appropriate title, that is what he would be called.

Sometimes we went on picnics on the lake - to an island where we were rowed in a caravan of little boats by footmen who then laid out white damask, wine buckets, delicious food, and waited on us at the water's edge. Michele came along to hold the parasol over the Contessa's head as she billowed in the water. No picnic has seemed worthy of the name since, no water more limpid or dappled with sunlight, no feast more luxurious, or wine more tantalising, no setting more idyllic.

In September, the fogs began swirling up and around the shores of the lake and down from the Alps, blanketing our little community in damp greyness. The Generals and the Barons began their farewells, relatives were remembered in cosier climates, and it became evident that we, too, must move on.

Other arrivals during that year, at other houses, as we moved slowly down Italy following the sun, were fraught with shock and despair, but none had been so complete as our first cold, damp night in our tower. But somehow, I look back upon our months at Fino Mornasco as calm, peaceful and regulated. I, too, remember the doves, and the peacocks pecking food from our table, the beauty of the park, the sunshine, and the delightful Contessa. I have forgotten the agony of worry caused by the tiny outside stone staircase and the sheer drop from the tower windows; the fieldmice in our beds and cots; the capricious water supply; the lethal stove; the mad Principessa. As we left Milano, I felt great sadness. Brunella looked back along the Autostrada: 'Mamma mia, Mrs Dalton. I leave plenty memory behind me here,' she said mournfully.

We took a hideous modern apartment next, at Sori, near Genova. The view was breathtaking and made up for the veneer of our dining room sideboard, Burmese gongs and three-piece suite. It was built on a bend of the coast, perched above the main coastal road, and nothing was to be seen from the windows but the sparkling sea and rocky cliffs. Peace was visual, not aural. Lambrettas and Lamborghinis shrieked round the bend below our windows night and day. Slower and more commodious vehicles had their radios on full blast. They hooted at each other incessantly. The children and Brunella slept at the front of the apartment directly above this parade; my bedroom was at the back in relative quiet. Until the night I was shaken awake by Brunella wailing, 'Mamma mia - come quick - house falling down - get children quick!' It did not seem to me inconceivable that we could in fact topple off our bit of cliff onto the road below, and so I sprang from bed expecting the ground to tremble beneath me. 'Where, Brunella? How?' I entreated as the ground remained remarkably firm. 'Big noise,' she cried, 'awful noise. Me fright.' There had indeed been a most appalling crash directly beneath her window: a huge lorry hung, headlights streaking far out to sea, half off the road edge - another crumpled van across the road; but to look out the window had been for Brunella far too fearsome a thing - far better to get me and retreat up the mountainside at our backs as best we could.

As the children had also to be propelled across this road if we wanted to reach the village or the beach far below us it was clear that Sori must be a temporary stop. It served to advance their swimming, begun in the concrete pool and now aided by rubber alligators in the Mediterranean. Seamus had his second birthday in a rowing boat, captained by a beautiful and insistent young Italian whom I had picked up, hopefully for Brunella, but whose object soon turned out to be to get me to the local dance hall. '*Perchè non ballare?*' he repeated plaintively day after day as he rowed me and the children out to sea and Brunella giggled on the shore.

The sun was retreating southwards - Brunella had not seen her family for more than a year - Capri was, to me, a picture postcard name, a place for youthful visits never taken but not a haven - but I agreed to go as far south as Positano and at least look at Capri. And so, granny knots tethering our belongings to roof racks once more, we went off. I installed us in a grand hotel in Sorrento where, in nearby Positano, I had a painter friend, Peter Ruta. The children went to bed: Brunella and I shared a luxurious room-service dinner at the foot of Seamus's cot. She was ecstatic. She had come home in great style.

The next day, Peter, Brunella, the children and I set off on a day trip to Capri. By the end of that day I had rented a four-bedroom house looking out towards via Tregara and the Faraglioni and had returned to Sorrento for our belongings. I left the car in a garage on the mainland and sent for a friend of Emmet's to come out and stay with us, drive the car home, and sell it. The equivalent of bridge-burning.

Capri was an instant seduction. I have never seen it in summer, but in autumn, winter and spring, it beguiled and charmed. Brunella had eleven brothers and sisters, a mother, father and various nieces and nephews on the island. I wanted for nothing: a sister sewed for me; a nephew delivered the vegetables;

a brother kept my evening table at a café in the square. The children made friends with the younger nephews and nieces; I made friends with a few charming residents; friends came out from England to stay; and here, I thought, I shall settle. The children will go to the local school and will grow up Italian.

I began to sense a permanence and stability in our lives there. There was a village school; there were new friends; there was Brunella. Perhaps the time had come to get Seamus christened as a good Italian Catholic. Emmet and I had never had the time between illnesses. And so Brunella was dispatched to the local priest, an appointment made, all of us interviewed, and a date and local godparents set.

Nearer the day, when a cake had been ordered and his putative godfather, a delightful Italian nobleman, 'Franchi' Lanfranchi, had organised the christening party, we had word from the priest cancelling the ceremony. It seemed that the Bishop of Naples, whose diocese we were in, refused to sanction it because I was neither a Catholic nor a guaranteed permanent resident.

Dr Cuomo was the only doctor on the island; so when Seamus developed a large lump in his neck gland and a daily fever, we all bundled off through the ferocious winter storms to Dr Cuomo. From Dr Cuomo we were sent to Naples on the churning winter sea to the International Hospital for X-rays; four trips across the bay; numerous trips to Dr Cuomo, when finally tuberculosis was diagnosed and Seamus was injected with fearsome doses of antibiotics. Dr Cuomo was far too grand to visit himself; so a fat and dirty woman appeared twice daily with a worn leather bag and a huge and dirty needle, which she plunged into Seamus' buttocks whilst she waddled to the window, filled the syringe, and screwed syringe into needle.

Three weeks of this and I was desperate for any remedy. The only other medical care on the island, and that most resorted to by the island people, was at the hands of the nuns. So one night Brunella smuggled (for Dr Cuomo was not to know) one of the nuns into the house. 'Pouff,' she said; a little ointment was all that was needed, and a jar emerged from her sleeve. Seamus' lump remained - the charms of Capri receded - I panicked into the arms of the P&O line and a ship from Naples to Australia. My children never grew up Italian. Nor Seamus a Roman Catholic.

chapter nineteen

The ship's doctor, blessedly English, asked to see Seamus for the injection minutes after sailing. 'Is that the patient?' he asked in disbelief as the chubby, rosy-cheeked little boy was produced. 'I've never heard such rot.' TB was never mentioned again.

On board the ship began the first of Brunella's romances since the unfortunate Forte. It began as the voyage ended – going down the gangway at Sydney Docks. The steward who had waited on her at table pressed a note into her palm as he helped her ashore and, the first of many, it was brought to me for translation. 'He wants you to go to the cinema tonight.' 'I go,' beamed Brunella. At midnight, she returned, engaged.

Ernie was twenty-one and in Sydney for five days before setting off round the world again. Brunella had four nights off and the promise of a ring on his return. The love letters which Ernie and I, in Brunella's name, wrote to each other did not mention the ring nor the impending marriage but were largely Ernie's impressions of foreign ports, foreign girls unfavourably compared to Brunella, and intimations of what he would like to be doing to Brunella. They were pages long. I skipped, in pidgin translation, and then settled, pen in hand, to reply. 'What do you want to say, Brunella?' 'You write, Mrs Dalton;

you write nice letter for me.' Brunella's life, or at least that part of it which she could safely relay to Ernie, did not compare with his for eventfulness, so the strain of invention was already becoming too much for me when Brunella finally became bored with the whole process and moved emotionally on.

His name was Roger - improbable I thought at the time for a Portuguese - and his English and Brunella's did not have much more in common than had hers with Forte. I dreamed of the days when she would meet a nice Italian boy. The one word on which she seemed to have a firm and rapid grasp was 'engaged'. 'Engaged' in Brunella's vocabulary meant a licence from distant Mamma in Capri, and ever-present priest around the corner. 'Engaged' meant good intention, both on behalf of Brunella and the current fiancé. A wedding band and a Papal blessing were absent only in question of time - before or after the union, a minor matter. And now, happily settled in Sydney, the need for written communication ceased and I was released from my role of ghost writer.

We, my father and I, were not released from the rows. We had all moved in with him and Brunella took on the task of cook-housekeeper to him in addition to that of cook-nanny to the children and myself. In return, we embraced her into the family and this meant intimate involvement in her love affairs. Although no letters now had to be written, the space in the flat available for Brunella's privacy was limited, and my father finally rebelled - just as years before he had rebelled in his own married life against a plethora of in-laws - when Roger chased Brunella around the flat, wielding a stick whilst Brunella jumped, shrieking and crying out to God and Mamma, over my father's legs, drowning out both sound and vision of the television set in front of which he was hopefully settled. He put his foot down, Brunella sulked, and I realised that the children had better be packed off to school for at least part of the day.

Seamus, just two and a half, had already bitten my father quite firmly on his calf, and so we thought he might conceivably handle himself with aplomb at school. The headmistress of the kindergarten at Ascham, to which Lisa had gone, consented to take him, albeit reluctantly. Unwisely as well, as it turned out, as his lusty yells were heard from the heights of Darling Point all the way down the hill to the water's edge at Double Bay. They commenced as we turned into the drive and continued until I appeared to retrieve him, and after three days he was expelled. Lisa continued doggedly at Ascham. I became a school mother - the days divided into the time for taking and fetching of children to school - a task which was to continue for years. Two parents can share these tasks. Two parents can share the tales of childish exploits. Two parents can laugh and cry together at childish pranks and childish tragedies. I assumed a double identity - proud mother and stern father. The administrator of spankings and the giver of the healing kiss, never to be allowed the luxury of leaving the room whilst one or the other took place.

I had had the chance of giving them a surrogate father but had rejected it. Together with Brunella, I had had my own shipboard romance, with a startlingly handsome pilot with Middle East Airlines, called John Cameron. In the three weeks of our acquaintance and before he left the ship at Fremantle, he had proposed marriage in the most delightful way. 'The more I hear of your circumstances,' he said, 'the more I think you'd better come on my payroll as soon as possible.' I had learnt enough to recognise that he was a very nice man. He was visiting his parents who had emigrated to Australia, but he cut short his visit to them in order to come to Sydney to marry me. The hurried preparations I made were, I now realise, undertaken in a daze of unreality, but my father, who must have been cast down by the thought of us leaving him again so soon, entered into the spirit of excitement in his customary jovial fashion, and made much of digging out the grey silk top hat bought for my wedding to John Spencer. My close friend Edmée Cameron came up from Tasmania to be whatever attendant seemed appropriate - witness, I expect - and I went off to the local authorities to obtain a licence and make an appointment. We were to be married on a Tuesday by a Mr Truelove. I still have the licence.

By Tuesday morning, the only items missing were John's divorce certificate, stuck in the post from England, and my resolve. The jokes, the top hat, John's niceness and handsome appeal, my children's precarious financial future, could not blind me to the gut feeling that I was Emmet's wife. His was the name to which I wished to cling and he was the husband to whom I had pledged my life. Death had diminished neither. But John had to get back to Beirut; so, promising to join him soon, I said goodbye, cancelled Mr Truelove and put the top hat back in its box. I had, regretfully, missed the experience of Beirut in its heyday, as I had missed Shanghai.

I got on with the business of being a single parent . . . at parents' days, sports days, plays, concerts, and work shows. My daughter, now a painter, must then have had her eye fixed on distant, more serious horizons, for not for her were the bright and painstaking inventions of her small friends at the art display. At the first end-of-year work table I moved hopefully along listening to the proud murmurs all around me as plasticine models, baskets of fruit, Snow White and the Seven Dwarfs, turreted castles were displayed above the names of my daughter's contemporaries. LISA DALTON I saw looming ahead of me and there, above her name, a solid hunk of plasticine, unshaped and unformed, resting like a cow's droppings on the waiting cardboard. GIANT'S HOUSE, proclaimed the label, GIANT RESTING INDOORS. There was no one to share what seemed to me then admirable evidence of contempt for time misspent, or possibly a lofty imagination - no one with whom to ponder if it might be one of these or, perhaps, dare one think it, evidence of a dull child?

I tried not to bore my friends, and above all not to bore my children, with the burden of my solitary thoughts. Mine never asked to be given another father; but once, after serious conclave between them, Seamus, aged five, announced that he and his sister hoped that I might have another baby. 'The only thing is,' he said thoughtfully, 'I'm worried you may not have enough breath left.'

So spoke the future doctor. The Giant's House was perhaps the first stirrings of the future artist.

chapter twenty

When we came back to England, leaving Brunella behind with the latest fiancé, after two years away in Italy and Australia, our London house seemed too large, certainly too expensive, and I was still being urged to move by well-meaning friends. Whilst contemplating this, the obvious temporary solution was to look for a lodger. I found him in the *Times* Personal Column: 'House-trained bachelor requires accommodation in sympathetic private house as close to Montagu Square as possible'. He took one look at the large front room which had been Emmet's consulting room, now to be converted to become his bed-sitting room; the small surgery next to it, transformed into a kitchen; and the ground floor bathroom, and moved in that day. I hardly saw him, as he left the house each morning around 9 a.m., not, I was to discover later, to go to work but to spend all and every day in Harrods' Central Hall. Before he left, a Moyses Stevens florist's van delivered a single red carnation for his buttonhole. He cooked quietly for himself each night, had no visitors, made no noise. I didn't know then that Harrods' Hall was a notorious homosexual hunting ground, so I expect he had had his fun for the day.

Slowly we became, if not friends, occasional companions.

I was invited in for the odd glass of sherry. I learnt that his last resting place had been a happy sojourn with another widow, who had lived in Montagu Square and whom he had christened Widow Twankey. I became Twank Two. Just before I sold the house and moved, he killed himself but not, for which I was grateful, in my house. Nor in Harrods.

The initial, instantaneous waking dread had subsided: it took about a year to awaken to an unclouded morning; but it happened.

It was lovely to see old friends again - picking up London life again, little seemed to have changed in my two years away and certainly the friends had not. Some of Emmet's more devoted patients also did their best to keep in touch with the children, amongst them Olwen Vaughan. She was a great, lamented, and largely unrecorded individual of the London bar and café scene of the forties and fifties - almost a muse to the raffish, literary, artistic odds and ends who were her regulars at the French Club. I had not been present at its inception but learnt that the French Club was formed and so named for the first of the French Resistance, and later Allied, officers of the war. Olwen had no French background, but was rumoured to have had a French lover or two and this was sufficient impetus for the recruitment of any French barmen or waitresses she could find; undeniably French - good and cheap - food; and a bistro atmosphere unique in the London of those years.

The Club was a narrow, pretty, terrace house in St James's Place. On the ground floor was the bar, presided over by Olwen and a series of barmen; tables and chairs; a piano; the regulars normally in various stages of inebriation, but matched drink for drink by Olwen. It was the scene of glorious, memorable rows - glasses thrown in faces, chairs overturned, the arguments usually about abstract or artistic points of view. Or a nasty review from one of the many journalist members, encountering their victim deep in alcoholic gloom.

Upstairs in the dining room, it was more orderly. The cooking remained extraordinarily good - the prices kept remarkably low. Olwen could never have made much profit and what she did was usually blown on her annual children's Christmas party. Drunks swept out, balloons, streamers, presents and conjurors took over. Members' children looked forward to it all year.

Above these premises Olwen lived and, we all feared, might eventually die - burnt to death by one of the several fires started by a cigarette falling from her drunken fingers in bed. She was an alcoholic and by that time had become part of my everyday life as she had also been Emmet's patient. He was fond of her, as were all of us, and had varying degrees of success in treating her addiction. During these periods of withdrawal into sobriety - and it must be said, as with most alcoholics, into a more mundane personality - Olwen retreated into our house, enjoyed the company of our children and stayed sober, occasionally for days at a time. From there, she went to Greece on holiday with a companion with whom she had a ferocious, heart attack-provoking row. It somehow seemed a fitting end.

Olwen's death seemed to herald the need for cutting ties with some of the past and contemplating a fresh start, and some possible occupation in life.

I reluctantly sold the house and moved to one in Putney. When Emmet had died his father had been the first to urge me to move, warning me of impending penury if I continued to live beyond my nonexistent means, and suggesting somewhere like Putney. Then I had replied, 'I'd rather go back to Australia', thereby voicing the next worst alternative. Now that I'd done one and it had not been all bad it seemed reasonable to try the other.

Whilst the new house was being rewired and re-roofed and

the new owners had moved into mine, we were homeless once more. Chula and Lisba lent me their flat at La Napoule on the Mediterranean coast; the writer Robert Ruark[14] and his wife Ginny lent me their superb apartment in Park Lane. Irish Mary agreed to come to Putney and Swiss and Italian mother's helps bridged the gaps between Brunella and school.

The Ruarks had been friends from holidays on the Costa Brava – I in a rented villa at Tamariu, Bob and Ginny in their beautiful beachfront house at Palamos, to which I went many days and nights for parties and games. One day I had to decline Ginny's invitation as it was 'nanny's' day out.

'Bring the kids,' she said.

I explained that, to a normal hostess, my then three-year-old Seamus would be a strain. To a childless couple, the male of whom professed to loathe children, he would be unbearable.

'Listen,' said Ginny, 'I've heard a lot about that child of yours. Bring him. I can cope with him!'

At the end of that long day, Seamus eventually having been coaxed down from the roof, Ginny was limp and beaten as I had never seen her. Bob had long since locked himself in his study. I prepared to leave. Ginny's farewell was, 'I always thought you were kidding when you told me about that child. That's no child. That is a shrunk Frank Packer.' (This remark will mean nothing to a generation and to a world who never knew Sydney's Sir Frank Packer. They may, however, have heard of his son Kerry, who sounds as if he may have inherited some of Frank's characteristics. They no longer seem evident in my now quiet and disciplined doctor son.)

Ginny is memorable because of her pithy comments. Once they came to drinks with me in London. Bob had given her a snow-leopard skin coat (shot, I regret to say, by himself) that day. I had left it in the downstairs hall whilst we were upstairs in the drawing room. Vanished, when we came down – front door ajar. Bob ran down the road and paused at the front entrance of the grand apartment block next door to ask the stately porter if he had seen anyone, adjacent house having been broken into.

'No, sir,' came the lofty reply, 'but I could pick any of those locks with my cock.'

When Bob returned, empty-handed, Ginny was immensely impressed.

'May I ask which porter?' she wanted to know.

We then acquired a much more permanent lodger, who was to stay in a succession of houses for four years: an Australian friend of my youth whom I'd re-met in Sydney, Hudson Henry.

Hudson, if one could afford him, was a luxury every woman should have in her life. Kind, generous, attentive, and above all funny, he fulfilled for me the role of major-domo, butler, surrogate father to my children, loving friend and protector; if he had lived in another time and place, a court jester. He had gone through one fortune in Australia, had got out just before the tax authorities had caught him, and landed in London on my doorstep to start a job at the *Daily Mirror* selling advertising space – a job I had persuaded Alex Mackay to give him. Hudson had never sold anything before but threw himself into expense account luncheons and the City with enthusiasm, selling a record amount of space along the way. I no longer wanted for an escort in London, or a companion on school holidays. The children adored him; the bookmakers adored him; my friends were intrigued by him; and his permanence in our lives only came to an end when he stole the cash from my widowed mother's pension which was lying on my desk, and tried to blame nine-year-old Seamus. My patience finally snapped. Until then, I had accepted the greengrocer's apologetic accounts rendered for bills I had asked Hudson to pay if I'd been away; the months of unpaid bills at the newsagent, cash similarly spent by Hudson on the horses; even the poor and somewhat simple milkman's tale of how Hudson had managed to extract sixty pounds in cash from him in two dud cheques. I had forgiven the time he came to see me in hospital, recovering from a minor operation, when his debt to me was touching the £6000 mark and his idea of cheering me up was to wheel me to the window in order to admire his gleaming new Jaguar parked outside. I even enjoyed driving around in this splendid prize, the result of one of his rare racecourse wins - Hudson ordering, as we turned left, 'Put your arm out, darl: you get six thou' for an arm.'

But the theft of £20 from my pension was the last straw. Hudson left. We did not see each other for a year or two. One night he telephoned, from the airport, en route to Spain where he'd landed a job selling cars. He'd embezzled the splendid expense account, and the *Mirror* had, reluctantly, had to say goodbye.

I asked him where he was, as I heard the pips of the pay phone: 'I'm one step ahead of the posse', and he was gone.

I was to see him twice more. Once he came to stay in Minorca, arriving very late one night, minus a front tooth and with a very drunk, very bewildered French Consul in tow, whom he had picked up in a bar in Mahon and persuaded to act as a chauffeur. He'd lost the tooth in another bar in Barcelona when he'd removed it (the real one having been lost years before in a fight) and put it on an adjoining bar stool. The woman who sat on the stool, on discovering a tooth embedded in her bottom, demanded the owner. Hudson left without claiming it.

The last time I saw him was in Sydney. He was in hospital, twitching with DTs, his liver destroyed. He clutched my arm and whispered, 'I've left everything to your kids. The family don't know - but my lawyer's got the will.'

He escaped one night from the Home where he was living, slipped down a rain culvert, broke too many bones, and died.

I was back in England when the lawyer contacted me. The will was indeed valid. I was the sole executor: my children sole beneficiaries. The estate was little but debts, but as executor, I paid for his funeral - even to the expensive headstone and lavish flowers ordered by his family, all of them heirs to their mother's fortune.

Once more, bizarre events had intervened to wrap the comforting blanket of laughter around loss. The sting of death has for me more often than not been swabbed with the antiseptic of comedy and, just as death had so often added a touch of melodrama, to offset any sorrow in my childhood, so it has managed to invest the remainder of my life with a similar tinge of freakish surprise.

None of us expected Roger Peronnier to leave us sitting gulping down our dry martinis in the Savoy Bar whilst he went upstairs and shot himself. Roger's death would have had nothing like the impact had we not been able to imagine his body upstairs in one of the River suites. The fact that Tam's £400 in notes were in his pocket certainly added to the shock. In the same way, when Blevins Davis, the American friend who had lent us our honeymoon car, died in the lift at Claridge's, the timing was as unfortunate as the event was sad. Blevins had been very rich indeed, but not by birth. He had grown up, alongside his closest friend Harry Truman, in Independence, Missouri, but fairly late in life had married the heiress to one of the great American railways. Marjorie was a kind and delightful drunk whose death on one of her own trains left Blevins a wealthy widower. It was reported that she slipped through one of the slats joining the carriages when on her way to the bar. Blevins's generosity thereafter with her money was spectacular and genuine. He was one of the original sponsors of the American Ballet Theatre, the money behind the production of *Porgy and Bess* which toured Europe in the forties, the dispenser of lavish gifts to friends and charities alike. During the fifties he suddenly and dramatically lost all his money, was declared bankrupt by the US Internal Revenue Service, was forced to sell his magnificent mansion in Independence, his palatial flat in Grosvenor Square, his Rolls-Royce in London, and skip to Lima, Peru, where, by some quirk of careless fate, he had bought, forgotten, and failed to declare in his overall estate, an iron ore mine - barren, but in existence. The nine years he subsequently spent, penniless, in Peru were tough ones. We sent each other cards at Christmas but the first I was to hear from him directly was a telephone call from Claridge's in the 1960s. He sounded jubilant.

'Come to lunch. I have exciting news for you,' he said.

It was lovely to see him again, thinner and fitter and full of the stories of his climb back to prosperity. It had taken nine years to find a partner, raise sufficient cash to commence operating the mine, come back to London, and start his life again. He had retained few friends. Most had deserted him. I was one of the few who had not.

'I wanted to tell you that the mine will be worth a fortune and as I have no family I want to see that your children are well provided for. I am going to my lawyer on Monday to make a new will in their favour.' I left Claridge's on air: not only was darling Blevins back in my life but that life began to look immeasurably easier. It was a Saturday. On Sunday at 12.45 the manager of Claridge's telephoned me. Blevins had dropped dead in the lift on his way to lunch. He had blocked the entrance to the lift, and had no doubt given the other guests a nasty turn. The US Ambassador at the time was Walter Annenberg, who showed no sign of displeasure when I telephoned him at home for help. All was done swiftly and expertly for Blevins. He was not, however, able to keep his appointment with his lawyer. And my children were not to grow up rich.

chapter twenty-one

To jump back in time again: on our return to England, with children at last, unprotesting and relatively contained, at school most of the day; time on my hands, and precious little money in the bank, I looked around for something to do which would free me for the school holiday travels. I had re-met my teenage sweetheart, in Australia, then successfully running an advertising agency. We thought it would be a tremendous joke if I did a television commercial for him and it was even more of a joke that the product was a mattress. The mattress was called Don. On a very hot day in Sydney in a very small studio, surrounded by an enthusiastic crew, I rolled around on one half of a rumpled double bed on the other side of which was prominently displayed a pipe and a crumpled pillow. I had to look towards the camera mouthing in the sultriest tones I could muster, 'It *must* be a *Don*!', writhing a bit under the sheets. The company won the advertising award of the year. I was told that everyone stayed at home on the nights it was shown and it ran for a year. Sadly, it was then scrapped.

However, this now gave me the idea that I could perhaps claim experience as a TV performer.

Having a few friends in the industry, I telephoned around

and I think it was Peter Willes, then Head of Drama at Associated Rediffusion, who put me in touch with a nice woman running their advertising section. Commercial TV had just started; therefore, although they could produce programmes, they had nothing with which to pay for the programmes – that is, advertisers. So, in between the sparse advertising slots there were big black gaps during which nobody said anything and nobody was paying for that blank space. Something termed Advertising Fillers was born and I think that I was born to fill them. I very soon discovered that given a microphone I would talk quite happily until someone pressed a button to stop me. I talked about a variety of things: a programme on travelling with young children, for which I was very well equipped; reviewing books – semi-equipped, if one overlooked training and substituted a certain amount of taste, plus some literary grounding thanks to my grandmother's guidance in childhood; a series of programmes like wine-tasting for which I believed I was well equipped but knowing not nearly as much as I pretended to know. A good deal more, however, than your average viewer in 1960. I must have been quite proficient at it as they got into the habit of telephoning me the night before a slot had to be filled saying, 'Can you fill in two minutes for us tomorrow?' – or five, sometimes ten, sometimes only a minute. This recurred about once a month. Could I regard it as a career? It didn't exactly pay the rent but it paid for the odd luxury and encouraged me to feel that an abyss was not about to confront me. More important I thoroughly enjoyed it. I forgot about trying to be someone's housekeeper. It has since, perhaps, served as good training.

Then, without a thought or plan, I became a literary agent by a similar set of fortuitous circumstances as those which had made me an agent for a foreign government. I was equally ill-equipped and inexperienced but, as with South-East Asian affairs, I did not get found out until I had had time to learn a little, and by that time I had also learnt that ignorance, coupled with confidence and femininity, could prove a positive bonus. The fear of making a fool of oneself doesn't hold one back if unaware of the depth of one's ignorance.

As nearly everyone not connected with the world of writing asks what on earth a literary agent actually does, it obviously possesses some sort of mystique for the layman. The simplest reply is that one sells writers and the product of their labours in the same way as an estate agent sells houses. It doesn't help to make such a simple equation and one gets very tired of being asked. I was lucky enough to ask someone who told me clearly and concisely what a good literary agent should do just before I became one, which meant I started off with high ideals, totally unrealistic aims, and the supreme certainty that it would all be easy, because desirable.

I was at a loss as to how to progress from the erratic TV appearances when at eleven o'clock one night Leslie Linder telephoned.[15] He had been looking for me, he said, for five years; he had never forgotten me; and he wondered what I was doing and if I wanted a job.

I had not forgotten him but I had not thought about him since leaving England. His two-and-a-half year old son had attended the same nursery school as our three-year-old daughter. He and his wife lived nearby; he and my husband shared the school run in the mornings and I had seen him occasionally as a face at the door. When Emmet died he had offered to take the children every day. He had begged me not to be alone over Christmas and to come and have a drink. He had asked me if I had future plans.

Emmet had written and published a book, under a pseudonym, and was halfway through another when he died. The British Medical Association frown on true medical reminiscences, hence the pseudonym; the second was to be a novel, and, as in many first novels, was very thinly disguised autobiography. It was his view of our meeting, our marriage, and his disability. It was never to be finished, and, in retrospect, death was its natural ending, but Emmet had asked me if I would finish it should he die. This, I told Leslie, was my future plan. Leslie was, he explained, a literary agent, and so I gave him the manuscript and subsequently lunched with him in order to discuss it. I didn't know what a literary agent did, but at the end of our lunch Leslie told me he thought I possessed all the desirable attributes and that if I ever wanted a job to telephone him.

Italy intervened. I could not finish Emmet's book, but in isolation in my tower jotted down the diary for my children which was to become my own little book. Leslie Linder had been forgotten and I am grateful to him for remembering me. At that time, he was a director of John Redway & Associates, and an appointment was made for me to meet Mr Redway. His agency dealt with theatre, films and television, with a thriving literary department run by two of the best agents ever to operate in England, Richard Gregson and Gareth Wigan. They had, however, just left, taking with them almost all the clients.

The night before my interview I dined with a friend, Bill Holden, then in publishing, and later owner of the Strathmore Bookshop. It was Bill who primed me as to the aims of a good agent, and the current need for one who lived up to these aims. Thinking back, these had mostly to do with energy and initiative and a lot of creative thinking. Of course he was right, and I totally bewildered Mr Redway with my crusading zeal and Bill's utopian dreams of how I would transform his agency. I think we both had a good time at the meeting, but as he didn't get much of a chance to speak we agreed that another meeting would be needed. Leslie telephoned to say I had made a terrific impression.

I started to read book reviews furiously, even sending off for the books, and wondered whom I would choose as a client. John Redway's secretary rang to make another appointment. Three times. It was the winter of 1961 and we were snowbound, or it seemed that Mr Redway was snowbound as he kept cancelling the appointments. My excitement waned and Leslie became impatient.

'I want you to meet someone else,' he said. 'He'd be much better for you than John and if John can't be bothered to move quickly I think you had better meet him. He's just started as an agent and wants to establish a literary department, and he's much younger. His name is John Heyman and he'd like you to lunch with him at the White Elephant tomorrow.'

At my second interview I had much less time to get into my stride. John was late, ate little, said less, and left me to finish my lunch alone. He gave no indication of any interest in me, the job, or indeed his business. As he got up to go he said, 'By the way, when can you start and how much do you want?'

I gulped 'Monday' with alacrity, and 'What about £2000 a year?' tentatively. It seemed a fortune.

'See you Monday,' he said.

The office was three rooms and a tiny reception area in a fairly grotty building in Great Portland Street. In one of the rooms, the work, such as it was, was done by an actor's agent called John Mahoney, and a variety agent called Tony Lewis. In one of them John Heyman spent his time on the telephone, feet on the desk, or having his hair cut and dreaming up grandiose schemes - all of which, in arguably different forms, have since come true. In the third room I sat, staring out the window and listening to the conversations from the other rooms. I had a desk, a chair, a row of empty bookshelves, four books - the A to Z of the telephone directory, but no telephone. I had no clients and absolutely no idea how to go about getting them, or what I should do with them if, miraculously, they should appear.

The conversation I heard from the next room didn't seem

to offer much scope for the sort of literary plans I had so confidently broached to Mr Redway. The clients seemed to be Hughie Green, Diana Dors, and in some mysterious and remote way - at arm's length - Elizabeth Taylor and Richard Burton. These two, it appeared, were to be 'serviced' when in England by John. I had not the remotest idea what being 'serviced' meant but it formed the basis of nearly all the lengthy long-distance telephone calls I heard. I could not see how, or why, or when I was to fit into this scheme of things and I began, due to my princely £2000 per annum, to feel exceedingly guilty as I stared at the empty bookshelves and dusty desktop. Sometimes when John was in an expansive mood he remembered I was there and we did indeed talk. I was able to air my ideas for transforming the entertainment world, starting with my desk; and together we hatched up some lovely plans. Once or twice, in a burst of creative euphoria, the receptionist would be sent to Selfridge's for a pot of caviar and an onion, and we continued our imaginative planning through a windowsill luncheon, wielding a spoon each. Once he put his arm on my shoulders as we got into the lift and sighed contentedly, 'We've had a bloody good day - we've made at least a quarter of a million today.' Of course, what we had done was plan how a quarter of a million could be made - bouncing ideas off each other - and by 10 a.m. the next day, those would be yesterday's ideas, John would be back on the telephone, and I would be back in my empty cubicle. Guilt and boredom escalated.[16]

After several weeks it seemed that the conversations from the next office had developed a pattern and a tension and that both could be linked with the frequent visits to the office of a large man called Lloyd Williams. Both John and Lloyd Williams sounded harassed. Franco was mentioned with increasing exasperation - and the ex-King of Spain (or, more accurately, having abdicated before accession), Don Juan, now the Count of

Barcelona. Lloyd was constantly just leaving for Madrid, or just arriving from Madrid. The problem seemed to be that a film was to be made in Spain for which interviews with both Franco and Don Juan were essential, and despite Lloyd's frequent visits no progress was being made. A first-class crew were standing by, on full pay; a script had been written, and presumably paid for, by the historian A. J. P. Taylor - and the film was to be the pilot in a series made for television about monarchy, past and present, in its various stages of insecurity - *The Uneasy Crown*. But the initial unease was in getting close to the Crown in the first place.

It wasn't quite what I had had in mind when I had immersed myself in the *Times Literary Supplement* but at least I might be able to justify my presence. It needed some courage to interrupt, but one day I managed to stick my head round John's door at a time when he was not on the telephone. 'Maybe I could help? I don't exactly know Franco but I have a lot of Spanish friends who do, and I could certainly help you with Don Juan,' I said. My years of brushing with Royalty might finally be put to good use.

It was about midday on a Friday. By five-thirty I was on a plane to Madrid. In the meantime I had spent an hour with an old friend, Bud Ornstein, then running the London office of United Artists but better known for long years in Spain, his Spanish decorations, and his passion for the country. I had read Taylor's alarmingly left-wing treatment, from which it was clear that Lloyd Williams had been lucky not to be stopped at the airport. I had a long list of addresses from Bud of technical experts in the Spanish film industry. I had left instructions with the nanny, picked up the children from school, packed a bag, and telephoned one or two Spanish friends. I had never been to Madrid before.

I had also never met a film crew or read a script. The original hand-picked crew had grown tired of hanging around and had gone on to more concrete projects, and it was understood that should I manage to get the required interviews a new crew would have to be hired at very short notice. Taylor's treatment had first to be put in the wastebasket of my bedroom at the Ritz Hotel and a new one had to be concocted. Far more sympathetic views of Franco were given to me, along with a lot of hard facts, by Spanish friends and I was quickly introduced to Señor Fraga Iribarne, then the most promising young politician close to Franco, Minister of Information, Head of Public Relations, future Ambassador to the UK, and full of charm. Doors flew open: if Franco himself could not be available, Señor Fraga would allow himself to be interviewed – by me; and, as he was being confidently tipped as Franco's successor, this would suit the purposes of the film, providing I could also procure an interview with Don Juan. This proved even easier: telephone calls were made by close friends of the *soi-disant* King and he would be delighted to receive me, and the crew, at his house in Estoril the following week.

The scene was set for the arrival of the crew.

Lloyd had had a hard time getting together a new one, and a motley lot arrived. Their equipment was swiftly confiscated. Nobody had thought to get something called a 'stock clearance'. Terms such as this, and first-hand knowledge of all the hazards of importing a crew, cameras and film into a foreign country became part of my experience in a matter of traumatic hours. My Spanish friends, old and new, rallied. The crew moved into their various quarters; whilst Lloyd and I set about arranging the interviews, they set about exploring Madrid. It became clear that, in the absence of a script, adequate preparation and an entirely sober crew, sixty minutes of screen time were going to be hard to fill. In the government archives was footage of the Spanish Civil War, including the siege of Toledo, never before released, and unlimited material on every aspect of the political history of Spain from the end of Alfonso

XIII's reign to the present. All of this was given to us, free, by Fraga; in return he asked only that the finished film would not be hostile to the regime.

The remainder of the week was fun. Thanks to the generous gift of stock footage the actual shooting schedule was relaxed. I interviewed Fraga, and we were all shot on a sunny day in Toledo, subsequently to be intercut with harrowing scenes of the real thing. At the end of the week, Lloyd and I moved down to Portugal - the plan being to shoot Don Juan's interview with a Portuguese crew. After two days Lloyd left me: with the crew, no command of Portuguese, and puzzling out what 'zoom lens' and 'tracking shot' could possibly mean, even in English. The wires of the camera and lights got horribly tangled with Don Juan's Aubusson, but somehow a few shots were obtained which served our purpose.

Triumphant, I arrived back in London. I thought that John might be pleased with me. However, a fresh crisis had arisen. Richard Burton had been contracted to read the text. There was no text; there was, in fact, no film - only a lot of unrelated footage. There was also a week to go before the Saturday morning booked for his recording.

I cannot remember by what series of mishaps Lloyd Williams and any tattered remnants of the crew had now become unavailable, but I remained as the only survivor of our Spanish journey. It is to this that I owe the memory of a thoroughly enjoyable week spent in a tiny cutting room in Soho, perched on a stool peering into a 'movieola' with a lovely editor called Ray who had the worst stutter I've ever encountered. I had a pad and pencil; Ray had the tools of his trade; and between us we concocted a film. Due to the generosity of the Spanish Government we managed our sixty minutes, with only one or two torn frames littering the cutting room floor. I went home and wrote the commentary to fit our efforts and, immensely proud and happy, presented it to John.

The following week I was back in my empty office. My commentary was largely rewritten by John - not so well, I couldn't help thinking. My voice was dubbed in the interviews. The film was sold and shown on BBC2. The credits read 'Script by A. J. P. Taylor' and somewhere near the end in small letters 'Research by Robin Dalton'. I had learnt my first lesson in film-making, and in the whimsicality of credits. I still had nothing to do.

chapter twenty-two

The weather had, however, improved. Snow had given way to spring, and Mr Redway had emerged, along with the crocus. Three months after our broken appointments he rang me up.

John Redway always gave one the impression that he was actually smiling down the telephone. He positively beamed compliments at me. He had, he said, been hearing wonderful things about me, and realised he had been foolish not to grab my services when he had had the chance, but would now welcome a second chance, if I was not entirely happy with my present situation.

I had been entirely happy working on our little film, but I was not only unhappy back in an empty office doing nothing but feeling, for the first time in my life, both insecure and redundant. I could see no signs that the writers were going to flock to my door; not many signs that John Heyman was aware of my existence; and the promised TV series designed to follow the pilot had not been mentioned again. I liked what I saw of John Heyman very much, but I found him both quixotic and intimidating, and both these qualities prevented me from seeing much of him at all. I felt a nuisance.

I will never know whether he felt that I was or not. He

took the news of my departure, of which it had needed three weeks to find the courage to announce, with characteristic laconism.

At John Redway's I had a proper office, a secretary, a telephone, several dusty scripts and a couple of disgruntled clients left behind by Richard and Gareth - by intent, I assumed. I also had unlimited time, energy, and a clean slate: I had not yet offended anyone in the business. I was therefore able to use this time and energy to concentrate on these two people who needed selling, and to telephone and meet as many possible buyers as I could glean names. The clients thought I had miraculous powers; the producers thought I had such boundless enthusiasm for what I was trying to sell that I must be right.

I now realise that this energy is the first step to take in becoming a good literary agent, or at least in gaining a reputation for being a good one. It helps to be able to read. In the beginning, be sure you have only one or two clients and that you give them all your attention. At least one of them should have talent beyond question, or be commercially orientated enough to warrant the telephone calls you will make on their behalf. They will also, presumably, have one or two colleagues to whom they will have praised you. They, with luck, will also have some talent, and something saleable. They will probably also have an agent, who may be thoroughly tired, either of them or of the business. Soon your telephone will start to ring and it will all seem tremendously exciting. And it is. In my case, the excitement lasted about ten years, and the interest another five. After fifteen, it became, by and large, a job, albeit an absorbing one.

There are good agents, and not so good agents. There are also caring agents, and more cynical and less caring agents. I don't think you ever totally develop a protective skin if you are one who cares, or that cynicism or disengagement of the heart can be truly assumed. I believe I was a very good agent - at least for the first fifteen years - but I know I was always an excessively caring one, and if I were to advise someone about to embark on an agent's job I would advise them never to start if they cannot achieve the necessary detachment. If you can't achieve that, you are forever pulling yourself apart.

As I have never been able to regard anything or anybody with even the amount of detachment commensurate with sanity, I embraced vulnerability. My first few geese were swans to me in no time, as indeed were nearly all those who were to follow. If they stubbornly remained geese in my eyes through no fault of their own, for they were doubtless unaware of their metamorphosis taking place deep in my consciousness, I could not sell them to anyone else; but a very few clients failed to get a grip on my emotions. Not all of them tried, or indeed wanted, the surrogate mother they discovered lurking behind the brisk businesswoman. Without the emotional link, in a very few cases, we parted company. The majority remained, and soon friendship patterns re-formed in my life. I found no lessening of affection for old friends but the days were full and long and hard, and at the end of them I seldom, and during them never, had the time, energy, or interest left over for chat, gossip, or much of the world not encapsulated between pages. Clients swiftly became friends to the exclusion of old intimacies. We had more of the present in common, if not the past, and, above all, we had in common a fervent wish for their wellbeing.

My telephone rang constantly at all hours. A very few clients respected the professional nature of our relationship and tried to telephone during office hours, but it was I who so eagerly swept away the boundaries and so joyfully cooked dinners for those for whom earlier in the day I had negotiated contracts. Scraps of paper lay in every drawer and handbag on which were scribbled the minutiae of my life: 'ten per cent of one hundred per cent of gross profits and no cut-off after first draft' sandwiched in between 'one dozen eggs and make dental appointments for half-term weekend'.

In those days - 1965 or thereabouts - films were being made out of Europe; Spain and England being the two most vibrant centres of the English-speaking film industry. Many of the successful writers, directors, and producers from Los Angeles had made their homes in London and there seemed no reason for them to return. Some of them, like Lester Cole, Carl Foreman and Jo Losey, had been victims of McCarthy in Hollywood. They were initially helped by the man who by now had become my father-in-law, J. Emmet Dalton. He had exchanged his career as a distinguished leading Irish soldier and politician for that of a film producer in London; a most unlikely and, as later proven, unsuitable occupation for one possessed of equal degrees of stubbornness and integrity. He gave Carl and Jo their first jobs in Europe, writing and editing films for him under pseudonyms, and was until his death the UK director of Carl's company. So, through him, I had a tenuous connection with the film world.

Through Tam and Margaret Williams I had made many friends in the theatre and television world, and so it seemed logical that I would continue the tradition of John Redway's literary department in concentrating on film, TV and dramatic writing and leave the publishing side to others. I was so lucky, and so ignorant of the standard approach, that my first piece of concluded business happened effortlessly during my first week. Reading a single small paragraph review of a novel in the literary pages of a newspaper, I liked both the sound of the plot and the title, *The Bitter Lollipop*, published by Collins. I rang Collins; they gave me the name and address of the author and sent me the book. I read it overnight; I telephoned the author, John Quigley, in Scotland the next day. No, he did not have an agent (this possibility had not actually occurred to me); yes, he would love to sell the film rights.

I knew who Bryan Forbes was - vaguely. He seemed to be the most in-demand director around and either then, or shortly thereafter, was to take over the running of EMI, the British studios, so I telephoned him, too, and sent him the book. Bryan bought it outright, within days (never made: still on a shelf somewhere: still, no doubt, a wonderful story). Beginner's luck - how incredibly enjoyable and easy it seemed to be a literary agent!

At John Redway's there remained only one client, Howard Clewes, who was successful, and therefore could be classified under the dreadful term 'commercial', and he possessed an ego commensurate with his talent: not overpowering but solid. The appetite of this ego found in me an answering void. I had very little to do, and was delighted to find in Howard's professional life a gap anxious to be filled with my questing energy. Howard had published several successful novels: what he needed was to sell the film rights of these works and to be engaged as a screenwriter. I worked almost solely on his behalf and within a short time gained the reputation of being one of the best agents in town. Howard, never slow to blow his own trumpet, took delight in blowing mine.

'Town' in these terms meant, as it still does to a lesser degree, a small patch of Soho streets and one or two show-business restaurants and clubs in which it was possible to conclude a good day's work walking down the street towards lunch, doing a deal on a street corner, concluding another with a luncheon partner, initiating still one more over a chance encounter at the bar, and a third on one's return journey - not unlike the Los Angeles network today, except that the deals held fast, the films got made, and it was rarely necessary to move outside London.

I also had the added advantage of being one of the few women active in the agency world in those days. I was young enough, comely enough, to feel no hesitation in approaching the giants of our London hierarchy. I was also unattached, which in some cases made the approaches welcome. I used my femininity shamelessly but I didn't stay unattached for long.

Howard invited me to a dinner at which he proudly proffered a carrot: I would meet there one William Fairchild. He didn't need the carrot: he had an excellent cook, a charming wife, a comfortable house. But John Redway's eyes gleamed and his smile was of anticipatory triumph when I told him. He was sure I might be about to lure William Fairchild as my client. Such was not my aim (I had never heard of him in any event, being too new in the business), but as a result of the dinner meeting Bill eventually became my client and the companion of the last thirty years of my life. It was also largely through him that my reputation as a literary agent in the film world grew.

Elmo Williams was running the 20th Century Fox London office. David Brown was the head of Fox's literary department in Los Angeles.[17] Darryl Zanuck still reigned supreme, albeit from his suite at the Georges V in Paris. Most of the other studios were still run by film-makers rather than ex-agents or accountants, and most of the London offices had Los Angeles executives manning them. A client of mine, John Burke, was the story editor at Fox. A very old friend from holidays spent in Spain, Bud Ornstein, ran United Artists. Old friends of my father-in-law and ex-patients of my husband headed the other London offices. There was no need to cross the Atlantic: enough of Los Angeles came to London.

The most talked about potential blockbuster in the late sixties was the Robert Wise-Fox film *Star!*, about the life of Gertrude Lawrence. Julie Andrews had just starred in *The Sound of Music* for Robert Wise and was to play Gertie, and Wise arrived in London to find a writer. Our office was across the street from Claridge's, so it took only a few yards' walk and a telephone call from the lobby to tell Mr Wise my name, announce my presence downstairs in his hotel, and the fact that I had the perfect writer for him – William Fairchild. I expect that 'coup', as it was to be perceived (John Redway's grin threatened to split his face), was the beginning of my reputation as an intrepid deal-maker, whereas I was unaware that less direct methods of approach might be the norm.

Like the war years in Sydney and the immediate post-war years in London, it was a golden time for me. The people in the film industry seemed nicer – was it because they were more secure? We certainly had more fun.

John Redway's office wasn't high in the fun stakes but it was a pleasant enough place in which to work. I remember my time there mostly because of the friendships and happy associations formed in those early days – with Denis Selinger across the hall, with Mel Frank and Norman Panama then working out of London[18], and Mel working his way through all the available females, with a young actor called Michael Caine who used to stop by my office on his way from seeing Denis to see if I had anything interesting 'to read'; and with a band of young writers represented by Warren Tute and Elspeth Cochrane's agency Theatrework, whose list included Arnold Wesker, John Arden and N. F. Simpson. I began to represent the film interests of their list, and so a new chapter opened.

After two and a half years I was still earning my £2000; I was also generating a lot of business for John Redway. No financial appreciation of this was offered, nor did it occur to me to ask for any. However, having negotiated impressive contracts for Bill, I did badly want to accompany him to Los Angeles. This John would not hear of. Warren Tute asked me to join him; the incentive was a promised trip with Bill; the result a few years working with Warren, which was immensely enjoyable, ending in costly disaster. But his promise was kept and I left John just in time to go to Los Angeles.

On our first trip to Los Angeles, we thought it would be nice to rent a house. Old friends of Bill's, Margaret Leighton and Michael Wilding, let us theirs in Harold Way in the Hollywood Hills. It had been Mike's when he was married to Elizabeth Taylor and some of the furniture had been Maggy's during her marriage to Larry Harvey. The dining table, in particular, loomed large in the list of taboos we were given over dinner in New York by Maggy. She had managed to salvage it from the marriage, a bone of contention, and lived in terror of Larry discovering its whereabouts and somehow spiriting it away. We were on no account to allow him into the house.

As it happened, the dining table faded into insignificance beside the other dramas the house had to offer, most of them connected to modern American life, and its machines.

My stubborn refusal to cope with machinery is now too deeply ingrained to erase. It is part fear, part impatience, part laziness. It is easier to say I cannot cope than to learn. I could almost have survived to the end, having mastered a typewriter in my twenties, a fax machine quite recently and the bare essentials of a motor car, if science and time had not come up with computers, e-mail, websites, the Internet (are they perhaps the same thing?), and many other inventions too frightening and too multitudinous for my mind to encompass.

The American-accented voice on my Japanese answer-machine greets me with a repetitive *You have a malfunction . . . you have a malfunction . . .* He does not tell me which particular malfunction plagues me and I don't know how to shut him up beyond crawling on the floor behind and under my bed, muttering angrily 'Shut up' or 'Fuck you', whilst scrabbling through the labyrinth of twisted wires from the bedside light, through hot blanket and telephone to the hated voice and disconnecting myself entirely from the outside world.

I can, with imagined hindsight, just work out how I came to lose my Filofax for one long traumatic day, and find it at dinner time under the grill; to discover after three puzzled weeks and a quick trip to Peter Jones, my iron at the back of the refrigerator; but I shall never learn to distinguish a speedometer from a rev-counter, how to operate the newest gas lighters, tin openers, deadlocks, or ticket-vending machines. There is no future for me in the machine age. I recollect fondly the ice man coming up the back stairs of my mother's house with the hessian sack dripping over his shoulder; the wall-mounted telephone which, when the handle was given a vigorous turn, responded with a friendly voice; the man behind the counter who not only sold you a ticket but told you where to find the train, bus, ferry, aeroplane; the milkman whose delivery obviated the necessity of wrestling with the cardboard obstacle course. I miss people.

When I set up house in Los Angeles in the 1970s I had never been to a supermarket, encountered a deep freeze or a waste disposal unit, lived with air-conditioning, or tended a swimming pool. I gave short shrift to these Californian aids to gracious living. The supermarket provided the cartons of eggs which I put in what appeared to be one of two huge gleaming refrigerators. Being the deep freeze, it transformed the eggs in no time into a mountain of meringue which billowed forth in the kitchen when the door was opened. The waste disposal unit chose the evening of our first dinner party to relentlessly disgorge its contents over the kitchen floor - corn cob after corn cob churning up and out. It only took the flick of a switch for me to blow up the air-conditioning. Terence Stamp had been the previous tenant and when we discovered rats playing with his jockstrap in the garage, and the swimming pool overflowed and flooded the next house down the hill, we thought a hotel might suit me better.

From then on, the Hotel Bel Air became our headquarters.

Perhaps because I was in love, perhaps because I was young and female, perhaps because the powerbrokers in the film industry had actually had some experience of film-making, like

Darryl Zanuck in Hollywood and Alexander Korda in London, I found Los Angeles in those days enjoyable and exciting.

Bill was for a few exhilarating years the 'hottest' writer in town: *Star!* not yet released but the buzz about it around town leading to more offers than he could accept; a dish named after him in the Fox commissary – the ultimate accolade – never mind that it was almost inedible. The Americans I had met in London, now back home, gave extravagant parties for us – Mervyn Le Roy, George Cukor, Frank Sinatra, Ross Hunter, Alan Ladd's widow, Sue. I swam around the Bel Air pool each day, intrigued to be summoned by the pool attendant to a telephone at pool's edge – no mobile telephones in those days, only one's name constantly on the loudspeaker. I didn't think I had much ego but I discovered one then.

Darryl Zanuck summoned us both to his suite in Paris to discuss subsequent films; on one occasion flying us separately, and so I flew from London accompanied, in my terror of flying, by both David Brown from Los Angeles and Andre Hakim (then head of the London office) so that I had two arms to clutch. David, I remember, had a single room at the Georges V and Bill and I had a suite each. David says he still has the suit with a sleeve missing from my clutches.

My children embraced my work, made friends with the clients and, depending on their ages as the years went by, entered a world which may have appeared more glamorous than the circles in which the parents of their peers moved, except that my daughter's school friends were a fair cross-section of London showbusiness – a hotbed, in fact, into which I had not known I was tipping her, of the offspring of Peter Hall, Edna O'Brien, Peter Sellers, Stanley Baker, Ferdy Mayne, Sean Connery. She was overheard by Ellen Baker holding forth to her group: 'Well, *my* mother's gone to Paris to tell Darryl Zanuck what she thinks of him' – in an effort, no doubt, at one-upmanship. Now that I was able to make the longed-for trips with Bill, it helped that my absences from the children during these periods also contained an aura of excitement for them. They felt involved.

Bill was asked to rewrite a film in deep, deep trouble in Colombia – Gillo Pontecorvo's *Quemada* (since become a classic – retitled *Burn!*) – the trouble being the incompatibility of the director, Pontecorvo; the star, Marlon Brando; and the incomprehensible script. That remains Bill's story: my triumph was that from two weeks work in Cartagena I was able to negotiate from United Artists sufficient excess baggage allowance for the trip to get us happily round the world for the next year on the vouchers.

The fact that *Star!*, although a well-made film, was a monumental flop in the United States (Gertie who?) didn't dampen either Bill's or my then successful rise through the Hollywood jungle. Bill remained rather proud of the fact of his involvement in an enterprise which was to single-handedly fell Fox. (*Star!* has now become a 'cult' film: on laser disc, continually shown on TV, remembered fondly by Robert Wise, and has, no doubt, been proved as not such a disaster after all.) Both of us coasted through the next few years after the making of *Star!* on his reputation, mine shimmering in his reflected glory. He wrote several very good screenplays and I made the appropriate deals.

At the outset of my work in the international film world, I was to hear the name of Charlie Feldman mentioned often as an influential player in the Hollywood game. On my first trip to Hollywood, I telephoned ex-fiancé Torbert, who, having married ex-actress Phyllis Brooks, might be able to supply some introductions.

'Well,' said Torbert, 'you remember Charlie Feldman?'

Indeed I did not, but he soon enlightened me.

Now, I do dimly remember a persistent hanger-on at our dinners and parties that 1948 Côte d'Azur summer, a sort of

Kennedy court jester from whom we could never escape. Torbert reminded me that one night over dinner at La Bonne Auberge I had said to Jack, 'Either I go or Charlie Feldman must go: he's an Olympic-class bore'; and that Jack had turned to Charlie and said, 'You heard the lady, Charlie - go.' It seems that Charlie went - to Hollywood and a pinnacle of power which I now aspired to climb.

I never telephoned him.

I managed, however, to survive in the rarefied air of Los Angeles without Charlie. Emmet's sister lived there, some of the instant friends made in the early days remained friends, and the Hotel Bel Air remained a welcoming womb in which to crawl on arrival in that fearsome place.

Expulsion from the womb was traumatic, but did not occur until many years later, over many happy visits. On that occasion, arrival was a Friday evening after a nineteen-hour flight from Australia. A beautiful basket of fruit awaited me in our beautiful room; a cheery note from the Assistant Manager said: 'Welcome back - Phil'. Hot bath, dinner in bed, tray put outside door: groggy but at peace.

Diary: *Ten minutes later a knock on the door 'Room Service'. Bill rather crossly says we've finished: a courteous voice asks if he may remove any stray plates. Jet-lagged as I am, the wish to waken to pristine order wins out and I wearily say 'Let him in'. Bill looks through spy-hole and sees man holding tray. The next thing he sees as he opens door is two more men leaping round the corner, three guns flashing and one of them crashing between his eyes. What I see is one man leaping on top of me on the bed before my face is covered with the sheet; something hard and, I suspect, nasty is pressed against my forehead.*

What I hear is Bill groaning softly in corner, from which I deduce he is not yet dead, and an urgent voice repeating in my ear: 'Where's the money?' 'Where's the jewels?'

I hear my own voice, decidedly governessy in tone to my own incredulous ears, saying, 'I'll tell you where everything is but I've just got off an aeroplane from Australia: I've been nineteen hours in the air: I'm very, very jet-lagged and I can't possibly tell you until you remove this sheet from my face because I can't see.'

Bill on knees in corner (with, I learn later, gun pressed to back of his neck) thinks: 'Jesus! She's going to give them her flight number next.' I think, as sheet is removed, how very silly I was to insist on seeing because I've now seen the hard object: my very first close encounter with a gun barrel. Also, as police later tell me, my assailant's face. However, I am able to identify beautifully tidy flight bag containing jewel case, and beside it, handbag with bulging wallet. I carefully tell them the colour of everything. I wait to be raped – slashed – shot.

Instead, I hear Bill being ordered to crawl into the bathroom, head down. Then, I am ordered to crawl into the bathroom, head down. They have called me 'ma'am'. We will be shot in the bathroom because it's cleaner, I think.

I see in the dim light of the bathroom a figure on the floor facing me, covered in blood. I ask, 'Darling, what have they done to you?' 'I'm perfectly all right,' whispers the blood-stained figure. We crouch, like two James Thurber dogs. But we seem to be alone. Cautiously, we peer out and crawl to the telephone to summon help. The room resembles a horror movie but it is all blood – not tomato ketchup.

We ask for a doctor. Five minutes later the security man arrives. He, too, has a gun. He says 'Shit' eight times, from which we deduce he is worried about his job. He asks three questions: 'Were they black?' to which the answer is 'Yes'; 'Did they have guns?' – another 'Yes' – and 'Which way did they go?' to which there is only one possible answer, 'Out'. He goes out, too.

After ten minutes two policemen come. They write down long statements about our birthdays, places of residence and other vital statistics. They ask me three questions: 'What weight would you say the man was who sat on you?'; 'What calibre gun?'; and, rather sweetly because no one else ever did, not even Phil of the Fruit Basket, 'Are you all right?'. I answer 'Yes', for which answer I am later chastised by the lawyer to whom we are guided, but I explain that one says yes because one is British. He thinks I am mad.

Eventually the 'paramedics' come, 'Nasty gash that – you'll need stitching.' The ambulance, however, is for life-or-death cases: if you can walk, a taxi will do.

The battle with the night desk continues. There is, I am assured, absolutely no one in the entire hotel who can possibly accompany profusely bleeding victim to hospital by taxi – a five-minute ride. I ask for Phil's number – it is 'totally restricted'.

We were attacked at 11.10 p.m. At 1.15 a.m. I finally locate a kind friend who comes to transport victim to UCLA where he has twelve stitches and is lovingly looked after. I, left alone in bloody battlefield, am not. Not even a cup of tea is offered, let alone a concerned voice. At 4.15 a.m. he returns and, full of pills, we sleep.

The next morning we confidently await messages, phone calls, flowers, Phil. At 11.00, we hesitantly ask. Phil has been, and gone, for the weekend. The Manager has left for the weekend; nobody seems aware that we exist. I ask for the blood to be cleaned from the bathroom. No one warns the maid who arrives smiling, and falls back, crossing herself. She obviously thinks we have been trying to kill each other in the night. We demand to move rooms.

After pressure, we are moved to what they think may be a 'safe' room because it is above the front desk. On Monday the Manager returns. We call him: he does not call us. When cornered he says he is deeply shocked. When asked if that is all he can say and will we be charged for the experience of staying in his beautiful hotel, he says we will not be charged for that night. That night, it seems, for the Bel Air did not exist.

Unlike most other Los Angeles hotels, beautiful Bel Air had no warning notices to guests not to open doors, no chains on those doors so that they could be banged closed in the faces of intruders, no main entrance through which all must pass. Swans swim serenely in the lake around which many of the rooms are dotted behind glass doors opening onto their private patios. It is like a private palace and so one assumes, because one is in a dangerous city, that there must be a policeman behind every tree or a hidden TV camera behind every bush - that such a grand hotel prefers to keep its security discreet. But beautiful Bel Air had one security guard on June 4 that year (1982), and now had two less clients: one with a nasty head wound and various other pains and aches, and one with no jewellery, a nervous twitch and many lost illusions.

After the experience I was taken aside by a kindly lady (actress): 'Don't you think you should go to a counsellor?' The victim is confused. I have only just learnt to call a lawyer an attorney, and wonder if this is yet another terminology. '*No - no* - a counsellor - to help you get rid of your rage.' I attempt to explain that I feel only deep gratitude - to fate, to God - not my attackers - for having survived relatively unharmed. Actress is now convinced I am deeply nutty. We do, however, succumb to universal advice and seek out a lawyer - reluctantly, as the British do not on the whole sue. I doubt we would have if I had ever been offered a cup of comforting tea.

We dropped our subsequent case because I am neither traumatised nor in therapy. Only British. We settled out of court for a fraction of the value of my jewellery, partly because our lawyer changed jobs and started work for the defendants (the insurance firm), partly because after five years we were bored, and partly because our - now their - lawyer intimated that the Bel Air could sue *us* - for defamation?

We learnt, later, that the hotel was in the process of being sold. All is different now: secure, but the result for me is a reluctance to stay in any American hotel and a dislike of having to walk down any long empty corridor. The Bel Air has recently been voted the best hotel in the world.

chapter twenty-three

But back in London, and back in time, our first trip completed, Warren's office was in direct contrast to John's. We were tucked away in a small street behind Harrods but what we lacked in impressive surroundings we compensated for in stylish living. For the first time, I had an expense account. At Redway's it seemed that only John went out to lunch. I had jolly luncheons with Warren when I wasn't having them with the clients, and business blossomed. Warren dispensed with an office accountant; indeed, he spent most of his time hunched over the books whilst I was out and about and abroad doing deals. Clients dropped in, champagne flowed, informality flourished.

One Christmas morning in my third year, I was dressing the children for our office Christmas Tree party when Warren telephoned. He sounded suicidal.

'Something awful has happened.'

I looked around, in automatic response – both my children were alive and well – it must be Warren's, or his wife.

'No, no,' he said. 'I've been up all night, with a new accountant. There's a problem with the accounts. I have to find over £20 000 in the next few weeks or we are ruined.' Nearly thirty years ago, £20 000 was quite a lot, but my relief

Thursday Club cricket lunch, 1948: The crime novelist Margery Allingham-Carter at the head of her table; on left, RD, Simon the dog, David and Prince Philip; on right, Vasco Lazzolo, plus other members and their wives. We were allowed 'in' once a year.

Thursday Club cricket match, 1948 – Baron and Prince Philip in top hats.

One of Baron's weekly portraits for my 'column'– I do not appear to be taking it too seriously.

At Madame Arthur's, Paris, 1947 – with 'Pino', 'Henrietta' and Wolfgang – in one of *the* hats.

Paris, 1948 – with Eric McIlree and David – halfway through the first aeroplane, but Eric seems happy.

Outside my country cottage with actor Kenneth More, Elspeth March (Granger) and Violet Eaton, 1948.

Chula and Lisba at Queen Elizabeth's Coronation – Lisba wearing Granny's Belt.

The household at Tredethy in 1951, in Bira's Trophy bar: Shura and Nan Rahm, Stanley Haynes, Lisba and Chula, Chelita (Bira's second wife), RD and Bira.

Wedding to Emmet, 1 May 1953: Baron, bride and groom, and Kay Walsh (then Mrs David Lean).

Our only posed family photograph, 1957 – with Emmet, Lisa and Seamus.

Thai government dinner party, 1955 – only I speak.

Villa Tagliaferri, 1957 – our tower is on the left.

was enormous - only money! So I reassured him that we would manage that somehow and he could tell me all about it under the Christmas tree. Warren cheered up immediately; telling me I was splendid, he mentally put his burden on my shoulders and we had a carefree day. When, after the full story emerged, it appeared that Warren's busyness with the books was not solely an economic measure. It also masked the fact that we did not have a clients' account. (I had no idea what this meant, anyway, being content with my jolly luncheons, my US trips, and my weekly salary cheque.) The earnings of John Arden, Philip Broadley, Eleanor Bron, Peter Draper, and a few more, had been paid into the Theatrework general account, in some cases being left there at the client's request against a subsequent lean year's earnings. Hence the champagne, the trips, the parties and, one presumes, the gilded lifestyle of Warren. The new accountant had uncovered this, and had threatened to report it unless the funds were immediately replaced. Elspeth Cochrane had already parted company with Warren; there remained an actor's agent, David White, and myself. David and I vowed to stand firm and do our best to bolster Warren over the next few weeks whilst hoping the money would appear from somewhere, but as fresh horrors emerged from the filing cabinets it seemed obvious that all would sink, including the clients, who were begging us to continue or they would be left with no agent, and, in some cases, no money.

We gave it six weeks. When we could go on no longer I found a temporary office in Conduit Street; we moved files overnight and I became, without intent, business experience, or forethought, an independent literary agent, Robin Dalton Associates, with a stable of clients, no capital, no idea how to run a business; indeed, no Associates: but with the knowledge of what was a clients' account.

The old Theatrework clients followed. So from being purely an agent in film deals, I was forced to learn very quickly how to manage clients' affairs in theatre and television and, gradually, publishing. The Royal Court was at the pinnacle of its early, great days – John Osborne, Arnold Wesker, N. F. (Wally) Simpson, were all writing their plays for it. David Storey was one of the 'new' boys, and all of them became, then or later, my clients. Tony Richardson was dividing his time between the stage and film; the directors were Anthony Page, Lindsay Anderson, Bill Gaskill, and John Dexter, and the bar was presided over nightly by Helen Montagu.

The Conduit Street offices tided me over the transition, but more permanent premises had to be found. The theatrical impresario Oscar Lewenstein, then Artistic Director of the Royal Court, telephoned me one day. A little house in Goodwins Court was becoming vacant, quite the most desirable residence for anyone working in the theatre, and an enclave impossible to break into – would I care to take over the lease?

If I could have moved children, bed, dog, cats and budgerigars into my enchanting little house I would have. It was one of the prettier ones – perfect seventeenth-century architecture, in a cobbled seventeenth-century walkway, and the twin brothers who owned the freehold of the entire Court lived in two tiny doll's houses spanning the archway at one end. They had identical little grey Tweedledee and Tweedledum beards; before assigning a lease, one was bidden to a glass of sherry, a morning biscuit, and a beady-eyed vetting. Having passed the test, I, the files, my faithful staff of three and the clients moved in. Those were the best days. I left one home each day in order to journey to another.

Almost simultaneously, I had acquired another new home. After four years of battling with my sinking spirits as the car turned the corner into our prim little Putney street, I moved into the most elegant, beautiful, life-enhancing house in St John's Wood, where we stayed for sixteen happy years. Steven Runciman, ever the fairy godfather, had, with his brother, sold their Isle of Eigg off the west coast of Scotland. Steven had bought a delicious pink Scottish castle and a London apartment and had given me the lease of this wonderful house.

Opposite me in Goodwins Court, her house not as pretty as mine, but distinguished by a board projecting into our alleyway like a pub sign blowing in the breeze, presided the doyenne of literary agents, the great Margaret Ramsay, at No. 14. We had never met. A week after my arrival the first of many fat, handwritten letters was pushed under my door: somewhat hysterically requesting me to vacate the court.

I sent a courteous but bewildered reply. In what did my offence lie?

Whenever I stepped out my front door a furious dog shot out of Peggy's, undergoing training, or so it seemed to me, in leg-biting. Its lips curled back in a vicious snarl, it barked at me all the way along the alley. Shortly afterwards Oscar Lewenstein telephoned.

'Please, for God's sake, do something about Peggy. Send her some flowers to pacify her. She refuses to speak to me and holds me responsible for you being in the Court.'

By then, I had had another three or four letters. I could not see why Miss Ramsay thought she owned Goodwins Court, and therefore why I should send her flowers. If any flowers were to be sent, surely it should be the other way round.

This situation continued for some months. My clientele and consequently my files grew. Robin Dalton Associates now had an associate. I had 'imported' from Paris a colleague, Alain Bernheim, with the intention of combining our two agencies and so the little house became too little. Above Peggy's office and using the same stairway was a floor which became vacant. Frank Dunlop, the outgoing tenant, offered it to me. It saved the space problem and so my files moved into No. 14a. This was altogether too much for Peggy. Her letters now accused me of trying to identify myself with her, of trapping her clients on the stairs, and I began to suspect tripwire laid across them, the dog having tired of trying to connect.

One of my clients, the director Peter Medak, who, like many people who knew her, adored Peggy, tried to bridge the gap.

'It's ridiculous, darling: you are so alike and you would love each other,' and so he wrote to Peggy saying it all had gone far enough and that he felt he should effect a luncheon meeting between us. Peggy's subsequent letter was directed at Peter, rather than at me.

MARGARET RAMSAY LTD
PLAY AGENT

Margaret Ramsay (Managing Director) *14 Godwins Court*
St Martins Lane
Telephone 01 - 240 0691 *London W.C.2*
01 - 836 7483

Cables: Ramsyplay, London, W.C.2 *(Reg. Offices 96 Britten Street E.C.1)*

Dear Peter;

This is a rather badly self typed letter. It had better be confidential, or I will find myself sued.

I want to explain why I didn't think it a good idea to have you arrange a meeting between Mrs Dalton and myself. In the first place, in the years we have been agents we never happen to have met, as we don't frequent the same ambiances – (for instance, I refuse to go to a restaurant like THE WHITE ELEPHANT, *which is full of agents spending the money taken from their clients, but behaving as if they are the important people, not their clients.) Secondly, I was a bit upset when she first moved into a Court where I've been the only agent for ten years, but of course I had no right to complain about that. However, no soon had I learned that she was taking number five, that I heard she was actually also proposing to move into this very house. I rang Frank Dunlop, who was letting the floor, and told him I had no idea it was to let, and that I would very much like to take it, particularly since another play-agent was moving in. He was terribly upset, as he hadn't known who he was getting it to, and he immediately asked his lawyer to deal with mine, as nothing whatever had been done by Mrs Daltons lawyer yet. However, he was informed, and Frank was immediately told that if he offered me the floor, Mrs Dalton would sue him for breach of contract (even though no contract had been made, and the lawyers hadn't even exchanged views.) Frank's Company own the floor below, and he was frightened to get his Company mixed up in a court case, so he reluctantly told me the position, which I had to accept. But before I even spoke to Frank, and the moment I heard of Mrs Daltons intention to move into this house, I wrote and asked her if I could please take the floor and I would pay all and any of the expenses etc. She replied that it was quite impossible as it was essential for her to have these extra offices as she couldn't possible run her agency without all the rooms.*

During the year she has been here, she has of course hardly used these offices. So she wasn't telling the truth, it seems. So – I deduce that Mrs Dalton is fairly ruthless, fairly selfish, and not very sensitive. These attributes (or negative attributes) are, I'm sure, the best equipment possible to become a good agent, but the last thing you want to find in your friends – and you were suggesting that we should become friends. I think after all she did that its even more insensitive of her to even suggest it. Does she really think I want to be her friend? I just don't want to think bout her at all. She is always asking people to effect an introduction – WHY?

Oddly enough Oscar thinks I'm being over-sensitive, but then I think he obviously doesn't understand about how people tick. And he doesn't understand how disagreeable the very idea of the agent "metier" is, as far as I am concerned. The behaviour I received from Mrs Dalton epitomises my whole idea of the vulgarity of the agency business.

So – it was sweet of you, and I hope you don't mind my not wanting to have to meet people, just because they happen to be in the Court.

Love, Peg

He gave up. I was driven to reply:

4 Goodwins Court
St Martin's Lane, WC2

Dear Miss Ramsay,

I am sick to death of hearing your scurrilously untrue version of 'l'affaire *Goodwins Court' and of hearing myself slandered in this and every other area.*

I have no intention of trying to sue you, or anything so laughable. I also have very little wish to meet you (which I have never suggested – people are always suggesting it to me, because they think we are so alike, God forbid!) but I have over the months thought it a great pity that our relationship is so strained that I would find it embarrassing should I have occasion to telephone you on business. For that reason only, I hoped that you had simmered down sufficiently to see the facts as they truly happened, or it would be indeed unpleasant were we to even meet on the stairs.

However, now so many people have repeated to me your version of our dealings and various other remarks that I'm bloody fed up and wish you to READ CAREFULLY *the following precis of* THE TRUTH.

1) *When you wrote and asked me not to take the rooms I replied that I needed them badly, although mainly for storage, but that,* TO HELP YOU *(at subsequent inconvenience to myself) I would use it personally as little as possible, would not have mail sent there, or any name displayed.*
2) *You replied asking if we might share it.*
3) *I replied saying that at first sight I doubted this could work, but might I come over and discuss it with you.*
4) *You replied 'Forget it' (fairly insultingly, I might add).*
5) *My contracts were on the verge of signature when you attempted to put pressure on Frank Dunlop and I would not have been advised by my lawyers that I could sue for breach of contract had they not been at this stage. A far more advanced stage of proceedings than you would have people believe.*
6) *I have, indeed, not used the full space during this year and could perhaps have lent you some of it (which is what I was prepared to discuss at the proposed meeting). But the portion I have lent (not let, as you claim) is very small and on a very temporary basis.*

Some general comments:

1) *I have lunched at the White Elephant perhaps once or twice in the past year and not by my own choice – always as a guest. So you should get your facts straight before quoting people's haunts (or even type of).*
2) *I can't imagine why you thought I could possibly interfere in your affairs? Do you think I am so eager*

for clients, or are you so insecure, that you imagine me planting an ambush on the stairs of 14a to catch them on their way up – or way down, perhaps?

Yours sincerely,

Robin Dalton

We continued to manage to avoid each other. But the day came when two of our clients – writer and director – were to work together. Somehow, communication between us had to be achieved.

I telephoned her. I suggested lunch at the pub opposite, the Salisbury, still smarting from accusations of White Elephant extravagance.

One got a very good pub lunch at the Salisbury, perched on bar stools. Peggy and I decided we loved each other almost at once.

'But of course he's an absolute shit, darling,' Peggy's theatrically trained vowels bounced off the bar mirror as we relished our exchanged gossip and viewpoints about first one, then another, of our shared business acquaintances. Two hours later we reluctantly prepared to part. On the next stool to mine was a solitary chap. As we disentwined our legs from the bar, he took my arm. 'I don't know who you two ladies are,' he said, 'but I must tell you I've seldom enjoyed a lunch more.'

After that, peace reigned in the Court. The dog wagged its tail. Whenever we needed mutual help, or advice (although taking advice was contrary to Peggy's nature), we telephoned each other. An old client and friend of mine, Rodney Ackland, had long since drifted out of my life, as he drifted out of everyone's when he felt he owed them too much money to borrow any more and therefore the point of retaining contact had vanished. He was a much undervalued and neglected playwright, and one of his unperformed plays had failed to find an audience. Although I no longer represented him, I felt it should be done – somehow or somewhere. Frith Banbury and I put our heads together and I bullied all the subsidised theatres, the National, the Royal Shakespeare Company, the Court and any regional theatres sufficiently endowed to support its vast cast. I rang Peggy: she enthusiastically offered her support, and she, Frith and I joined forces in attempting to find a home for *The Pink Room*, as the play was then called. Rodney never knew or, if he did, paid much attention. Anthony Page was then my client. He never forgot the play and some twelve or fifteen years later, thanks to Anthony, it was produced by the BBC as *Absolute Hell*. Rodney lived just long enough to see the finished version on video but not to read the glowing reviews. Nor to see its subsequent life at the National Theatre, again directed by Anthony – Judi Dench in both venues, and based, in part, on the French Club and Olwen Vaughan.

The move to Conduit Street with the files, and the subsequent more substantial one to Goodwins Court, had happened so quickly, the business had grown so rapidly, and my own commercial sense was so shaky that I had failed to realise that I was doing rather well. In the beginning, my main concern had been how to pay the rent. Believing that I was no businesswoman I had assumed that I needed backing. This was swiftly and reassuringly offered by Tom Mashler and Graham Greene, then running Jonathan Cape Ltd, and was thankfully seized upon by me. Months of negotiations followed – friendly evening sessions with them and my lawyer working out the amount of capital I would require and the percentage of profits I would retain of my business. After eight months my lawyer expressed his concern to me.

'How are you managing financially whilst this deal is being discussed?' he asked me.

I rang my bank manager. I was very handsomely in profit,

it seemed. My lawyer brought negotiations to a speedy close. I didn't need backers. Tom and Graham were exceedingly gracious about our wasted meetings, and I was able to concentrate exclusively on my clients' concerns, rather than my own.

It has never ceased to amaze my clients, myself, and certainly Bill that I should combine a hard head for business and an undoubted gift for driving spectacular bargains on behalf of others with a total incompetence where my own financial affairs are concerned. This is not a pose: it is only too horribly, disastrously, scattily real. I am sure a psychiatrist would not have to delve too deep to interpret it. As for myself, it is far easier to accept than correct. One morning, upon opening my personal mail, before my business persona took over at the office, a closely typewritten page of figures ended with what appeared to be a huge total. 'Bill,' I gasped, 'my widow's pension has *shot* up - it's enormous - look!'

'That,' he said, 'is your telephone bill.'

chapter twenty-four

Agents' memoirs can only be truly interesting if names are named, confidences breached, enemies made, half destroyed files gone through. In my life, notes lie on slips of paper, half-filled notebooks in every drawer, partly muddled up with the event- and people-filled years of a life in which no coherent records were kept. Whole people have slipped down the plughole of oblivion in my overcrowded mind, but my clients were the larger part of that life for twenty-five years.

What to say about them? I was their servant and in nearly every instance, I was also – and am – their friend. Amusing tales might be a betrayal, particularly with a writer, one of those beings whose subconscious, if not conscious, mind would have absorbed those tales into their own membranes of memory. And in the doing, possibly transformed them.

To quote postcards and letters is to steal their copyright – to recount joint memories to intrude on their material. I allow myself only brief insights into some of their characters – the occasional longer anecdote to amuse, perhaps. These recollections are chosen, if not quite at random, then due to some capricious chance of having found letters, documents, photographs. Not because these clients were more important to me than others but only because I don't think in these instances I am transgressing any privacy.

Out of the rollcall of illustrious names whose careers I am proud to have been a part of - Mike Leigh, Hugh Hudson, Anthony Page, Waris Hussein, Peter Weir among the directors, Bernice Rubens, Ruth Prawer Jhabvala, Jon Cleary among the writers, to name but a few - I select the following flashes only in the hope that these tiny observations may shed a light on some salient characteristics. Food seems to be a link with many - I was able to do deals for them by day and cook for them at night.

The American clients I came to represent in England only, through my reciprocal arrangements with the US agents - the great 'ladies of the corridor' as they were known in the New York office of what was then IFA, with whom I was to merge: Kay Brown, through whom I represented Arthur Miller; Audrey Wood - Tennessee Williams, Bill Inge, Christopher Isherwood; and in Los Angeles 'Zig' of Ziegler-Ross - through him the director Richard Donner; from Robby Lantz in New York, Milos Forman. When Alain Berheim joined me from Paris, I absorbed Gore Vidal, Louis Malle, Irwin Shaw, Jules Dassin, Larry Gelbart. Most of them were my charges at one remove, looking after them in the UK; never such intimacy as with my native English brood.

I did not represent actors, nor did I wish to, apart from two or three - one, Lalla Ward, the daughter of a friend, Jill Bennett briefly, and then Joan Collins.

On the flyleaf of Joan's last book she has written: 'Darling Robin - you are part of my life always'. That life is a triumph. A triumph over adversity, tragedy, the bumps and grinds of surviving fame in Hollywood, occasional ridicule at home, four less than perfect marriages, and recently - splendid news - the bestowal of an OBE in England. I am happy I shall always be part of her life because these things are easy to forget and it seems to be much easier for actors. Not Joan. She is, above all, loyal and down to earth and what I was part of was a crucial stage in that earthing.

I started to represent Joan because she was then married to Ron Kass and I was dealing professionally with Ron, as a producer. Ron asked me if I could not help to lift Joan out of the rut of second-rate films and TV shows into which she had slipped. I like to think that I did; helping to have her recognised once more as a talented actress. During those years I steered her into quality television opposite John Gielgud and the like; lucrative TV commercials with Leonard Rossiter; a few not too memorable films; and finally the stage at Chichester in *The Last of Mrs Cheyney*.

During the run of this, Bill and I went down to Chichester for the eighth birthday party of her adored daughter, Katy. A happy afternoon - just the four of us and a friend of Katy's. I remember Joan saying, 'I am in love with Katy. I adore all my children; but I am in love with Katy.' Days later, Katy was to have the car accident about which Joan has written.

Joan asked us if we would visit Katy in hospital. The hospital, just outside central London, is the main public (teaching) hospital for serious nerve injuries. We were led into a ward in which were six narrow beds. In the other five lay pathetic little creatures who most resembled battered animals - animals left whimpering by a roadside, conscious but not cognisant.

Katy lay in a coma, tubes attached to every orifice, every part of her: still and white. Her pillows were pink, ruffled. Her bed was surrounded by hundreds of cards, photographs, toys, ribbons fluttering merrily in myriad colours. At the end of the bed was a television set on which flickered her favourite show. Beside her bed sat her father and busying herself constantly around it was her mother - tireless, sleepless, unmade-up face, scraped-back hair, cheerful smile, laughing voice - talking, talking, talking to the stiff little body on the bed. Outside the window was a caravan, a far cry from the luxury 'trailer' all movie stars demand on set, this one fairly basic with two bunks on which Joan and Ron took four-hour shifts to sleep, climb back through the window to take up their bedside vigil.

'Katy!' called Joan. 'Look who has come to see you.' I took my cue, leant over and kissed the still, unconscious face and pinned on the pillow beside it a bunch of lavender. Joan continued, 'And look what Robin has brought you; it smells lovely.' And so she went on, never silent, never still, touching, talking, literally breathing and willing life into her child.

I was there the day Katy's toe was seen to flicker: a tiny tremor of movement. She had been propped up amidst her tubes on her father's knee. Neither Ron nor Joan stopped talking to her, playing with her, for days, weeks. I watched Joan bring Katy back to life. Joan would give all credit to the doctors and to the hospital and has, indeed, devoted much time, energy, and money to support them but I don't believe that medical science alone could have supplied that life force.

So – no amusing Joan Collins anecdotes. Only praise for her spirit, her loyalty, her guts and her professionalism. In the days of the numerous unmemorable movies, one memory stands out: the times producer after producer (with whom I had invariably fought over her fee) would telephone me at film's end to voice their thanks and appreciation for the hard work of a real 'trouper'.

Another actor, whom I represented for about a month, was old friend Stewart (Jimmy) Granger. A trifle rueful at the sight of his contemporary, James Mason, having made the transition from romantic leading man to distinguished character actor, he asked me if I could not perform the same service for him and cast him in a new mould, if I should come across a suitable script. I did – I had one – a perfect role for the fifty-year-old Jimmy.

'There's no money in it,' I enthused. 'It's a tiny budget film but it's a wonderful part.'

'Well,' said Jimmy, 'you're a silly cunt, aren't you. I love money, and I hate acting.'

That was the end of our professional relationship, although not our friendship.

I am gobbling up everyone else's memoirs. Everyone, I should say, whom I know. Joan's has stimulated memory and now I read in the painter Jeffrey Smart's of his meeting with Moura Budberg. This leads in turn to my memories, not only of Moura, but of the Australian writer Hal Porter. Like many writers, he stole other people's memories, and savaged mine. One of the disillusionments, although not without enjoyment, of combining client with friend.

I rate the first two volumes of his autobiography, *The Watcher on the Cast Iron Balcony* and *The Paper Chase*, as amongst the best of the genre. Hal was also a poet. He aspired to be a playwright and through that avenue came to London and into my life with his play *The Professor*. He was vastly attractive, unreliable, amusing: I was intrigued by him. We had what I suppose was a flirtation - some suggestively loving letters, a tantalising unspoken promise of some deeper relationship. I lent many of his letters to me to Mary Lord, his biographer, and have since found many more. Hal's accounts in Australia of his London productions, his London successes and near-misses do not tally with my literary agent's records, but it is his distorting of my friendship with Moura in a subsequent volume of short stories, *Mr Butterfry*, that I find hard to forgive.

Moura, the Baroness Budberg, was a substantial figure both in life and in literary London. She was Russian, had married first an Estonian, Count von Benckendorf, and after his murder by revolutionaries, a German, Baron Budberg. Her lovers were usually writers - but all of them famous: Bruce Lockhart, Maxim Gorky, H. G. Wells and Alexander Korda. It was always said, on introduction to Moura, that three of them had 'died in her arms'. In probability, this could be narrowed down to two - Gorky and Wells. I don't remember how we became friends but we were close for thirty years, until her death, and I loved her company, as did everyone. She lived in a vast flat on the Cromwell Road, noisy, cluttered and fairly dusty, where one drank minute frozen vodkas at dusk with half of literary London. Moura continued to review books almost until the end, and she loved a party well into her eighties. It was at one of mine, a garden party in my house in St John's Wood, that Hal's betrayal occurred.

Hal was in the garden - just arrived from Australia, and knew no one. He asked about the old lady holding court under a tree. I told him her name and the salient facts about Moura which could be fitted into a few sentences - her departed lovers, her 'salon', her charm - and explained that more court was being paid than usual by her many friends and acquaintances in a show of loyalty and support because she had recently appeared on page one of most of the tabloids as BARONESS ARRESTED FOR SHOPLIFTING. Everyone knew Moura was a dedicated kleptomaniac. One tried to hide particularly treasured possessions but the chances of swapping them back at a later date with another victim were not unlikely, as she stole to give. Somebody's silver ashtray at Christmas could, if one was lucky, be exchanged back for one's own Dresden figurine, and a happy Christmas had by all. We all valued Moura more than the belongings. All she had 'lifted' this time were books, from Hatchards, of which she had no need.

I stupidly told Hal a little of this in a brief résumé of Moura's life before introducing them. He spent some time with her before leaving. He did not, for once, send me a copy of his next book. Here is an extract from the story 'The Two Baronesses':

The Russian baroness I met a couple of days after arriving in London from Japan.

Lisa Eaton, a beautiful and witty Australian widow, asked me to a late-afternoon party. She lived in Elm Tree Road, NW8, slap-bang next to Lord's in that Lisson Grove area once fashionable with such lickerous scions of the Victorian nobility as could afford Gaiety Girl mistresses. It was in the discreet and charming streets hereabouts that stripling dukes used to lease for their demi-mondaines bijou houses concealed behind walls of gladiolus-coloured brick, and secretive gardens of laburnum and delphiniums and moss roses. Lisa's house might well, in its day, have served as one of these love-nests, or as the retreat of a superannuated courtesan of the Lily Langtry kind, grateful to be becalmed at last with a rake-off of ruby bracelets and pendants, with her Turkish cigarettes, M. E. Braddon novels, and a silver saucepan in which to boil milk for December nightcaps of Schweitzer's Cocoatina.

. . . Lisa's party was held out-of-doors on a day of dead-calm Indian summer weather. The giant plane-trees behind the Members' Stand of Lord's, towering over her garden wall, could have been the outskirts of the Forest of Arden: As You Like It *was in the translucent air. For the rest it was all very English: the apple tree growing out of the lawn was as arthritic and bebunioned as an Arthur Rackham one; a Mermaid rose looped itself about the wrought-iron railing of the steps to the house with pre-Raphaelite intemperance; the hired stewards spoke in cockney or stage-butlerese; twilight lingered and lingered and lingered; doubtless a nightingale somewhere in the fragile upper galleries of the planes contemplated an aria.*

Something always gets added to a crowd, no matter whom

it is composed of or what it has come together for, something that one cannot and does not really want to stroke one's hand across, although one clearly sees oneself wanting to. The something that hovered like an invisible mist, a scentless fragrance, about Lisa's gathering of the famous, the up-and-coming, and the merely dazzling - poets and poetesses, novelists, actors, socially amphibious and extrovert blue-bloods - endowed them with the incandescence and piquancy of imperfection-proof immortals. Under the lofty branches borrowed from Lord's they drank champagne as though they had not experienced and were never to experience petty thoughts, moral headaches, unnecessary lusts, or outbursts of spite.

Lisa, vividly circulating, ultimately came to me with her 'Darling, I must snatch you away from these fascinating wretches - you haven't met my favourite baroness yet.' As she led me off she said from the corner of her mouth, 'I'll tell you more about her later, but she's a fabulous darling. She used to be Maxim Gorky's mistress. He died in her arms . . .' By this time we had reached the apple tree near which stood several people with the air of those small and kneeling donors one sees on the outer panels of devotional triptychs and, rearing imperially as Melancholia, as it were in the centre of the central panel, the Baroness –' . . .

. . . As we reached her, her face, that seemed to have grown pallid and sorrowfully blank in the obscurity of disreputable palaces haunted by the back-fire of balalaikas and the snarling of tzigane love-songs, resurrected itself, and expressed unmistakable relief at the sight of Lisa. She drained her brandy, sea-horse and all, like Catherine the Great playing Cossack.

'For you, dear Lisa, I shall smile,' she cried in a voice of operatic floridity, and smiled.

. . . Before she did go she had freely offered me her manner to Lisa rather than her imperious manner to the others, and had invited me to come with Lisa to her flat in Queen's Gate

the next day for eleven o'clock hairs of the dog. Invited? Summoned is a more exact word. Refusal, I felt, could have meant the salt-mines or the knout . . .

Just before she moved off and away from the apple tree with the stateliness of Helen pacing along the Trojan ramparts, she said, 'Have you told him, dear Lisa, that I have been a model of wickedness? No? Then tell him behind my back so that he will drink with us tomorrow without ignorance of me. Tell. Tell. Tell.' The thrice-uttered word, each with its special intonation, seemed to suggest that three, at least, visions were possible. She departed, leaving to stand in her shape in the twilit English garden an unseen statue of some musky Persian scent like Otto of Roses.

Later that night, indoors, when most guests had gone, and only a hard-core seven or eight Australians were finishing off the party, Lisa presented a champagne-enlarged résumé of the Baroness's life. The idea remains with me that not only Gorky had died in her arms but several other famous literary lovers – was H. G. Wells one? Famous names were everywhere scrawled across the pages of her doings: Chaliapin, Melba, Katherine Mansfield, Emil Jannings, Isadora Duncan, Fritz Lang, Marie Corelli, Augustus John, Conrad Veidt. Now, over seventy, still volted with life, and looking no older than fifty-something, she earned her living by translating Russian and French works for publishers, the BBC, for West End theatres.

The story is a good one – well written. But he distorted the introduction, changed and vulgarised my words. He had not bothered to hide my address, the description of my house, or even to cloak my identity. 'Lisa' is my daughter's name. None of these details added anything to the story: they simply served to point the finger at my own indiscretion (disloyalty?) should it be read by Moura. The story went on to record the kleptomania; I lived in terror of someone sending her the book to review. But not too long after, she died: not the death she would have wished but drugged against pain. I remembered a remark she had made to me once, when we were talking about death some years before.

'I want to enjoy my death. I have enjoyed my life and I do not wish to be robbed of the experience. I want to know all about it.'

In the 1970s, Ben Travers, a legendary name in the British theatre dating from what were known as the Aldwych farces – four truly great examples of the genre: *Rookery Nook*, *Cuckoo in the Nest*, *Thark* and *Plunder* – had become only a name. Very few had heard of him for over thirty years. But suddenly he wrote a new play – a sparkling, witty, gloriously original play.

He was brought to see me by my client, director Anthony Page, and Helen Montagu of the Royal Court, after they read this play, *The Bed Before Yesterday*. They thought he should have an agent before they put it on at the Court. Within half an hour Ben and I discovered that my mother's childhood friend, and my sometime honorary godmother, was the mother of the woman he had lived with for twenty or so years after his wife's death, and on whom he had loosely modelled the lead character in *The Bed*.

Ben has written his account of our first meeting and our friendship in his own autobiography, *A Sitting on a Gate*. He described our meeting as a miracle. There was, for me, something both miraculous and transporting in discovering and cherishing a close, exhilarating and life-enhancing friend as he entered his eighty-eighth year. With Ben, age was irrelevant. We were to have nearly six years of one of the merriest relationships of my life before he died on the eve of his ninety-fourth birthday. In those last years he had the excitement of seeing three of his plays running simultaneously in the West End: *The Bed*

Before Yesterday, written in his late eighties, at the Lyric, revivals of *Plunder* at the National, and *Banana Ridge* at the Queen's. And he worked on all three. Rewriting during rehearsals of *The Bed*; attending rehearsals and advising on *Plunder*, and rewriting and restructuring an entire act of *Banana Ridge* - nightly - on his way home by train from Guildford where it was tried out. At the same time, Alan Ayckbourn staged a revival of *Rookery Nook* at his theatre in Scarborough. This meant a train trip up for the night, a picnic hamper on the train provided by me and two bottles of chilled champagne with which to wash it down by Ben, another bottle to greet us in our rooms provided by Alan, and a champagne supper with the cast afterwards. We dined at the Garrick Club when we weren't at one of the theatres - and I laughed as I had not laughed since my parents died.

Helen Montagu invited him to *Side by Side with Sondheim*. He didn't really want to go - an evening far removed from his theatrical gods of Pinero and Galsworthy, but it was a huge success, nice of Helen to invite him, and I rather wanted to see it. We had house seats - bang in the middle. The house was packed. The curtain rose and nice Ned Sherrin walked to the footlights and began to address the audience. After a very few minutes, Ben, in the heavy hiss of the deaf, exclaimed: 'Who's that chap? He's awful!'

'Ssh, darling - it's Ned Sherrin.'

'Yes, but who *is* he?'

Trying to whisper, into a deaf and irritated ear, the lengthy and somewhat complicated biography of the multi-talented Ned, in as few but telling words as possible is not simple. 'Well,' I began, 'he sprang to fame in the 1960s in a show called *That Was the Week . . .*' This wasn't going to work. I'd lost both his attention and my own thread.

'What? What?' Ben was now speaking in hissing bellows. People in front were turning heads; those on either side lifting eyebrows.

I tried a new tack. 'He writes. He's a sort of partner of Caryl Brahms . . .'

'Good God!' A positive explosion from my side. 'Do you mean to say my darling Coral lets *him* fuck her?'

'No - no,' hurriedly from me. By now, I too am hissing quite loudly and people are getting cross. 'Not Coral Browne - *Caryl Brahms*.'

'Oh, well,' Ben sounded relieved, 'she's bloody lucky if anyone fucks her.'

He subsided into silence for the rest of the first act. Ned carried on entertaining me and everyone else, until interval.

'Well, now,' says Ben at the bar, 'do you think we have to go back?'

As we are Helen's guests and in prominent house seats (and I am enjoying myself), I explain that I think we would be missed and therefore be insulting, and that, yes, we must. We settle into our seats. The house lights dim. Ned once more walks to the footlights.

'Ladies and gentlemen,' he begins. I see a curve of spotlight arching up from the gods, slowly descending. 'We are honoured to have in our midst tonight a man who is a legend in his lifetime . . .' The spot has passed over the boxes, the heads of the first few rows and is clearly coming our way.

'My God,' Ben bellows, no longer hissing, 'is that bloody bounder talking about *me*?'

He got up and made his bow. I can't remember if he subsequently met Ned - and to meet him is to like him - but I hope that he did.

The year before he died, Ben agreed to write a little book of cricket reminiscences for Roger Houghton of Elm Tree Books. He had a deep love for the game, could remember when he was seven seeing W. G. Grace bat, and went as far afield as Australia to see a test match. With his phenomenal memory, he could recount the great moments as well as the scores. The book was to be called *94 Not Out* and was to appear on his ninety-fourth birthday.

Just before publication Ben went to a ball, drank and ate rather too much, stayed up rather too late and spent the night throwing up on the bathroom floor, where he was discovered next morning by his cleaning lady. A violent stomach upset at ninety-three is not to be ignored, so he was whisked off to hospital in an ambulance for tests. The following night he was due to appear on Michael Parkinson's television show, standing on his head - his favourite party trick. All day he begged the doctors to send for me, so that I could call Michael Parkinson, and assure him that Ben would be well enough to appear. By nightfall, anger that no one would do this brought on a heart attack and he died.

The publishers were in a dilemma. Dustjackets had been printed for the cricket book. I suggested the alternative title *94 Declared*.

I was also able to see Ben's last wish carried out.

'Promise me,' he had said one day, 'that my epitaph shall be "THIS IS WHERE THE REAL FUN BEGINS".'

After his death, the agency to which I had now sold myself - dragging with me unwilling and complaining clients - embraced Ben's memory to the extent of digging out portraits of him from my personal files, sticking his signature on the bottom, cut out, no doubt, from some redundant contract, and hanging it in pride of place in their front office. I don't think Ben would appreciate it. He chose never to remember the names of my successors and rejoiced in saying that as I had dropped my own name from letterheads he was now under the roof of people called Arriviste and Parvenu.

John Osborne asked me to lunch at the Ritz for our first meeting: I was later to discover a typically civilised gesture. I think we were both a little nervous and shy. Shyness is foreign to me but John's managed to cross over and infect me. His manners were, as always, impeccable (except when offence was intentional). Soon we became the closest of friends, travelling companions, Christmas and birthday sharers, recipients of the most carefully thought out gifts from each other. Joint refugees from failed marriages (his) and traumatic love affairs (mine), we scurried to shelter in each other's houses. Too close, I now see, for the pattern of John's relationships, always rushing headlong towards the U-bend. It took ten to fifteen years, however, and they were good years.

John derived much amusement in finding new 'names' for me. 'Mrs Fuckwit' was a favourite – slightly edged out by 'Madame Hulot'[19] after staying with us in France. The fact that I was Australian gave him particular pleasure, thus affording him ammunition for his yearly invitations.

CHRISTMAS PLACE, MARSH GREEN, Nr. EDENBRIDGE, KENT

John and Helen Osborne
invite you to

CRANMER'S SUMMER BALL

Sunday August 30th
Noon Onwards

(General Synod Burned in Effigy 3.0 p.m.)

Swimsuits (1662 only)

Kids welcome, Social Workers, Guardian Women and Australians admitted

R.S.V.P.

These invitations were the spar to further contributions from his guests. From Ben Travers the following:

28 Wyndham Street
London W1H 1DD

Cranmer? Ah, yes – my senile mind recalls
That bloke; he was with me at school at Morecambe
In 1500. Organises balls
Does he? He only used to talk 'em.

I never saw him since we both were boarders
At Morecambe (he was the maths-master's fairy)
Then I believe he took to holy orders
And finally fell foul of Bloody Mary.

My god, she was a bitch; I lose my nerve
And turned R.C. But Cranmer got her goat.
But what a joy to hear that you preserve
His balls, to keep his honoured name afloat.

But dance? You taunt me. Oh, those nights again,
The rumba, conga, Charleston, hokey-coke.
Spurred on by Carroll Gibbons or Jack Payne,
And blissful prospects of an odds-on poke.

Gosh, I'd accept, if only half alive,
Your gracious bidding in a brace of ticks,
Ambitious to secure Prize number Five,
Or, more ambitious yet, Prize number Six.

I love your dear endeavour to provide
A light to pierce my circling winter's haze,
And haunt once more my lingering eventide
With dreamland raptures of my dancing days.

We first met through his then wife, Jill Bennett, whom I had agreed to represent. Jill and John not only shared a battle-scarred marriage; a secretary-cum-assistant, cum-confidante and buffer; but now an agent, so that jealousy and competition proliferated in even more areas. Jill was wickedly manipulative and acidly funny, but in the beginning she seemed to care for John. It was she who had suggested that he, too, move to my care, and it was she who telephoned me and suggested possible ways of lifting John out of his deep depression, and some years of unproduced plays, the key way being the possibility of directing.

It was not easy. A West End theatre was out of the question as all possible managements had already rejected the two unperformed plays, *Dorian Gray* and *The End of Me Old Cigar*. It had to be repertory, ideally in London, and Greenwich, under the direction of Ewan Hooper, seemed to be the answer. Greenwich agreed to mount a season of three Osborne plays, the main attraction being a revival of *The Entertainer*, with Max Wall playing the Laurence Olivier lead, John directing. This meant that it would be the original complete version as written, with not a word deleted. *Dorian Gray*, which John had originally thought might be played by a woman (Jill, naturally), was played by Michael Kitchen and *The End of Me Old Cigar* proved to be a pyrotechnical battleground between Jill and Rachel Roberts, who flew in, drunk and combative, from New York. The series was not a success: on the whole reviews were lukewarm, and a good deal of money was lost by Greenwich. But John had both his new plays performed, earned a little money, was able to try his hand at directing, and harboured a deep resentment towards me thereafter, hidden until the bubble burst, for having battled to give him this opportunity. It also lifted him, temporarily, out of his depression and out of relative and temporary obscurity.

His life entered a sunnier phase when he was to meet his

subsequent wife, Helen. I encountered, briefly, my second most exclusive club, through Helen. The Wednesday Club was certainly the most exclusive, being limited to two members, but through Helen I was allowed occasional access to the Wash-Out Wives Club. This, like the Wednesday, was a luncheon club, our meetings being dictated by the availability on a given date of sufficient members: these being the wives of writers, mostly in the theatre, who were not necessarily wash-outs as wives but considered so in contrast to the glow of their husbands' halos. Peter Nicoll's wife, Thelma; Christopher Hampton's wife, Laura; John Mortimer's wife, Penny; Charles Wood's wife, Valerie, were amongst them and I was only accepted as an honorary member as being a fully occupied literary agent could not rightfully qualify as a wash-out. I was allowed in occasionally, however, when I pointed out that I was the biggest wash-out of all: I was not even legally a *wife*.

Years later, when John was happily married to Helen, and at the height of our loving intimacy, the Osbornes suggested that we might convert a beautiful outbuilding in their grounds and live there. They had moved from their cosy, rambling house in Kent, where Bill and I had spent many happy Christmases, Easters, weekends and parties, into a huge and far grander house in Shropshire. As always, financial doom had dictated the move and once a new roof had been added, and several walls had been restored, there was precious little left over for furnishing on so grand a scale. Happy to be able to help, I managed to buy for them a few pieces of lovely furniture from the estate of a recently dead acquaintance, at a risible price. I, too, bought a huge bed, sofa and armchairs from the estate, destined for our own holiday home in Biarritz. Due to inspired timing, I was to leave my own relatively grand house in London for a small apartment. The furniture I could not house, in addition to these, would have gone to my daughter or to a saleroom, but it seemed a splendid chance to lend it to John and Helen until they got settled and gradually bought their own; thus also giving myself a chance to decide what to do with it eventually. It was a trouble-free arrangement for some two and a half years - the bed, sofa and chairs being installed in a spare room christened by the Osbornes 'The Dalton Suite' and in which slept their houseboys and subsequent guests (but never a Dalton).

The day came, much more suddenly than I would have chosen, when I had the opportunity to share in a load of furniture being transported to France - if I could have it ready within the week it would go for a fraction of the normal price. It was, indeed, short notice in which to remove a bed, even after more than two years - a bed in which I later discovered guests were to spend the weekend - but remove it I did, with suitable and genuine regret. I was not, I was told later by one of the house guests, the 'flavour of the month'.

It became immediately evident that John had decided that our long years of happy personal and professional association had not been at all what he had wanted. I had become in his mind a rotten agent, whom he had suffered all these years. Deals I had instigated for which he had praised me now became areas of, if not incompetence, feminine sloppiness; feisty fighting on his behalf for which he had expressed gratitude now seemed proof of mild hysteria. We no longer needed to speak on the telephone professionally, as the transition of my clients to the offices of Arriviste and Parvenu were proceeding, but Helen and I continued to chat every Sunday night and she continued to write me funny and affectionate letters. I assumed John was in a period of depression - maybe he was missing the bed? The fact remains that we hardly spoke again.

It didn't take him long to turn on my successor as his agent who was so horrified that he brought me a sheaf of letters to read. My gossipy morning letter from Helen had suggested that we lunch one day soon and amongst the sheaf presented to me that afternoon was one from her describing me as 'that stupid woman who is nothing more than an indolent meddler'. Stupid being an objective judgement with which I couldn't argue, I questioned the coupling of 'indolent' and 'meddler' and rushed to the dictionary. *Indolent*: lazy, idle, disliking work or effort; and *Meddler*: to involve oneself officiously. It would seem to demand a certain amount of effort on the part of an indolent person to achieve the interference demanded by a meddlesome one. In another letter I am referred to as 'the office girl'. I did not follow up the invitation for lunch. I miss Helen.

And I miss John dreadfully. I miss his humour, his wit, his generosity, his company. I miss what I mistook for his genuine affection.

My link with Sonia Orwell, George Orwell's widow, was definitely food - the love of it and the excitement of cooking it. I first met her socially at Edna O'Brien's, and then through the agent who handled the Orwell estate for publishing, Mark Hamilton. It was decided that I should look after all dramatic rights in the books. Without the years of adventurous shared meals this might have been a thankless task, as Sonia's main preoccupation was to prevent any adaptation of any of them, thereby preserving the integrity of the original, and making me quite a few enemies - Melvyn Bragg probably amongst them - when, at Sonia's bidding, I had to refuse permission for a stage adaptation, television version, or film treatment, written speculatively and handed over for seal of approval. Sonia invariably - possibly rightly - said no. She was certainly pretentious, breaking into French at the slightest hint of opportunity - exercising literary judgement ruthlessly - but she was intelligent and perceptive.

She was cruel, and she was kind. Her cruelty led her to indulge in public humiliation by a cutting tongue of some unfortunate, and usually shy and insecure, young acolyte. The kindness was shown in innumerable acts of silent generosity and thoughtfulness where she saw need.

She was, above all, courageous. Dying painfully and protestingly of cancer, she insisted on being taken to luncheon at La Tante Claire, just opened as the best and most talked about restaurant in London, by the American producer to whom we finally, possibly mistakenly, had entrusted the film rights of *1984*. He was desperately trying to impress her with his sincerity: he wanted to be thought a nice fellow. Sonia was just able to walk a few steps and was mostly confined to bed when not undergoing distressing treatments. But a meal at La Tante Claire would get her up, even if she could hardly swallow the food. It was for her an affirmation of life.

By this time, Mark, Sonia and I had hit upon the idea of forming a company to be called George Orwell Productions through which we would control the rights and be involved ourselves in any production. Sonia asked her accountant to finalise the necessary paperwork and join us on the board. The 'board' and the board meetings were a springboard for monthly luncheons, cooked alternately by me and by Sonia. We had a marvellous time planning our menus and surprising our fellow board members, and luncheons went on far into the afternoon. Of actual business done, I only remember agreeing to let the American buy *1984* providing I was his co-producer. Deal done, we decided that Sonia now needed a new lawyer, someone familiar with the film world.

A happy choice was Sam Lyons. I did the deal for the film; all other paperwork involving our new company was handed over to Sam. But Sonia had by now very reluctantly sold her pretty London house and was living in Paris in what one would consider romantic surroundings if one was still a student. A semi-basement hovel with a board over the bath serving as kitchen table but with a French door leading to tiny patio and entrance. The romantic side of this dwelling was that once you had taken the two steps to the patio you were facing onto the Luxembourg Gardens. The dismal side was that Sonia's cooking was now confined to a gas ring in the bathroom, chopping over the bath, and washing-up bowl emptied down the lavatory. It was not romantic leanings which had driven Sonia out of her London house and into this relative penury, but her accountant - our fellow board member. In fact, it was his father who not only controlled the firm but, as Sam Lyons peeled away the layers of deception, controlled the entire Orwell estate.

He had told Sonia that she could no longer afford to live in London and that, on the small allowance the estate was able to pay her, she would be able to exist in her beloved Paris, speaking French to her heart's content, whilst he looked after the trickle of royalties coming in from the books. Due to the formation of our adventurous new company and Mr Rosenbloom from Chicago, with whom I was now in close correspondence, it seemed that the sale of the film rights of *1984* and the financial involvement of our production company might enable Sonia to move to more agreeable surroundings and afford the occasional hotel stay in London. The cancer had not yet attacked her.

One day Sam Lyons telephoned me. He had been to lunch in the country and one of his fellow guests had been the accountant - senior. Not knowing of Sam's representation of Sonia, then in its initial stages, he had indulged in some conversational bragging about his Orwell connections. It was possible, he said, that a film of *1984* was going to be made and he personally owned seventy per cent of all George Orwell's works through a company he had formed at Orwell's death - George Orwell Productions.

It did not take long for Sam to uncover the facts. Unknown to Sonia, Orwell had indeed formed the company with his accountant, just before his death. Over the intervening thirty or so years, many of the documents he had given Sonia to sign, none of which she had even glanced at, were giving him ever-increasing percentages of ownership so that it had now reached the point where Sonia's portion was a very minor one. All the documents were legal.

We discovered that our company, George Orwell Productions #2, had never been formed by Accountant Junior. He had had many bounteous luncheons. If Sonia had not developed her cancer almost immediately, she might have fought on, but just before she died a settlement of sorts was reached: the accountants were paid off, thereby retaining what they had gained over the years plus a little bit more but freeing the enormous revenue which continues to pour into the estate - to the best of my knowledge, to Orwell's adopted son.

The first time I met Edna O'Brien was at lunch at Prunier's. Edna was looking for a new agent, someone had suggested me and she had telephoned, inviting me to lunch. Only Edna would invite the agent to lunch, rather than expecting the reverse. Typically Edna chose Prunier's - the current elegant restaurant of those days. Our friendship - and our professional relationship - was born during that lunch. I expect we drank champagne; we have been drinking it together ever since in good times and bad times, and have agreed on our own formula for priorities when the bank balance allows for no more luxuries: champagne and baked potatoes. We have our private jokes from shared memories: small phrases which summon up private meanings. Once she was to meet Louis Malle. Anxiety surrounded her attire. She described a new frock to me, debating its suitability. It seems, like Mussolini, that I gave it decent consideration before posing the pregnant question: 'How *long* is the frock?' Although, unlike Mussolini, the length of the frock had little bearing on the situation. Once, when staying with us in France, she discovered a new (French) word - *froideur*. A new word for Edna can be a shining gift. When people know we are friends they often ask me what she is really like. Let her public persona speak for itself, and Edna with her writing. For me, her essence is champagne and a baked potato. Priorities.

Arnold Wesker was one of my clients with whom I forged the strongest personal link and that, too, started with food. The first time I took him to lunch, at Mario and Franco's, then almost the first of the 'fashionable' Italian restaurants in Soho, we discovered our mutual love of puddings. Lunch consisted of three each. Through over thirty years I have fought with Arnold, eaten with Arnold, battled on his behalf (no thanks for *this*!), watched him doggedly almost destroy himself and his family, seen him and his wife, Dusty, become godparents to my granddaughter and finally almost given him up in despair. But of all my famous playwright clients, I still believe that Arnold's early plays are those which may survive changing fashions longest. Like Ibsen, he touches on universal themes and imbues them with an unerring sense of theatre. *Roots*, *The Kitchen*, *Chips with Everything* - surely no accident that the last two are resonant of eating in their titles. He goes even further with *Chicken Soup with Barley*.

I met Iris Murdoch at a dinner arranged by her publisher, Barley Alison, who thought the combination would be a happy one, which it was to be. But the first intimation that we were to share some of the same passions came when I drove Iris home from dinner. Our contact was sealed when two huge, heavy sacks of stones were hauled out of Barley's bedroom to be lifted into the boot of my car. Iris had been staying with Barley in Spain. The stones, pebbles, occasional rocks, were treasures gathered by Iris from Barley's beach and they nestled appropriately into the sandy debris left by my stones recently lugged up from our own beach in Biarritz, where I had begun to spend my summers. Neither Iris nor I could long be happy away from the sea - sea smells, sea creatures, sea structure. We knew we would get on.

Iris also loved food but cooked not at all. To open the occasional tin of sardines was to her a major culinary event, but we shared a most robust and appreciative greed. We could talk about food for hours, whereas to cook for her and to watch her childlike delight in the results was a supremely rewarding experience.

Margaret Drabble literally fell into my life.

At a crowded cocktail party, I was squashed in a corner with a charming young woman who, mid-sentence, dissolved in an unconscious heap at my feet. Nobody turned their heads. Nobody helped as I half carried, half pulled her into the bathroom, splashed cold water in her face, held her head as she was sick, and introduced myself. Maggy, pregnant and prone to fainting spells, became my client through childbirth. I felt an instant affinity because of our shared, obsessively protective concern for our children. Maggy is the only other woman I have ever met who would blanch at the sound of an ambulance and instinctively rush to follow it before realising that her children were in another city.

David Storey was alone among my clients in approaching me with meticulous planning. His wonderful play *The Changing Room* had just been made into a wonderful film by Lindsay Anderson. He was among the brightest stars in London's literary heavens. I had never met - nor even seen - him. One day I received a telephone call.

'Is this Robin Dalton? I am looking for an agent. I wonder if I could come and see you? My name is David Storey.'

Well, it couldn't be *the* David Storey, but nor could I decline this gentle, tentative telephone request, so I made an appointment to meet David Storey's namesake.

He looked just like the photographs I had seen in theatre foyers. We spent an hour together. I was totally enthralled by this exceptional man. The hour flew by. I was overjoyed at the prospect of representing him, clasped his hand at the door and was about to say how delighted I was when chilling words stopped my open mouth.

'Well, I'll be in touch. Thank you for seeing me,' and he was gone. Oh, my God, what did I do wrong? I thought. I couldn't believe it.

After three days I could stand the suspense no longer. I rang Mark Hamilton, his long-time publishing agent (as opposed to screen and theatre – until then my special fields).

'He liked you very much,' said Mark, 'but he is seeing twelve to fourteen agents, which will take some time, but I'm sure he'll let you know.'

I spent the next three weeks trying to count twelve or fourteen literary agents in London – failing – there simply could not be so many whom David might think of seeing, and he simply couldn't have so much time to spare. At the end of the month, I decided I had nothing to lose except some pride, one of the seven deadly sins? So I rang him.

He was mildly surprised. 'I thought you realised I would like you to represent me,' he said 'We'll meet again soon.'

Not clients, but memories.

Of Rodney Ackland, years before he became a client or I an agent. Years and years earlier, a bogus little doctor called Dr Engels had held a surgery in Harley Street every Thursday. I have no proven basis for labelling him 'bogus' except that the cures he offered were distinctly suspect. There was not much wrong with me – still in my twenties – except for neck pains, diagnosed as fibrositis, a then fashionable complaint that has been dropped from the 'in' list of diseases. But lots of theatrical friends managed to produce enough alarming symptoms to fill Dr Engels's surgery with half the neurotics of Shaftesbury Avenue every Thursday. He taught me to inject myself (through a raincoat) in the thigh with, I now suspect, water. It had no effects, ill or otherwise. But I convinced Rodney Ackland that Dr Engels might hold the key to his perpetually cold hands.

Yes, we did go to doctors in Harley Street in the 1940s with no more grave complaint than cold hands.

Rodney was assured by Dr Engels that he could cure him in one session. The cure was to be produced the following Thursday, having been brought up from Sevenoaks. It came in a solid black box. Rodney bared his arms expectantly. Dr Engels opened the box. It was full of squirming black leeches. They were to relieve Rodney of some of the excess of blood which Dr Engels told him was draining the normal supply from his fingertips.

Rodney ran all the way down Harley Street, his shirt cuffs still flapping open.

Emlyn and Molly Williams were great friends of the Hoschschilds and were almost the first people I met in London. Everyone has written their own account of Emlyn's witticisms, published or unpublished, wicked or - seldom - benign. It was he who first said, of Daphne Rye, then more or less managing Binkie Beaumont's theatrical empire at H. M. Tennant: 'It's the first known case of the ship leaving the sinking rat', when she left. It was he who, on seeing Joyce Carey and Noël Coward entering the Ivy at a time when a homosexual witch-hunt was sweeping London, and dear loving Joycie had not been averse to encouraging rumours of her impending marriage to Noël to circulate: 'There goes the future Miss Joyce Carey'. And it was Emlyn who, on seeing Jill Bennett tackling a corn on the cob at the Caprice, remarked: 'Now I see what Godfrey Tearle saw in her'.

Few people, however, know that he once tried to kill Lillian Hellman by pushing her under a Number 9 bus on a wet night in the Strand. I know because I met a shaken Lillian shortly afterwards. It took quite a lot to shake Lillian. Emlyn was directing and performing in a play of hers. Memory fails me as to the play, although I rather think it was *Watchers on the Rhine*. Binkie Beaumont, the Sinking Rat, had found Emlyn intractable over his interpretation of the second act, and in desperation had sent for Lillian who, as the author, had enough authority to insist on her own text as written. They all attended a rehearsal at the Savoy. Binkie hissed to Lillian that she should tell Emlyn she thought the second act very badly tampered with. They were walking from the Savoy to Simpson's along the pavement, Lillian on the outside, when she delivered this judgement to Emlyn. He gave her an almighty shove towards the gutter and the bus driver braked to avoid her body by inches.

Lillian had many enemies who might readily have pushed her under a bus, but to me she was the contrary to her perceived persona, and nearly everyone else's experience. I was naïve, perhaps, but I found her loyal, generous, and good company. I was much younger, could benefit her not at all, and yet met her over the years with ease and enjoyment. During clothes rationing she would post me clothes from New York. I don't expect everyone else on record can be wrong in describing Lillian as a monster – a mean, vicious and self-serving liar. Everyone must have a good side and I was lucky enough to experience Lillian only at her best. I neglected and forgot her in the last sad years of her life: it was I, not she, who failed in our relationship . . . And I *have* kept her letters.

Memories of clients should be balanced by at least one memory of their counterparts – the producers.

One of the resident Americans of the 1960s and 1970s who gave birth to the most anachronistic stories was Hal Chester. As a child he had been one of the famous 'Our Gang' screen actors of the 1930s. He had not changed much.

One day a colleague met him in the street. 'Hi, Hally, what are you doing lately?'

'Well,' said Hal, 'you know that of every ten movies made only one makes any money. *Somebody* has to make the other nine. I'm pretty busy.'

chapter twenty-five

Twenty-five years on, I was slowly extricating myself from the agency. It was a gradual process and, in many ways, a painful decision. As always, the desire for more freedom came into it. I longed to be out of reach of the eternal telephones just occasionally. I was rediscovering the joys of reading for pleasure, and so discrimination sharpened, whilst, on the other hand, the few tastes of disillusionment had left scars. I began to want to produce myself those books and scripts in which I believed but had been unable to sell. I had had to sign a seven-year agreement with my new colleagues guaranteeing that I would more or less hang around in the background until clients were 'weaned', and so I had more time to relax, to think about producing, to travel without guilt.

Once more, moving house coincided with changing work. Leaving my splendid house in St John's Wood, just as with Emmet's and my house, was both a wrench and a mistake. Wrong priorities. I could have turned my commodious garden-floor, housing kitchen, pantry and servants' quarters, into a self-contained and lucrative letting proposition. I could have adjusted my life so that living-in servants no longer seemed essential. I could have had more courage.

However, most of those servants had earned their places

amongst the memorable eccentrics of my youth; most of them foreign, many Marias amongst them. Outstanding in her impact was a Spanish Maria whose brevity of tenure resonated long after her departure.

Not all the wine was drunk in the immediate years after Emmet's death. Some twelve years later, settled in the larger and grander, but cellarless, St John's Wood house, I kept a stock of everyday 'drinking' wines in the proverbial cupboard (although a basement cupboard) under the stairs and the dwindling stock of first-growth clarets in a wholly unsuitable walk-in cupboard in one of the unused attic rooms. There were some of the 1945s, most of the 1961s, all of them first-growth clarets, and four precious bottles of d'Yquem 1937.

We had an Irish couple of some incompetence both as cook/general and gardener/*homme à tout faire*, but of seeming honesty and undoubted good humour. The Spanish daily had just left and a new one engaged as we set off on holiday. A month later we came home, to find a clean house, but were greeted by Mr O'Leary with the news that they didn't hold much store by this new daily - yet another Maria - as she spent most of her time gossiping at the kitchen table from which vantage point she had frequently offered them a glass of wine.

'Mrs O'Leary and I, we never touch the stuff,' he stoutly professed.

What stuff? I wondered idly. The wine cupboard did not seem depleted to me. Mr O'Leary simply sniffed when interrogated further. It wasn't until the next day that I thought of the attic cupboard, soon found empty. Sixty-six irreplaceable bottles had gone. It was a Friday. Maria would not appear again until the Monday morning, but the first people I thought of were my insurance company. They immediately notified the police. It was out of my hands and reluctantly and feeling both foolish and unkind, I gave them Maria's address, the O'Learys having repeated to them their saga of the kitchen-table orgies.

Maria and her husband were flabbergasted. All those old bottles had been covered in dust and cobwebs – obviously forgotten and of no value to anyone. No wine could possibly cost more than 50p per bottle when new and presentable. There was nothing left to salvage, except a stack of empty bottles outside their door.

To their eternal credit, the insurance company paid up, the first time in their history they had had such a claim. We settled eventually on the sum of an average of £11 per bottle. I suppose in the 1970s this was a fair price. Similar bottles now fetch thousands in auctions but I dare say I would have found yet more unworthy but eager gullets by now and should instead count myself lucky to have had the £700. I would rather have the diamond brooches I had sold years before.

Following Maria, there was the one with an illegitimate baby whom we got from the nuns and the visiting uncle who turned out to be its father; another whose illegitimate offspring was, she told us, a surviving Siamese twin; Mary, both deaf and dumb but full of affectionate grunts; the Chinese cook, U Moi, who speared her exquisitely rolled veal paupiettes – presented on small wooden sticks – with large black hairpins at our first formal dinner party; and, worthy of a saga to herself, our first and last experiment in Filipino maids.

I had answered an advertisement, exchanged photographs and references, paid for her fare to England and waited three months for her arrival. The references had stated that she was a good cook, seamstress, waitress, and spoke English. We signed a two-year contract, and she was to let me know in advance of her arrival. Christmas Day was, of course, cold. I was preparing Christmas dinner for ten when an irritated immigration official telephoned from Heathrow. Nelida was there, waiting to be collected. Turkey in oven, I rushed to fetch her. She was shivering in flimsy cotton pyjamas, with no teeth and no English. No acquaintance with a bed, either, I was to discover, as I ushered her into her room and made lying-down gestures. She slept only on the floor. This did not encourage her to make beds for the rest of us. She had not been told that the earth turned, so when she had not reappeared by five o'clock and I attempted to waken her, she cowered behind her locked door, believing that she was in danger of attack in the middle of the night, and she did not emerge until dawn - winter dawn, which meant breakfast time for the children.

Laying a table was an equal challenge. Nelida's only endearing act in her brief three months' stay with us was, having learnt from me how to lay a table for dinner, to prepare the kitchen table for the children's breakfast (I having bought her a clock and explained about the winter solstice) complete with open bottle of wine and lit candles. Arnold Wesker has even immortalised this action in a short story.

I had, immediately on arrival, taken her to a dentist and to Marks and Spencer so that she now had teeth and warm clothing. Plus, gradually, a very few words of English. Her cooking remained a Filipino 'fry-up' - chiefly salmon and chicken, thrown together in a pan with much rice and vegetables in vast quantities of oil. This took place in her bedroom on her days off - the smells wafting throughout our street - and fed eight to ten chattering Filipino friends appearing from the St John's Wood branch of that particular mafia.

A better paid job at a hospital was the main topic on the agenda of these bi-weekly convocations, and the first I knew of it was a call from the housekeeper of the hospital near us asking for a reference for Nelida, who intended starting work for her the following week. I told the woman of my two-year contract, but also gave her my blessing to break it. The housekeeper demurred. Nelida and her coven descended upon her and danced around her in a circle, invoking Filipino curses, in particular the death of herself and all her family. The housekeeper's mother died the next day, her dog three days later and she had a nervous breakdown. I had the perfect excuse to say farewell to Nelida and she departed with her winter wardrobe, spitting at me through her new teeth. This final experience helped me to accept the lack of a servant living in.

But I did mourn the fact that there would be no more garden parties for hundreds. No more dinner parties for thirty. No more attics in which to store everything now thrown out. I see now that I was going through a period of stress, before the word was coined to describe what is now the universal condition. The stress manifested itself dramatically. A bout of flu and a week in bed had left me weak and light-headed but a French film director was flying in from Paris that morning to discuss a deal with me, so I gingerly bathed, dressed and got as far as my garage before thinking better of it, and calling a cab. It was a beautiful sunny day and the cab driver whistled merrily as we turned into Regent's Park. In the back a strange tingling sensation started in my fingertips. By the time it had spread to my wrists it had started in my toes and was spreading rapidly upwards.

The driver was still whistling when he pulled up outside my office and turned round for his fare – a whistle which died in his throat. A seemingly normal woman had got into his cab; he had done nothing wrong, no lightning had struck us, and now curled up on his back seat in a foetal position was a gurgling bent twig. Unable to move, I could just gibber, 'Auk me ouup stairs – uup, uup . . .' Poor man. He carried me up as quickly as he could, dumped me on the floor and ran.

My secretary loosened clothes, called the doctor and Bill – both luckily at home. My doctor, when he arrived, went pale, gave me a massive injection and called Middlesex Hospital Casualty, and an ambulance. Although I could not speak, I could hear: 'Urgent. This is an emergency. I have a patient in tetany'. 'That's what we used to call lockjaw,' I thought. 'That's why I can't speak.' Gradually, my limbs straightened, speech came back, and Bill arrived, going pale too. I gave detailed instructions about contacting schools and notifying them of my death. The ambulancemen arrived and I was whisked down the winding stairs, gently vomiting over the red blanket. The French film director chose this moment to appear, and on being told that the figure on the stretcher was me, rushed into the street, bought a single red rose from the corner flower-seller and laid it on my chest as the stretcher slid into the van. I heard the siren, worried briefly that it was for one of my children and nodded off again. Four hours of anti-climatic testing later, I was sent home again, alive. Two weeks of trudging up and down Harley Street for more tests, I was diagnosed as having had a carpo-paedal spasm of unknown cause. My doctor told me he had never seen one before, and when I learnt that Elizabeth Taylor had experienced just that when she had had her windpipe opened and a tube inserted to breathe, I felt rather special.

It left me, however, with rampant claustrophobia in case it should happen again and no hypodermic handy. So small boats in the middle of large lakes, whose engines might stop, trains going through long tunnels ditto, lifts which might stick, and any locked door induce panic. The door need not even be locked from the outside. Keys can stick. I perch on lavatories in public places, with one hand outstretched uncomfortably pressed against the unlocked door. As for locking the lavatory door in an aeroplane – unthinkable – a double trap.

chapter twenty-six

I had, in addition to *No Hard Shoulder*, considered calling this memoir *Double Agent*, thus joining a band of predecessors and giving a false impression. Literary agent certainly, but intelligence agent hardly, despite the brushes with government bodies. Not only Thai and the aborted British, but on the sidelines the FBI. I did not discover this last, tenuous connection until years after the event, but I suppose it was my second foray into espionage.

The connection was Alfred Wells, an American diplomat, with whom I had a brief romance during which I had accompanied him to many parties, luncheons and dinners - and unbeknownst to me, to lunch with some of the key figures in the Profumo case, as it became known, and generally acknowledged as the bullet which shot down the Macmillan Government. I had known Jack Profumo and Stephen Ward, but only as occasional fellow guests of common hosts - neither intimately. I now only vaguely remember a luncheon with Alfred, Stephen Ward, and two of the men who were to share the headlines in the case - Tom Corbally and Billy Hitchcock. I have little recollection of these two and none of our lunchtime conversation but I do wonder at my presence. Was I taken by Alfred as some sort of social smokescreen? As with the Thai job and the possibly bewildered political journalists, the British Foreign Office and its equally bewildered intermediary for my services, I wonder what these three gentlemen made of my presence and what significance I was given in the subsequent FBI report. It sounds, on reading, as if my sole identifying factor was as an Australian female. I expect, somewhere in intelligence files all over the world, I still have a listing – but as what?

I was sent the report in 1986 by the author of a book, one of many, on the Profumo case, in the hopes, to use his words, that 'the report will jog your memory of the recorded events . . . no matter how insignificant they may appear to you'. Poor man: all I could remember was that the luncheon probably was held at Simpson's in the Strand, because of a magnificent silver trolley of roast beef and Yorkshire pudding, although my correspondent believed it was at the American Services Club. Not long after this, my romance with Alfred foundered, bitten in the bud on a beach in Tamariu.

My third brush substantiated my suspicion that 'intelligence agent' was a misnomer. All of mine have been characterised by a supreme dottiness. As a literary agent, I was approached by one Greville Wynne. He was famous for having been recruited by MI5 whilst on business in Russia, and caught and imprisoned; but was somewhat eclipsed in notoriety by the better-known names of George Blake, the Rosenbergs, Fuchs, and our own Burgess and Maclean. He wanted my help with his memoirs but our meetings caused him grave concern. He would slink up my drive (always home – never the office), sidle sideways round my drawing room door with furtive backward glances, seat himself extremely close to me on the sofa, and furiously whisper. My house, he told me, was bugged; my telephone tapped. I was now, because of him, under surveillance. He believed this so strongly that I might have had a frisson of unease had it not been for my memories of the man in the submarine and the luncheon so important in the annals of the FBI.

chapter twenty-seven

When I was seventeen I visited my first fortune-teller – in Bayswater Road in Sydney. Two of her predictions stuck in my mind: 'You will spend your life travelling,' she said, 'and you will have three husbands and two children.' Only the first two struck me as both unusual and possibly desirable at the time, but all three have come true, if an uprooting from one's country of birth counts as travel and a live-in companion spanning almost thirty years can count as a third husband, if not in the eyes of the law and the Church, then certainly in the cloudy depths of the crystal ball. But it was proven correct: in the thirtieth year we got married.

The travel is, to one born under the sign of Sagittarius, a drug. Too long in any one place is a drenching of the spirit; to arrive, excitement; to anticipate departure, a fillip; and the path has usually been beset by adventure. If Emmet had lived, perhaps we might not have voyaged so much, or, if we had, would not have had so many adventures, being removed from my sole influence. When I travel, trains go on strike, aeroplanes crash (usually the one just before mine), ships are fog-bound or sink, farmers revolt and block the motorways with dead cows or rotting tomatoes. All of these have happened to me with alarming regularity. My family no longer choose to accompany me if other means of transport are readily available, because at least one of these happenings is more likely than not.

I have run out of petrol over the French Alps with Bira, his second wife praying in the seat in front; I have slipped anchor in a fierce Mediterranean storm at night and joined Bira on watch on deck, as we veered wildly from rockface to rockface on either side of the bay where we were anchored, same wife praying below, '*Seigneur*, *Seigneur*, protect me from this man!'; I have been The Lady Vanishes in a train becalmed in a French field by thick fog, the frightened face of a cow pressed against the window when I pulled the blind of my sleeper, expecting Vevey railway station; Bill alerting police in two countries when I did not alight at the station, assuming I had slept on until Istanbul.

I caught the first TGV (express) train to traverse Europe - a flag-hoisting event. As we pulled out of our station, a lady jumping aboard was caught in the automatic door - her arm firmly trapped half in and half outside the train, but saved from pulp by the slightly larger bulk of her suitcase clutched in her hand. The driver refused to stop. We arrived on the dot, to the accompaniment of her shrieks. I once drove, alone, to catch the Santander–Plymouth ferry, nervous of finding my ticket, the correct dock, the appropriate queue. All were in place, except the boat itself. It had just sunk, majestically, in dock. We waited all day for a replacement - a much grander ship, *The Prince of Brittany*. Because of the delay we were due to arrive in Plymouth late at night instead of early morning, so my plans to motor immediately to London seemed foolhardy. My friends, Ian and Margaret Farquhar, lived close to Plymouth so perhaps I could invite myself for the night. On the bridge, the radio operator took their telephone number whilst I waited patiently beside him. 'Sorry,' he said, 'they don't wish to accept the call.' When I finally insisted he try again, I snatched the telephone and having arrived safely at the

Farquhar house learnt the reaction to the first call. Eight people at dinner - Margaret is approached by her butler who has the radio operator on the line. It is an inconvenient moment. 'Ian,' she calls down the table, 'do we *know* the Prince of Brittany?' They did not.

Bill and I have had five marvellously enjoyable and luxurious trips to New York on the *QE2* - tremendous VIP treatment, caviar all the way - all free in exchange for giving a 'lecture' each, the latter equally enjoyable and easy. However, we did manage to hit the worst trip in the history of that doomed, unlucky ship - a hole staved in her bows mid-Atlantic, engines stopped, four hundred miles off course to avoid icebergs, TV sets sheering off walls in the cabins, the morgue full (our waiter telling us the last body had had to be put in the deep freeze just as we watched a little old lady keel over at the central table in the grill room: dead), and we finally limped into Baltimore a day late as we couldn't make it to New York. Four hours hanging over the rails watching the coffins being off-loaded before passengers allowed off, and all 'bussed' to New York with our packed luncheons, courtesy of Cunard, on our laps. No accident that I was aboard.

Once, having tea in New York with a friend whose apartment was, to me, in the seamier streets, I voiced nervousness at braving the street on my own in search of a cab. As she came out with me, scoffing, 'Don't be ridiculous - nothing can possibly happen to you here', she was brushed aside by a respectable-looking middle-aged lady advancing towards us who thrust her angry face close to mine and spat forcefully in my eye before continuing on her way. Things can, and do, happen to me *everywhere*.

Running parallel to my work, I had juggled with the peaks of school holidays; changing mother's helps; childhood illnesses; my own romances. Women alone with small children used to attract favours, extract chivalry, excite sympathy -

before the world was full of single mothers. A midnight wait, luggage-laden, on Cannes railway station, desperate for a sleeping compartment, none booked and train full, can bring great good fortune if the luggage is overwhelming enough, the children small enough, and the chance taken. Once, when so laden, hearing the roar of the approaching train, I entreated three-year-old Seamus, perilously near the edge of the platform, 'Hold tight to Mummy, darling', and like an answer to a prayer came from behind me an American-accented, 'Please may I hold tight to Mummy, too?'. His sleeper given to us, our luggage stowed away, our American Sir Galahad bore us through the night. Today, I expect, mother, if not children, might be raped, luggage rifled, but it wasn't always so.

But when the children were small and unable to refuse to travel with me, there was nearly always what passed for a nanny - a succession of pleasant, jolly, and usually competent foreign girls - Spanish, Italian, Austrian - who shared our journeys.

Despite the unforeseen dramas, car journeys across Europe were exciting expeditions, children acclimatised to strange hotels, exotic foods, elastic hours, foreign tongues; in retrospect always companions, never liabilities. Lisa spoke perfect French, Seamus the remnants of his babyhood Italian. Spanish picked up by both from a succession of mother's helps. They became accustomed at an early age to a mother inclined to lose tickets, passports, and the way. Lisa learnt young to be organised, Seamus to read maps. They learnt very young indeed never to trust my sense of direction in a car and never to sit next to me on an aeroplane. On our first visit to Spain, Hudson was coming with us to help with the driving. We reached Southampton and I left him to put the car on board whilst I put the children to bed. I found our cabin, changed Seamus's nappy, brushed Lisa's teeth, was tucking them into bed when a bewildered lady appeared at the door claiming her cabin. 'E4' said her ticket, but so did mine. The cabin steward was sent for and verified both numbers, but also pointed out that mine was on the boat sailing for le Havre, whilst the boat we were on was sailing for Cherbourg – at any moment. Just time to snatch children, pots, wet nappies, and, so laden, totter down the gangway and onto the ship in the next berth where already installed were car and companion. Not a confidence-building exercise for my children.

Each summer holiday was dictated by term-times. This vice-like constriction appears endless during those also seemingly endless school years. Memories of August are dramatic to me: to each child they must carry a separate flavour. To Seamus, I imagine, it is the food he ate; to Lisa the best-looking waiter. Portugal was whitewashed walls, rock-pools and pebbles, Seamus investigating one more taste in his gastronomic journey through life, bugs and shortage of water. Our villa, found for me by the Williams, was picturesque and comfortable, but Albufeira, before both the tourist invasion and the Portuguese revolution, was not equipped for the summer influx. The pipes groaned and gurgled, and the town, taking pity on protesting nature, turned the water off each day from ten in the morning. Unfortunately they did not announce the fact, nor the time of reconnection. So, the first night without water, the children and I sampled one of the local restaurants and came home to a flood. All the taps which I had angrily turned on to no avail in the morning were happily responding, and in the resulting flood of swirling water, on our floor floated rubber ducks and old tin-openers, discarded beach sandals, spent matches, lumps of dislodged dirt, dead cockroaches and large, live, swimming spiders. The children sat fascinated on the stairs, watching as I struggled to bail us out with saucepans. Bored at last, they began, as always, to hit each other. Tethers ended, I claimed childhood as my domain and burst into screaming sobs. I had had, I told them, enough of them. Swimming spiders were sufficient to bear without this added burden of my own making.

Thoroughly shocked, they stopped fighting at once, relieved me of the buckets, and sloshed happily through the sodden house, making it habitable, whilst I retired to bed. Seven and nine, they had taken over, and from then onwards assumed a protective role when it seemed appropriate.

Another villa, in Minorca, of breathtaking beauty and inordinate discomfort, is remembered by the children as one of the best holidays of their lives, and by me as one of the worst. Minorca, too, was in the first year of being discovered by tourists. Totally unprepared, there was not enough food in the markets. After a few days of inventing new ways to cook pasta, we settled for the local taverna in the bay, which served only lobster, freshly caught each morning in the sea below, and so spent the remainder of the month luxuriously broke. Carlo and Sasha Gebler, Edna O'Brien's two sons, came to stay. Carlo had just been given some shares for his birthday and his daily requirement was the *Financial Times*. Ciudadella was five miles distant, along a deeply rutted dirt track; not only did we have to travel it each day for whatever meagre rations we could grab from the market, but once there, embark on the hunt for the newspaper. Our somewhat reluctant male companion on this trip was Bill, who had transported us in his new Rover, and had brought with him his essential typewriter. The new Rover shuddered along the dirt tracks, the owner shuddered with it, and each time he touched his typewriter he received an electric shock. He departed on the first available boat, leaving us with the name by which Minorca is known in our family, Little-Shitville-on-Sea.

Tamariu, on the Costa Brava, was the scene of my wrecked romance with Alfred, my American diplomat, divorced, with an adored only daughter. The daughter was twelve, Lisa nine, Seamus six. It seemed politic, if we were considering marriage, that the children should get to know each other. I had already rented the villa and gone ahead with the children. The daughter's idea of fun, when she had arrived and surveyed the possibilities, was to scare the wits out of Seamus with recounting of ghost stories once lights were out. He had circles under his eyes each morning and clung to my side at bedtime. She bloomed, and basked in her father's besotted regard. Seamus rebelled, and my romance came to an abrupt end on the day he finally bit her and drew blood. It was at lunch: I was in the kitchen when I heard her screams, her father's outraged bellow, 'He's *bitten* Gully!', and Seamus's answering yells as he was dragged from the table. Amid the general uproar as I attempted to shut him in the kitchen, averting my eyes from the blood, and Alfred's shocked accusation – 'in *five* places' – Seamus, through righteous sobs, managed to gulp, 'Well, I did bite her, but the *blood* is from where I stuck a fork into her'. At least no fangs, I thankfully thought as I mopped up the mess. But our family of three did not merge into five.

Tuscany was a blissful rescue from a disaster at Eze-sur-mer. The villa I had rented there from an agency sounded perfect – a few hundred yards from the sea, four bedrooms, a fortune in rent, payable in advance. The diplomat having departed from my life with his daughter, I had met Bill, but our relationship was in its infancy – although ripe, I thought, for full exposure to my children. He came with us, and so I did not have to bear the cold shock and horror of that unspeakable villa alone. There were dangling naked lightbulbs, huge flaking patches of plaster peeling from walls, a dirt-encrusted kitchen, primitive plumbing, piles of damp grey sheets on lumpy beds, cobwebs everywhere, four weeks' rent paid. We battled to the beach. The few hundred yards lay across the main railway line; the beach was a strip of dark grey shingle, littered with rubbish and broken bottles, probably tossed out of the passing trains. We dined, swatting mosquitoes, on a minuscule terrace, and distributed ourselves into the cleanest-looking beds, exhausted. At least, I was spending my first night under a shared roof with my lover. We knew we couldn't stand it for four weeks, but we could make the best of one night.

Lights out, moonlight filtering through shutters, I tried to imagine the villa back into the promised paradise of the brochure. A terrible howl from the open door put paid to all such thoughts - in the doorway staggered the white-clad figure of my daughter, wild-eyed, drenched in blood; blood literally pouring, it seemed, from both ends of her.

'I'm bleeding!' she howled, unnecessarily. She had always been prone to nose bleeds, but Eze-sur-mer had brought on one of Niagaran proportions, the blood spurting down her nightdress where it seemed to mingle with a series of pools on the rented linoleum.

'Aah - aah!' yelled Lisa. 'I'm bleeding from *everywhere*!' Thoroughly frightened, I expect, but not so startled as my poor chap. It was an intensely dramatic onset of puberty.

I had little compunction about leaving the bloodstained sheets in the morning. We drove straight to Montreux, children singing all the way, spent the morning discovering the French for sanitary towel, the evening with Noël Coward in his house on the mountain top, the night in *grand luxe* at the Palace Hotel, and the next day set off for Tuscany, to one of the loveliest hotels in the world, the Tenuta di Ricavo. Here Lisa discovered *Gone With the Wind* and her own burgeoning femininity.

As Bill had survived Minorca and Eze-sur-mer with us, I started to long for a villa of our own: no more of someone else's bent wire coathangers and capricious ovens. The first of our acquisitions was in Switzerland, chosen partly because of the proximity of friends - Noël, and of course his companions, 'Coley' and Graham Payne; James Mason and later his new wife, Clarissa; Eric and Joan Ambler; Jack Cardiff and wife. Apart from the friends already living there, we would never have thought of Switzerland in the first place - nor could we have afforded it - had I not had a preparatory adventure.

A close friend had invited me to luncheon - her tone on the telephone urgent - could I come that same day - and I was Australian, wasn't I, with a genuine passport? Luncheon was not its usual gossipy and languid affair: her husband, nervous at the best of times, kept jumping and pacing; his knuckles which he chewed on relentlessly were ragged and bloody. The story matched the urgency. His extremely rich mother had recently died, leaving intact her husband's famed and priceless collection of antique French furniture. Her son had quickly spirited out of the house the most spectacular items (pedigrees of pieces were well logged in art houses around the world), and had sold them, for cash, to a newly rich and media-famous businessman, in the process of acquiring his own ancestral pile, along with some ancestors.

Some months elapsed. Probate granted on the remaining contents of the house, the husband developed the habit of whipping off to Geneva most weekends. My friend, his wife, assumed a lady must be the reason and asked no questions. The businessman, new owner of fabled furniture, died dramatically. Probate would now have to be assessed on *his* assets, amongst which would now be the famous pieces of furniture with no record of him having bought them - but all of their provenances catalogued.

The Swiss weekends had been the method by which my knuckle-biting friend had disposed of the proceeds - weekly in cash, to a Swiss bank in Lausanne. Soon, he feared, questions would be asked; furniture traced back to his collector father; how had it ended up in a new castle, and where was the money - indeed, why was it not declared in his mother's estate? The cash now had to be brought back, put in his bank and a mistake over the probate question admitted. Not nearly such a serious offence as money smuggling. Could he have it sent to me, an Australian living in London, quite normally, via bank transfer? As I was a UK resident this wouldn't work. I, too, paid British taxes, and my bank account was conceivably open to scrutiny. Their faces fell and more blood dripped from the knuckles.

It seemed to me that the simplest solution was for me to go to Geneva, collect the cash and bring it back. No connection with my friends should I be intercepted; my own story to be worked out in due course. There was, it appeared, a very great deal of money: too much to get into or onto one individual. My friend had a Spanish lover; he was summoned from Madrid to be my companion. We stood in the street outside the bank whilst the husband went in with his empty suitcase, emerged with a full one and we all three went back to our hotel and emptied it onto my bed. I had never seen so much money in my life. He was a very *small* lover, and having a good Spanish tailor (a trim line) his suit fitted snugly and impeccably. We stuffed him as full as we could but could not manage more than a third. After an hour I could barely walk. If I did, I rustled alarmingly. I had banknotes inside my brassiere, my girdle, my shoes. The husband deposited us thankfully at Madrid airport. We waddled to Departures in reasonably good time to catch our plane, seated separately. Reasonable if the plane had not been delayed for four and a half hours by which time I was gasping for air, dying to pee (impossible), and fairly drunk. For practically the only time I had been on an aeroplane I was not consumed by worry that the plane was about to explode. It was I who was in danger of exploding.

My friend gave me a magnificent diamond brooch from Cartier. It was stolen in our Bel Air adventure. Poetic justice. And I gained a nodding acquaintance with a Swiss bank - an Australian domicile established - and therefore a legal right to use it, without which we would never have embarked on our Swiss sojourn.

From hotels we graduated to an apartment rented from James in the midst of vineyards above Vevey. We towed a small motorboat out from England and learnt lake life. From the lake we spotted an idyllic village, St Prex, and cruising in for a closer look, saw at the water's edge a sign saying: APPARTEMENTS A VENDRE. So we met our first Swiss architect, our first team of Swiss builders, and our first Swiss banker, and with incredible speed and efficiency, our dream house rose at lakeside. As the first buyers, we were able to choose the attic apartment, under the sloping roof, built to our specifications, and in keeping with the medieval village; the words *poutres apparentes* daily on our lips as the ceilings soared and we had a replica of a huge country barn under the rooftops, looking out over Lac Leman towards France. It was a stupendous apartment, when finished.

At first, we revelled in the things the Swiss do well: the cleanliness of our award-winning village; the solid quality of our apartment where every mahogany cupboard door closed noiselessly; every bathroom tile miraculously arranged in the exact size and colour ordered; every tap firmly turning; every window framing a picture postcard view of mountain and lake. Switzerland was, miraculously, full of Swiss efficiency. It was also, we were to discover, full of Swiss laws, duplicitous Swiss lawyers, unfriendly shopkeepers, and Swiss bores; and, four years later, we admitted defeat at their hands and, unable legally to become owners of our dream home, we had to relinquish it, at last, to the architect who, we suspected, had anticipated such a windfall from the outset.

We were to return to Switzerland on visits to James and Clarissa, heart-pangs as we passed the motorway turn-off to our village, but no more. The last time was for James's funeral. I flew out the morning he died – suddenly of a heart attack – followed the next day by Bill, who was to give the address at his funeral. We spent two days trying to help Clarissa decide between a burial and a cremation, during which time the bank manager, who was also a neighbour, came into his officious own. His overriding concern was, 'But who is going to flower the coffin?' Later, when, the flowers having been picked, great armfuls of them from James's beloved garden, I asked about vases. Rodolfo was incensed: 'But these flowers are not meant to *survive*.' His wife's concern was what she should wear. James's faithful servant's sister had come to stay from Spain. She, Carmina, slept on a mattress on the floor outside her sister's room, sharing a corridor with me. I fell on top of her in the night and Carmina made a noise like a disturbed bulldog.

We all go to the chapel where James's body lies, oblivious to the arguments regarding the manner of his disposal or the draping of his coffin. Carmina is very short, very fat and very curious. She grabs the side of the coffin in order to pull herself up sufficiently to peer in. The coffin tips over; Clarissa is obliged to hang onto the other side and they remain, like two survivors from a shipwreck, clinging onto either side of a rocking rowing boat.

chapter twenty-eight

Death, too, was weakening my links with Australia. My grandmother and father both dead, unspeaking to the end, I received only occasional news of friends - they, too, in thinning ranks. Australians tend to post their Christmas cards to Europe before our last autumn leaf has fallen and I was kept in touch yearly by a masseuse of my mother's, eager to send her version of Christmas cheer packaged with the year's events. Her name was Sylvia - Brunella's name for her 'Slap-a-da-face Sylvia' - and every Thursday a handful of my mother's friends had gathered, supine, in rows on our drawing room floor awaiting in turn Sylvia's attentions. My first Christmas card, arriving one such late November, gave news of them, words entwined around the jovial faces of cherubs, chirping robins, and festive holly:

Dearest Robin & children,

Just a few notes - Mrs Maiden has just had a major operation, this time very sick, but improving (but for how long?). Mrs Farley very big, and not very well at all. High pressure and all that follows it. Pauline very thin and living on nerves, and Tracy very difficult. Poor Russell! Pauline's sister 'Pam' was found dead in her unit about a month ago - heart. At this stage of our lives everybody seems to be cracking up. I wonder if you've heard - Miss Mackellar (Nutty) the fourth month in the Scottish Hospital as a vegetable (High Blood Pressure, Stroke and never shall be better).

With Every Good Wish for Christmas and the New Year

To you all the best of health;

With fondest love,

Sylvia

P.S. How's the world treating you? Still working very hard? How are the children?

Except for the brief flying visits always occasioned by deaths - my mother's, my husband's, my father's - after thirty-one years I had no thought of ever seeing Australia again. As for wishes, they were probably more negative than positive. A connection had been established through my son, Seamus, as a student doctor who had served his elective term in Sydney at my suggestion - frantic to keep him out of Third World danger spots. There, during his three-month stint, he had fallen in love with a nurse and had determined to return at the first opportunity. Some of the old friends had been exceedingly kind to him, so that when an opportunity came for me to return I grabbed it.

This was in the form of an invitation from the Arts Council of Australia to John Osborne, to preside at the Annual Playwrights Conference. John had recently separated from his fourth wife Jill, and was living with Helen. He professed to love Australians, having a few intimates in London, but never having been exposed to them en masse, certainly not the literary variety. He also, in those days, was inclined to love me. He had not yet 'turned' as he was almost invariably to turn, like ageing milk, if exposed to any close relationship for too long a period. So the invitation to Australia came at the right moment for him, and for our relationship, and he, Helen and I set out in high spirits, John having said he wished to travel with his agent.

We flew separately – I via Los Angeles, and John and Helen through the East, arriving a few days ahead of me. As soon as I had landed a frantic official of the Playwrights Association appeared.

'We've lost John Osborne. He's gone walkabout!'

Indeed, he had managed to do just that in a perfect simulation of Aboriginal customs, having been last sighted crossing the quadrangle of Canberra University in an interval between two discussions. His hosts had alerted all airports, checked out all the leading Sydney hotels, and were about to start on shipping lines when I appeared.

The public relations representative and I flew to Canberra together in search of clues. The hotel into which I, John and Helen had been booked was built in what I expect they imagined was an imitation of a Japanese inn; imitative invention having gone only so far as a brick walkway through gurgling water on which bobbed a few limp waterlilies. At the entrance door, inspiration had run out, and so, we were to discover later, had the money. The hotel was in receivership.

At the reception desk I was given a note with my key. 'Come and get me,' it said. 'Am in Chinese restaurant next door – John.'

They were in the darkest corner, stuffed with Chinese food and desperate for conversation. Thirty-odd journalists had met John as he stepped onto the tarmac, barring his way with microphones, and the inevitable query: 'What do you think of Australia?'

John had just published an acerbic article in the Sunday *Observer* lashing out against a certain trend in England's homosexual art mafia, so the second question followed smartly on the first: 'And did you know that "homos" have paid your fare out here?' His fellow writers in Canberra proved no more benign than the Sydney journalists. Two days had sufficed, in the wasteland that is Canberra, and so the Chinese restaurant afforded familiar solace; sweet and sour pork and spring rolls having a comforting universal familiarity.

But the PR chap, Paul Aamodt, turned out to be a twin soul, ended up a good friend and the next four days were spent in companionable hilarity. Trying to find our way to the lecture hall, Burton Hall, wasn't made easy by the fact that the letters 'B', 'T' and 'N' had fallen off BURTON. On our first hunt for it, cruising through the faceless, unpeopled, straight, dull streets of Canberra, John enquired of our dour driver, 'Where do the people live?'

'In the suburbs,' was the reply.

But the chip-on-shoulder resentment, coupled with needless awe, of his fellow playwrights and the lack of organisation proved too much for John – and he did indeed go 'walkabout'. Having performed his main function as the presenter of prizes, he and Helen left by the first available plane, bombarding me with hilarious postcards from Singapore, Bangkok and Rome. He subsequently 'borrowed' back his own cards: never to be returned, no doubt kept for his own memories – undoubtedly this time to heap venom on Australia.

But I stayed.

Landing at Sydney airport now, over the bays and the low skyline, life the last fifty years becomes an extended journey from which I have returned to base. The years between are misted over and reality is here.

Memories evoked by return are always activated by a geographical time slip. So: the cracks in the pavement are surely the same. This corner of a Double Bay street will lead, if I lift my eyes, to the large house and garden where I played after school with Georgie Cohen and where my mother came to play bridge with her mother, Dulcie. Providing I remain intent on the pavement I will not see the block of flats where once stood the Cohens' house, but will remember, as if yesterday, the scandal when Dulcie ran off with dashing English naval officer Hookie Bell in the war, leaving Leo and Georgie behind.

If I walk down a certain block in Pitt Street, I am on my way to the Liberty, then the newest, smartest, smallest cinema in Sydney. I see the round face and round brown eyes of the cinema manager, with whom I am passionately in love, leaping to open the door of the hired Buick as Nana, Great Aunt Juliet and my twelve-year-old self emerge to watch *Naughty Marietta* for the twenty-fourth time. I was more deeply in love with Nelson Eddy, but the cinema manager appeared more available.

Is it possible that the Capital Hotel in Darlinghurst Road at Kings Cross is large enough to inhabit the entire space of the Kings Cross Cinema, vast and cavernous in memory, where *The Perils of Pauline* ran every Saturday matinée, and the Wurlitzer organ played 'Tiptoe Through the Tulips' while we, proud in our Girl Guide uniforms, and newly stitched-on badges, sang in unison from the Dress Circle to the words rolling on the screen?

As I skim across the harbour by ferry, is it possible that the turreted mini-castle on the shore of Darling Point is really Carthona, quite unchanged since the days I went there to tea with the Bushell sisters? How can one particular place remain so perfectly in scale with memory when so much else has diminished? Mrs Bushell, immensely rich from Bushell's Tea, the mainstay of every good Australian household, trusted neither insurance companies nor the security of Carthona, as she went everywhere with a large carpet bag stuffed with her famous jewels (Marie Antoinette's emeralds? rubies? – here memory falters), which rested throughout lunch or tea under the restaurant table.

As I walk down the top half of Macleay Street, past the once glamorous entrance to Gowrie Gate apartments, I wonder what has happened to the chic abortionist on the ground floor to whose door came Sydney's wartime golden girls? Once, legs strapped up, I glanced at the newspaper-covered floor to see my own face and name staring up at me from last week's headlines: YOUNG DIVORCEE ANNOUNCES ENGAGEMENT TO AMERICAN AIRMAN. The US airman already being back in New Guinea, the young divorcee was temporarily deserted.

Palm Beach means the same sea, the same sand, the same palm-fringed hills behind. We are running along the beach one pink and blue dawn in the vain hope of finding Cam Jaquet's glass eye, lost in a midnight swim some hours earlier - and we find it!

I trudge up the hill from the top of the steps down to Rushcutters Bay to Kings Cross - but where was the newsagent's shop, en route, which my school friends Ros and Alison Bowman and I visited each day after school? I bribed them with sixpence per day to walk the extra half mile or so from their house in Elizabeth Bay to mine at the Cross so that they could engage the newsagent in conversation whilst I rifled through film magazines on the rack tearing out photographs of those stars in our current favour. Where did I get the then substantial sum of sixpence per day? I expect from Great Aunt Juliet.

Walking past the site of the house where I was born, now the Kings Cross Underground Station, resentment and sadness tinge the nostalgia. How can *this* have changed so much? Along these streets at night limped one of my first loves, a one-legged man, nameless in memory, who whistled under my window 'Goodnight Sweetheart' as I leant over the sill, wondering how I could meet him. I remember his face, good-looking and I suppose only a boy, for I finally managed to entice him indoors and further entice him to kiss me. I was fifteen. I remember the age because my grandfather had died that day: his body lay surrounded by candles and weeping women in the downstairs drawing room. I adored my grandfather. In memory, the excitement of the clandestine kiss upstairs in my mother's sitting room was the highlight of the day. I don't remember seeing the one-legged man again - a creature of the Kings Cross night, I wonder what he made of the precocious and seemingly heartless child. Fifteen was the age of a child in my youth. Somewhere, however, under the wilful coldness lurked a heart, or would I have remembered the kiss were it not for my loved, dead, Sammie?

The block of flats next door still stands but I must not glance at the doorway. Prostitutes and drug pushers bar the way to the remembered vision of the young girl who was me rushing up to spend a few minutes with the poetess Dame Mary Gilmore, to say goodbye to her forever. I have the book she gave me with its dedication: 'For Robin Eakin, to wish her life at its fullest' - and, written in her hand on the flyleaf that day, the poem:

I watch the doves
that, in the cold,
With bent knees rest
Upon their hearts
And brood. And as
I watch I think
How man, for all
His pride, is but
A feathered bird,
Where Life keeps warm
breasted upon
Its heart.

But the cracks in the pavement outside her door are the stronger heart pull.

I can look, but with amazement, up Cooper Street as the bus passes, for there, still painted white, unchanged, is the Masonic Hall, now behind the Post Office. Here on Friday nights happened the highlight of our young teenage week: Miss Penelope Kaye's dancing class. The boys lined up on one side of the room; the girls (is it possible I had a new dress every Friday night? Memory dictates that I did) on the other. The band struck up: was it a gramophone? One elderly pianist? In memory it was a band, and one hoped that the boy of one's choice was quickest across the separating parquet. 'Ackie' Davis, who always wore white gloves, was too short. 'Breezy' Gale a bit too tall – bliss if it was Harry Mitchell who gave me my first kiss at the Bowmans' dance. He was fourteen; I was twelve. This was the desired object of the dancing classes: the foxtrot and the waltz and the two-step and the new dresses only the preliminary rituals.

There are no longer trams or trolley buses, but the buses take a familiar route. We turn the corner from William Street into Elizabeth Street and there on my left should I bear to look was the then tallest building in Sydney, the T&G. Apart from the dentist, who wrecked my teeth forever, it meant for me a year of 'finishing' school. Miss Janet Stevens (could it really have been called Academy for Young Ladies?) had one room high up in the T&G where a handful of us went to be 'finished'. In what sense? We had hardly begun. Certainly not educated. I remember only the Current Events class in which we read aloud from that day's *Sydney Morning Herald*; French literature – a glancing blow, no more, at Flaubert and Baudelaire – the lessons petering out because, thanks to Mademoiselle Le Begue, my French governess, insisted upon by my grandmother in my infancy, I was the only pupil capable of reading the title page. I doubt the teacher – name and nationality forgotten – was capable of much more. Bridge, at which I proved totally inept; dressmaking, at which I made one dress, on the back of which the men in the Chinese garden pattern on the material stood on their heads; and cooking. Ah, the cooking! To whom did we think we would later feed the mountains of Russian toffee and cheese straws at which we became expert? We performed the physical task at the local Technical College, with whom Miss Stevens must have had an arrangement. We cooked for the students, forced to eat our morning's efforts at long trestle tables for their lunch. Nothing of what I learnt there remains. Joan McGrath's lovely long red fingernails were grated one day into the mince, so I vaguely remember a shepherd's pie.

Only the Rose Bay Surf Club at Bondi's north end seems unchanged. The showers still smell of the same faint disinfectant; the hooks on which you hang your bathers may be rusty but they are the same hooks; the steps to the verandah on which I posed at twelve with family and at twenty with a succession of American boyfriends are the same; and Pears soap still nestles in every soap dish. The drive home is still divided by a formal row of hideous red and yellow canna lilies that, I realise, is the image of Bondi which springs to my mind – not the perfect semicircle of sand and sea, overlaid now in memory by countless other beautiful beaches. None of them is approached through the serried rows of stiff, unlovely lilies.

George Street meant the Trocadero. The Trocadero meant dancing of a different brand to our normal shuffling. The newspaper cuttings I still have bring it back: 'At the charity show Robin danced with Aub Smart – short, square-shouldered and superbly blond – a tailor's cutter who hailed from Robin's home town, Kings Cross . . .' The charity show was the brainchild of Nuttie MacKeller – we were advertised as a clutch of debutantes – or 'society' girls – slumming it at the Troc; nobody seemed to mind or raise an eyebrow at the terminology. When my partner's parents, Mr and Mrs Smart, christened their beautiful blond baby 'Aubrey', they would surely have known, it being Australia, that he would be forever 'Aub', although they would certainly have had no idea that they would one day be reading about him in the society pages. I know he was a beautiful blond baby because he was a beautiful young man, his hair a helmet of burnished gold; and if we only came second at least I had the satisfaction of having captured such a god as my partner. I must have been dimly aware that, despite his beauty, Aub lacked sex appeal, or at least he did not find me sexy. There was no current between us as we danced, and dancing, in the 1940s, was all about current. We didn't need to be truly promiscuous when as much excitement as we needed was to be had on the dance floor. Clasped cheek to cheek, flank to flank, one simply exchanged one erection for another, and it never occurred to me that we were driving our partners crazy with frustration. There was an older man in the boys' team: he must have been nearly thirty. His name was Don Lucas and dancing with him certainly produced a current. After our charity competition, Don asked me to continue as a Trocadero regular, meet him for training and enter as a team for the State Waltzing Championships. I did and we won!

The dead boys – the boys who died in the deserts and jungles and skies of World War II – I remember as I glance down Martin Place and across to the corner of Castlereagh Street. Not too closely or I will miss with a sharp pang the Monterey Coffee Bar, our very first brush with American culture – a thrilling feeling that by its name, its ice-cream sundaes and hamburgers we were at last partaking of that glamorous film star-inhabited world across the Pacific. Or, next door, the chemist Eddie Samuels – a *real* American – the dispenser of Prairie Oysters and, rumour had it, much else besides. But the boys who whirled me round the dance floors of Prince's in Martin Place and Romano's in Castlereagh Street are remembered for their agile feet, the swinging ends of their coat-tails, the tunes we danced to. 'Wuzz' Stuart teaching me to dance on my mother's parquet floor to 'Night and Day'; Ian MacMaster on the revolving coloured glass floor of the 'old' Romano's in York Street; Wal Anderson, because he and Jocelyn Josephson looked so beautiful together . . . all three to be killed.

The war came. The boys we had grown up with left to fight. On leave from the camps before embarking they fought in the nightclubs. One night you could only go to Prince's because Geoff Moses had knocked someone down the stairs at Romano's the previous night and was barred from entry; that is, if you were unlucky enough to be with Geoff Moses. The next night if you were unlucky enough to be with Peter Glanville you would be barred from Prince's because he had been in a fight the previous night involving bowling the round flower bowls along the floor at his adversary. Physical violence was the norm. David Stewart-Dawson, he of the trestle tables provided for me in London, figured in a famous court case when he whipped out a pistol and shot George Mackay because he did not stand up for the National Anthem. The bullet is still lodged in George's spine . . . Australians behaved in that way in my youth; perhaps the blood has been somewhat diluted now.

News filtered down to us from the areas of war to which most of our chaps had been posted, chiefly the 9th and the 7th Divisions in the Middle East. Our dearest and oldest family friend, a rich, homosexual, sometime actor, Roger Barry, volunteered in the early days. As he had only one kidney, and an extremely dicey one at that, he was not acceptable for active service, but, knocking a few years off his age, managed to get posted to Malaya as Pat Levy's batman. A few days before the fall of Singapore, Roger's remaining kidney blew up, and he was invalided back to Australia.

Cam Jaquet, of the glass eye lost on Palm Beach, somehow

got through the initial, more eagle-eyed recruitment officers, although unable to last the full distance into certain internment and probable death. John Thompson told me, proudly but regretfully, of Cam: 'At least we got him as far as Tobruk', the fact that he was repatriated before capture regarded as a sad mishap.

Just as my childhood, thanks to my grandmother's determination, had been permeated by Dickens, Ibsen, Gilbert and Sullivan, and Shakespeare, my adolescent influences were shaped by Errol. Errol, after whom we had named a cat, was a bachelor friend who worked in shipping. Today's obituary would pinpoint him as a 'confirmed bachelor'. Every week he brought me the *New Yorker* and kept me supplied with proof copies of the published plays of Somerset Maugham, Dodie Smith and the like. I read them all - in retrospect my first exercise in script-reading. We never thought to ask how Errol's tastes had been gripped by these choices or how he came by the proofs but sophistication and sparkling style became, for me, mantled within the pages of the *New Yorker* and it is possible that I learnt to recognise something of craftsmanship from Maugham.

I think I was just a little bit in love with Errol, just as my first love, at about three, had been for our other dear homosexual friend Roger Barry; and my six- or seven-year-old idol, Lance Fairfax, star of *The Desert Song*, rampantly gay, whom my father sought to erase from my heart by telling me he wore red flannel binders under his trousers as a sort of warm corset. I wonder when I switched my affections to heterosexual men? Certainly not before Nelson Eddy, whose photographs, teeth prominent and gleaming just for me, surrounded my bed, and hid under my desk lid.

When I finally lost my technical virginity, on my eighteenth birthday in the bunker of the ninth hole of Collaroy Golf Course, I had fondly imagined that my young love and I had been 'doing it' for two years. What we had been doing must have been driving him crazy: skirts hitched up and brassiere discarded in the backs of cars after a dance; naked in bed, whispering, in his mother's beach house; once, sitting on his lap in full evening dress in the billiard room at Craigieburn, the staid country hotel, skirts demurely spread over his erect penis, whilst elderly guests strolled through; and, through it all, never entire penetration. Our main worry was how to avoid pregnancy and we were not too sure how to go about this. I had never heard of an orgasm, so I had no idea that I might be missing something. No one had ever told me that there was any connection between the delicious feeling one had induced in oneself from the childhood cot onwards, and the almost equally delicious feeling of close warm contact with one's passion of the moment. So, when penetration was finally achieved in the ninth bunker, the only indication I had that something unusual had happened was a sharp jab of pain, and a lot of blood on the taffeta lining of my gold lace ballgown when I got home. My mother also saw the blood, and my young beau was not thereafter welcomed by my parents.

As he was now barred from the house, our meetings were arranged with difficulty. I somehow stupidly got married to John Spencer who never got nearer to the war than camp in New South Wales (his war being restricted to eventually fighting me in the law courts) and I survived a brief marriage without ever learning what an orgasm was.

Half a century and more later, I am asked sometimes, as if I am an expert, my opinion of Australian men, in the context of the sexual gavotte: in what way I think they differ in their amatory - for want of a more apt word - approaches. Let me quote just one glorious example, my old friend George.

George was generally thought to be, in his day, one of Australia's richest men, his riches based on what was then the solid foundation of Australia's economy - wool. Good merino wool, endless acres; but all augmented by George's fertile business brain. He was never physically pleasing, and in our shallow pleasure-seeking teenage world to be avoided as he was prone to pounce. This was not always easy, as George believed in the most direct approach. Speech could be dispensed with if nubile flesh was within grabbing distance. I managed to escape being grabbed all through my Australian youth, but one day, living in London, George caught up with me. He telephoned daily and after a few weeks I realised I could not pretend a prior engagement every night, every week, every month. As he was living at the Dorchester, I thought that I would, at least, have a decent dinner. We met in his suite: my heart sank. A table was set for two, champagne in bucket, George at the ready. All through dinner (passable) I managed to get him to talk, and talk with interest, on his ruling passion - sheep. So far so good. I began to relax as I settled on the sofa for coffee. Not so George. Rubbing his palms together, hitching up his pants as at a starting post, he launched himself full length across me, pinning me to the sofa. I pushed him off, but he was not easy to shift, and determined to plead his case.

'Aw, come on - I've had my eye on you since you were seventeen. You were the most eligible virgin in town only John Spencer got there first [which of course, he hadn't] and from what I hear of that English boyfriend of yours, you could do with a good, virile Australian.' The English boyfriend was David.

Later that same week I learnt that, failing with me, George had managed to track down two other Australians living in London: his grabs were in taxis this time. To Valerie Fairfax, it was: 'Why didn't you tell me you'd gone on the sex wagon before I bought you a feed?' And to the other, upon being rebuffed, 'Don't tell me you've turned lezzo.'

George eventually married, produced a family, gave up the chase, but still, on his occasional visits to London, kept in touch. Years later he came for treatment for cancer and I visited him in the London Clinic.

'Come here,' said George, patting the bed. I came and perched on it. 'I've been trying to get a feel of your tits for thirty years. Now I'm dying do you think you could give me a feel?' I hitched open my blouse - George slipped his hand inside my brassiere and gave a contented sigh.

'I can die happy now.'

chapter twenty-nine

Coming back to Australia disturbed a pool of tentacles reaching far back into the past - a past which, never having been directly experienced, had failed to interest me. The house in which I was born had contained enough life - enough lives - to feed my childish roots and so I had never questioned nor explored their depths. But now I began to quest, and to question. My mother's cousin, Colyn, was still alive and through him I was able to live in imagination the lives of my antecedents with details never supplied by my grandmother. She seemed not to realise that, fascinating though the characters from Charles Dickens may have been, her family had thrown up their own store of relationships, event and emotion equally worthy of record. Was Peggotty any more memorable than Rosa, our cook? Or Mr Micawber than Tony our SP bookmaker?

I knew through her the dramatic story of how my Polish-Russian great-grandfather had escaped conscription in the Russian army by swimming the Vistula on the eve of his fifteenth birthday. I vaguely remember her telling me that he also spoke fourteen languages, but the details of why or to what use he had put this knowledge had never interested me. Now I discovered that he had, at a very young age, taught some of these languages at university in Birmingham, had sent for his parents, and eventually his siblings, and established them all in England before sailing to Australia, still only nineteen, to join the rush for gold. Out of this, he must have made his first fortune, enabling him to return home, marry, give birth to his first half-dozen or so children and return to Australia as a substantial citizen.

To be Australian in the late nineteenth century and into the twentieth was to be European - Irish or, if possible, English, but if not, then certainly to adopt the customs of England. I expect my great-grandfather possibly even embraced at an early age the Australian obsession with swimming. Having swum the Vistula, fully clothed, I don't imagine Sydney Harbour and beaches posed a threat - only sharks substituted for Russian soldiers. There were beautiful houses to be bought: my mother was born in what, now restored, displays itself as one of the loveliest, Rockwall in Rockwall Crescent. The arrival of more children and some of the married ones returning with their own families to the now widowed patriarch must have been the reason my great-grandfather moved from this lovely house to a far larger, grander, but less beautiful one, Maramanah. Life at Maramanah was the foundation on which my childhood memories were laid.

The house, altered by my great-grandfather to accommodate his brood, was to be centred around music, so the first priorities were to be the ballroom for concerts and the music room for practice. The all-white drawing room, even to a white grand piano, was a much discussed feature of the house, and in the ensuing excitement lavatories were temporarily forgotten. This led to a flurry of activity during which time the household no doubt learnt a certain amount of bladder and bowel control. Tennis court, croquet lawn and stables were installed and suitable servants engaged to care for them.

Through Colyn I learnt about Pasha, an Egyptian brought back from his travels by Great Uncle Spot and kitted out with turban and white satin knee-breeches. Pasha was reputed to be a eunuch, no doubt thought advisable in a household of single ladies and nubile maidservants. A puzzle is the fact that opposite was a brothel and Pasha was thought to have 'crossed the road' when syphilis was diagnosed. His duties thereafter were restricted to the outdoors: cleaning out the stables and sharpening the knives. Stable block and harness room had remained untouched, over which Pasha continued to reign with dignity. Censoriousness does not seem to have spread beyond a certain hygienic caution: Pasha was no longer required to clean the silver or wait on table.

Sex was, of course, seething and bubbling away under Maramanah's vast roofs. Long after all possibility of censorship by my grandmother had been removed, I learnt from Colyn that he had spotted Great Uncle Barley propped up in bed between Aunt Flo, his wife, and Lilla, his sister-in-law. 'To keep warm, darling,' he was told. Another surviving cousin tells me she opened a door to surprise the same Uncle Ba and Lilla in a passionate embrace. Great Uncle Spot was named as the co-respondent in a notorious divorce suit, was sued for damages and defended by his brother-in-law, Uncle John, then a QC, never to be paid for his services.

I learnt, too, some details of the lives of those married great-aunts whom I knew. My father had bowed to convention and attended Great Aunt Juliet's funeral, but when asked on his return what it was like, replied, 'Well, I was there but I can't tell you much because I was listening to the Test match on the radio.' Great Aunt Flo watched television in hospital when she was 103 (and in fine health). When her eighty-year-old daughter came to visit, she went on eating chicken sandwiches and champagne, but told her daughter to keep quiet as it interrupted her television.

Great Aunt Bertie, whom I loved, was, according to her son, a fairly harmless kleptomaniac. Her main target was sheet music which she would purloin from my mother's pile and which would then appear on Colyn's music stand, inscribed

'For darling Colyn with love from Mother'.

The four maiden great-aunts, vilified in his lifetime by my father, and ridiculed by me in a book, were, I now learnt, somewhat daring and dashing characters. They smoked cigarettes; they wore make-up; they were decidedly avant-garde. The house had the first electricity installed in the city, the first bell under the thirty-two seater dining table - and the first telephone. Although named Lilla, Minna, Netta and Anys - and by my father as Litter, Titter, Fritter and Anus - they had nicknames and strangely masculine ones at that: Mick, Bill, Pouff and Nett.

Netta, it seems, was 'not quite all there'. Family legend has it that she was in love with her first cousin, Percy, but was locked in her bedroom to prevent her seeing him. This was brought to its conclusion by the death of her father, over whose coffin she was forced to swear relinquishment of her passion for Percy. It was claimed that these shattering events unsettled Netta's mind henceforth.

They all seemed to shift their names at will, so perhaps my father was not the first. Another second cousin reported that her father claimed his mother's (my great-grandmother's) name was Hannah - listed as Annie on her birth certificate, but by death elevated to the more elegant Anne by her daughters. Dastardly rumour also has it that Lilla, Minna, Netta and Anys had begun life as Lily, Minnie, Nettie and Annie. I learnt how my forebear, the Polish rabbi, had come to be called Hollander. The family were rich timber merchants from Donetsk, whose main trade was downriver to Holland. A former ancestral home had been a castle on the Rhine, on their own island, Katzenelnbogen. This cousin, hopeful of catching out the aunts in pretension, had visited it: but it existed. What would have amused my father most of all, had he known, is the fact that visitors to the Jewish cemetery at Rookwood are now taken on a tour to view the graves of the Aunts up the Cross.

In the intervening years I have returned seven or eight times to Australia, always to work - on a film, or once for the publication of a book - veering wildly from love to hate on each trip; later, staring through a window into grey English skies with only the nostalgic longing for the landscape remembered, and the still memorable phrases ringing in my ears. From a particularly garrulous taxidriver, upon hearing of my literary and film interests: 'When I read a good book I feel a bit resentful: if someone else can entertain me by their imagination why can't I entertain myself?'

'I like real life people in films: I'm a normal, average human being . . . if I took a prisoner, in a war say, and he made a move I'd shoot him - no nonsense about reaching for cigarettes.'

'With a beautiful girl, I'd want to know straightaway - was it bed or not?'

'Films are better than books 'cos you can see round the sides. You've got all that scene-changing.'

'The ones with the small print are always the best books. There's more in them.'

On John Osborne: '*The Entertainer* was a pathetic sort of story - laugh, clown, laugh - that's all it's about, really. He was lucky to have had Olivier.'

The bus driver who with great patience explains directions and interprets coinage value whilst I am holding up the queue, and then beckons me back to present the ticket with a flourish and the admonition: 'Have a little souvenir of a joyous occasion'. The man behind the ticket desk at the ferry terminal from whom I inquire directions, in my very chic, new and expensive Josef outfit, with the obligatory seams on the outside: 'You've got your jumper on inside out, love.' A man talking about an acquaintance: 'He's so mean he wouldn't give a blind duck a shove into the pond.'

chapter thirty

Now, half a lifetime later, I have discovered the landscape of my childhood in another continent. Twenty-six years ago by miraculous chance we came to Biarritz in the corner of south-west France on impulse, and stayed to plant roots in its sand, sea and rocks. It has replaced Australia in my reveries as a balm to the rootless spirit. Perhaps I only love it because it is, geologically, the closest to Sydney I have found in Europe; it links me with earliest childhood – the light and sound and feel of Sydney; although the Basque country pulls always at the heart of all who have lived there. Michael Blakemore, Sydney childhood friend, discovered it first and had bought a house there. We were realising that Switzerland was coming to an end. At the close of one summer holiday in 1972, Michael sent me a telegram to St Prex: 'Come at once,' it said, 'the house of your dreams is for sale'. Coming at once meant a gigantic change of plans: Seamus to be put on a plane at Geneva for school – a rushed car drive across Europe for us. We arrived in a thunderstorm late at night. The approach to Biarritz closely resembles the approach to Eastbourne; the rain did not help. I thought Michael had lost his mind. Determined to leave at noon the next day, we fell into bed in the Blakemore house. We awoke to one of Biarritz's golden days. I was hooked.

Biarritz has golden days, days of pale sparkling sand and brilliant blue skies; the waves snow-speckled. It has silver evenings, pink and blue dawns, purple and orange sunsets, soft navy velvet nights. In twenty-four hours we sampled them all. It also has violent, grumbling days; huge steely seas; distant pale jade mountains turning to gunmetal grey; triumphant, roaring thunder and torrential rain. It has days of scudding cloud; sad, relentless, soft drizzle; tearing shutter-banging wind. All of these can also happen within twenty-four hours - sometimes the same twenty-four; but they did not, that first time, happen to us. Without that first, perfect day - the sea like a still, turquoise lake, with a tiny frill of white-edged breakers - I might never have fallen in love. Not until much later did I come to love the storms and the drama of the changing seas. The house of our dreams still sits on the cliffs overlooking the Côte des Basques, still an unrealised, though coveted, fantasy. It was falling down the cliff. Faint hearts and lawyers' warnings prevailed and we did not eventually buy it. Now restored and newly owned, it mocks our temerity.

We did, however, find an acceptable compromise: a spacious and beautiful apartment which was once the nursery floor of a grand old stone villa and from whose vast terraces I can still glimpse the sea.

The splendid old Hotel Victoria was being pulled down. Our painter was hired to help dismantle it. 'Dismantle' meant to spirit into his van and over to us anything that took our fancy, could be got out of the hotel and up our stairs, and be paid for in cash over a glass of wine at a local bar. So for a few thousand francs, our apartment began to take on an air of Edwardian solidity. The wardrobes have round ball feet, bevelled mirrors and mahogany shelves. The chests of drawers have marble tops. The vast mirror is topped with gilded 'HV' garlanded with cherubs and roses. Bedside commodes are stuffed into every niche.

One night, the painter appeared, panic-stricken, at our door. Someone in authority was due in the morning to inspect the work in progress. Everything must go back for the day. So back it all went - before it was deemed safe to take permanent possession.

Now it has grown gradually around us. There is furniture brought from Switzerland in a trailer - pictures piecemeal from England - stones and shells from the beach on every surface. A large coffee table covered in linen is a piece of hardboard resting on an empty champagne crate; this last a constant reminder of Tony Modet, our first Biarritz friend.

The day we became owners, although not yet inhabitants, we met him in the driveway. He had bought the elegant ground floor apartment, once the library of the great house, having hesitated about ours and rejected it on the grounds that the stairs would prove too much for his dead mother's friends to manage. Tony was the eldest son of a Spanish nobleman and a rich American. He had given away his title to his younger brother in order to please his sister-in-law but hung on to the money which, we learnt, came from Niagara Falls: a dramatic image as presented to us of a cent being earned by Tony every time someone flicked on a light switch in the USA. A prudent forebear had bought up the land surrounding the Falls and the electricity generated from its waters became part of the leasehold. Or so we were told over almost our first tea and cakes party in Biarritz. Tony's own life had not been without drama; an engineer by profession, he had earned a singular distinction when the company of which he was a director built two bridges of record-breaking dimensions - one in Argentina and one in Melbourne. I don't believe that Tony was personally responsible but in due, and not too distant, course they both collapsed. The casualties, and gruesome photographs, made world headlines; Tony retired from active professional life. His mother died, leaving him her piece of the Falls and thereafter he devoted his considerable inventive talents to the service of his hobby - carpentry and indeed any small problem requiring a brilliant handyman. Hence our coffee table.

We were, for the first year, without a telephone whilst we awaited the ministrations of France Telecom. Tony, under cover of darkness, nailed an extension lead underneath the ivy growing up the side of the house and provided us with a spare handset so that we were his telephonic house guests. The champagne crate was never intended to be a permanent fixture but a temporary stopgap whilst he knocked together our bookshelves. But it is the perfect dimension and now an endearing memento of Tony, now dead. It seems appropriate to my life's pattern that I found him dead one morning on his bedroom floor, halfway through his breakfast.

Biarritz has many beaches, just as Sydney has. To the right of the town there stretch the curves of the Chambre d'Amour - named for two lovers who were trapped and drowned by the incoming tide; beaches with romantic names, Sable d'Or, Le Corsair, La Madrague - and on up the coast to Bayonne. In the centre of town is the Grande Plage, perfectly symmetrical and, to me, perfectly horrible in summer with its bathing huts and visiting hordes, the Hôtel du Palais solidly perched in the centre and protected from the beach by its pool, cabanas, restaurant, lawns, and rich flesh. Once, before it was burnt down and rebuilt, the summer palace of the Empress Eugenie of France, precursor of all her royal relatives who gave Biarritz its early cachet.

But, to the left, towards Spain, lies my real Biarritz - the Port Vieux for swimming at high tide and the Côte des Basques at low tide. We are protected from swamping popularity by the capricious weather. It has the reputation of being frightful: in reality, it is simply unreliable, lending spice and excitement. Impossible to plan a picnic with equanimity or house guests without the risk of glum faces. The climate invites privacy. On 'our' beach the faces of the regular addicts are recognised afresh each September. The August bucket-and-spade brigade has gone: the beach now belongs to the surfboard riders; the man from Barclays Bank who was born here; the elegant, elderly woman with sombrero, walking stick and bikini, who walks the same half-mile of beach at low tide each day; the stocky red-faced local woman who bathes three or four times each day, winter and summer, racing down the steps with her plastic bag from Uniprix and who has never learnt to swim; the ice-cream lady in her kiosk, too busy to notice one in high season, greeting one as an old friend; the grey-haired man we have privately dubbed the 'horse-faced man' who only appears each year on the first of September. We greet each other smugly. The invaders have gone.

Strength, joy and peace come from this little stretch of sand, sea, sky and rocks: as I walk it each day I thank my own quaint God aloud for this blessing. I thank him quite loudly and sometimes look behind me to see if I have frightened a fisherman. I know nowhere so immediately accessible where I can talk to myself so very happily and loudly. The sea answers back - the clouds move - my voice does not meet an embarrassed silence.

Not for nothing is this stretch of coast known as the Côte des Foux. It seems entirely appropriate that the oldest firm of estate agents are Bliss et Fock and that the top half of the 'O' is peeling off; that three successive bank managers of the English section of Barclays have been Messrs Hope, Church, and d'Eath; that a retired English admiral built himself three artificial lakes stocked with rare and expensive duck, periodically eaten by polecats; that bombs explode almost unremarked in the portion of town most frequented by ETA, the Basque terrorist organisation, but that the biggest bang was caused by a bomb which blew up the empty Taxation Department at 3 a.m. - empty, that is, of all except taxation records; that the

CRS, the special police, double up, when stripped of guns, as lifeguards on the beaches.

The great houses are slowly closing down. As their owners die, few of their children are prepared to take on the responsibilities and expense, but the slowly narrowing circle who remain continue on their elegant round of luncheons, tea, cocktails and dinners.

My Australian ghosts now dance with my Biarritz ghosts, inhabiting my days and memories there. My diary jottings keep them alive.

Peggy is the widow of a very senior Belgian-French Prince and Duke – a child of Southern America, she is in her late eighties and she trots like a sparky sparrow through the town to the beach each morning. Once a week she takes the bus to San Sebastian, across the Spanish border ignoring the terrorist attacks, to buy olives, oil, nuts, a lethal drink called Chinchon, illegal in France, and to visit her dressmaker. Once a month she goes to Geneva to visit her banker. She has style: her apartment in Biarritz and her apartment in Paris are repositories of regal splendour, ancestral portraits on each inch of wall. When the banker in Geneva advises, an ancestor leaves the wall.

As we splash through the shallow water at a cracking pace she tells me how miserable she was some fifteen years ago when her husband died. Her masseuse, too, was very unhappy: life was not worth living. They make a suicide pact to jump off the Rocher de Vierge, hand in hand, but for this to have maximum effect the tides and the weather must be propitious. They look up the timetable of tides and fix a date. Five days before the appointed time, Peggy is summoned to Paris by her husband's lawyers to sign some important documents, but she tells Madame X not to worry – it will only take a day or so and she'll be back in plenty of time for their rendezvous. The lawyers keep her ten days in Paris. When she returns she immediately telephones Mme X, but there is no reply. She calls a mutual acquaintance to inquire and is told, 'But haven't you heard? Mme X jumped off the Rocher de Vierge five days ago.' Peggy takes this as a sign that she is not meant to kill herself.

Peggy asks me one day to explain the meaning of a 'toy boy'. When told they are usually good-looking young men who are always on call she is intrigued, 'Oh, good. Can you get me one or two of those?'

She says that Barclays Bank is now run exactly like the Galeries Lafayette. They are trained *to slam the doors in your face.*

Since writing this, Peggy has died - no longer need for anonymity. Her obituary gave her full titles of Duchesse de Nemours and Princesse d'Orléans, and we all discovered she was well into her nineties. She broke both hips - one in a fall running along the street, the other falling out of bed in the nursing home in Bayonne. Gradually, the enforced immobility broke her splendid spirit.

Susie Cleveland was a rich American - child of a former US Consul in the area. Susie developed cancer, and then her son killed himself - all in one year. She put all her papers in order, collected exactly the correct amount of pills and alcohol to do the job cleanly, chose a time when her maid would not be frightened or embarrassed - and settled down to the job. At the very last moment she remembered that her beautiful jewels, in particular her emeralds, were left in trust to her grandchildren, all minors, and meanwhile would doubtless be worn by her hated daughter-in-law. The thought was too much. She imagined her emerald ring on her daughter-in-law's finger. She cancelled her suicide; life was preferable.

Isabel d'Orizaba has become very 'confused' – an operation on something as minor as a tooth necessitating an anaesthetic has left her minus both toothache and her wits. Her beloved brother, Pepé de Santa Cruz, formerly Spanish Ambassador to the UK for eleven years, has died and his many friends are constantly consoling her. Far from being warmed by the affection shown him in death, to her confusion is added irritation and boredom. So, to every inquiry about the remaining male members of her family – son, son-in-law, brothers – she replies, 'Oh, he died two months ago'. Tout *Biarritz is in shock at the unprecedented string of disasters which seem to have befallen the family.*

Our greatest friend – very much alive, so I shall not give him his full name – is a Spanish Duke, of great charm and erudition. We walk along the sand and compare our dinners of the previous night. I have had a jolly, delicious, and cheap meal at the Bistrot with Isabel d'Orizaba and her brother, Pepé de Santa Cruz. The Duke and his wife have been to a very grand dinner at the Café de Paris – all 'grandees', he says, and very good company – the Albuquerques and the grandmother of Francisco Franco, the host a Prince, and a sprinkling of Bourbons in there somewhere. Women beautifully dressed; superb jewels; but the Café de Paris, we agree, is second-rate and not worth its three stars. He describes his meal in detail – a petite marmite, *veal kidneys, far too greasy, with cepes – the* spécialité, *a* gratin des fruits, *which turned out to be raspberries in a custard. Ah, but the wines! They were superb. A quite extraordinary Sauterne, so extraordinary that he had sent for the patron so that he might note down and remember the year and the vineyard of each wine.*

'And your host?' I inquire. 'What was his name?'

'My host?' The Duke stops short. We both stare out to sea as if hoping for inspiration. 'I cannot remember the name of

my host. The wines, yes, and the food – but what is the name of the poor man?'

It is no good. He can only remember the family name – an excellent and distinguished family – and that he is an Italian Prince, ruler of one of the Italian Principalities. And his excellent war record.

'Not on the same side as you, of course,' he says.

But the name is never recalled.

His wife has a phenomenal memory. Shakespeare, Verlaine, Goethe and Baudelaire are tucked away in quotation marks in her richly stocked mind, along with a fascinating variety of facts. She is talking about the problems of her son and his baby son whom he wishes to make 'tough' – at sixteen months – by taking him swimming at 7 a.m. and forbidding pyjamas. She thinks this is a little extreme. 'After all, poor little thing, why shouldn't he have pyjamas? It's not as if he's Alexander the Great, and even Alexander the Great slept in a leopardskin. He hasn't even got a leopardskin.'

One day Bill has toothache. We discuss possible Biarritz dentists and I voice concern over allowing one to pull out Bill's tooth. The Duchess says this is ridiculous – anyone can pull a tooth out *– Peter the Great did it all the time in the marketplace. It is putting one* in *for which one needs expertise.*

At Mass one day, she opens her prayer book and finds an old photograph of her eldest son. 'Poor man,' she sighs, 'I left him there.'

Another son visits with his wife. She leaves the house for a week, admonishing, wisely, as she leaves: 'Don't discuss your father with your wife, and don't discuss your wife with your father!' On her return she laments, 'But when I came back nobody was speaking to anyone and Alvaro and his wife had gone to the Argentine. Imagine! I can't even go to Dublin for one week.'

She recounts these facts with calm authority. She has a

remarkable gift for not wasting words, of choosing the apt phrase on her shafts to the point. When her sister's husband is taken ill in Madrid and her sister is visiting London and must be contacted, she telephones us in London and in two sentences makes her point in what one recognised, in the Duchess, as logical progression.

'My brother-in-law is dying. Do you know the telephone number of the Ritz?'

She asks me one day what the husband of a newly married friend is like. I tell her he is sixteen years younger than his wife. She looks thoughtful – finally: 'What a very good idea,' she reflects, 'when there are no porters at railway stations any more.'

Their servants move with them between their three houses – Biarritz, Madrid, and their principal country estate; the names, when translated, are Angel (the estate foreman), Faithful (his chauffeur), Perfect (the estate overseer) and Miracle (the cook). When not in their own houses, they descend on hoteliers who by now must have had some advance warnings on the international hotel intelligence line. The Duchess has set fire to two bathrooms by following her simple habit of ensuring a clean bath. Her mother travelled always with a small bottle of neat spirit, marvellously effective when thrown into a cast-iron bath and flambéed. She has not encountered problems in continuing this practice until baths in lesser and newer hotels than those of her youth became plastic and not sympathetic to heat treatment. At the first hotel in the Midlands country town, she emptied the bottle, threw in a lit match and the bath exploded. The Manager, summoned by the Duke in righteous anger (his wife, he explained, was simply removing her nail varnish whilst lighting a cigarette sitting on the edge of the bath) is stunned into abject apology. She is furious at this somewhat louche vision painted of her, particularly as she does not smoke. The builder is chastised, and the

Duke is triumphant when moved into a new suite and the bill for their two weeks' stay is cancelled.

It is explained to him by his friends that unless at Claridge's or the like one must be prepared for plastic, but the warning is forgotten and two years later a London bathroom in a lesser hotel goes up in flames. This time even the architect is blamed. No bill is presented. The Duchess still travels everywhere with her lethal spirits.

Once, having let the flat, we camp at their Biarritz villa for a few days.

The Duchess is away on a cruise. We and the servants have no common language. I sleep in the daughter's room, which resembles an extremely pretty nun's cell (the cell, not the nun). It is tiny and divinely decorated in the most chic of French papers and materials. The bed is about two feet wide. If you turn over you fall out. The dogs are all at sea because the Duchess is *at sea so they pee on the floor if the door is open for a second. The furniture consists of an exquisite little desk covered in exquisite* objets de vertu *– nonoperative Louis XVI clocks, etc. – no room on it to actually write; two minute and exquisite armchairs; a child's dressing table on which rests a gnome's mirror (period, therefore its glass blackened); an ormolu lamp (without a bulb); a bedside pedestal table of marble and gilt containing a Sèvres saucer which contains, in its turn, a crucifix; a small round inlaid gem of a table, supporting tray with water and glass; and a very inadequate hanging cupboard. There are delicious, fluffy blankets and inviting pillows, monograms and coronets everywhere, and absolutely nowhere where I can see to dress. Bill is in larger quarters down the hall. We have, however, a large and comfortable bathroom and two lavatories. Our first act is to flush both loos – mine won't go down and Bill's floods all over the floor. Luckily plumbers are in situ, installing a new kitchen (banging and drilling all day). Ordering meals is a problem –*

we are told to order what we like. The servants have no word for – or use for – butter, so the first day's breakfast was fairly dry, and we discover when Bill's tray is put on it that the gem of a small table in my room is designed for water and glass, and no more. Now, however, everybody orders everything and we are bloated and surfeited and long for our normal lunch of raw stuff on our terrace. We are like stuffed geese.

Last night as dinner was announced at 10 p.m., I am called to the telephone – there are three lines and they all ring in different places and the servants don't understand what anyone is saying. It is Lisa. She does not say, 'How are you?' or even, 'Hello, Mum'. She says, with some heat in her voice, 'You've given me the wrong number – I've been calling the wrong number for hours, and I've driven some poor French family mad, and what's more, Arnold Wesker's been trying to get you for hours and he's driven the poor French family mad' – and more in that vein, with increasingly bad temper. I try and tell her, with great restraint, to calm down and point out that she must have a *right number as she's just reached me (at an extremely inconvenient moment, which I do not add).*

'Well, that's the other *number,' she* spits. *We argue a bit along these lines before I think to ask why Arnold Wesker has been trying me. Some address he wants, she thinks, so I tell her to ring and correct the number; and go, apologetically, into the waiting dinner. The telephone rings. It is Arnold. He, too, launches straight into the tale* he *wishes to impart. 'You know how everything happens to you,' he begins, 'well, things happen to other people, too – just listen carefully to this.'*

The saga lasts all the way through the soup, but in essence it concerns a Japanese writer who has been staying chez *Wesker who has gone to Paris to fetch her daughter who has been staying with a friend who leaves and locks up her flat for the summer when the daughter leaves. The two Japanese ladies have arrived at the Spanish border to discover that the daughter's passport is at the Paris flat. They are huddled in a hotel on the border at Hendaye which has no front door or telephone and is seemingly suspicious. They have made arrangements to find someone in Paris to break into flat and procure passport but they now require, in Arnold's terminology, a 'safe house' to which the passport can be sent. He has been reading too much le Carré. Bill says that the last time we – the English – have used any in this area, he was having his bar mitzvah in the Old Kent Road. I explain that (a) I am no longer in my own house, (b) Hendaye is a good half-hour distant in bumper to bumper traffic, and (c) I am staying in a house which belongs to a highly eccentric Spanish Duke and that, although it could be termed 'safe', the arrangements could never be called reliable and the servants have no command of Japanese for when the ladies call from Hendaye.*

Arnold is not to be deflected. I weakly give the address to which the passport will be sent registered post, and return once more to the table.

*I tell the Duke, thinking it may amuse him. He looks reflective. 'This will pose problems,' he says. '*Not *insurmountable, but it will involve certain visits to the Post Office. It can be done but it will not be easy.' It seems the staff, even the gardener, all have strict instructions not, under any circumstances,* ever *to accept a registered letter. I don't enquire but I know him well enough to deduce that this has either some fiscal or legal connection. Not ETA bombs.*

He suggests I telephone Arnold back at once and tell him to have the passports sent Poste Restante to Hendaye. Arnold expresses amazement that he hadn't thought of it himself. When I come back to the table, the Duke says, 'Who is Arnold Wesker?' That takes up the rest of dinner.

The Duke invites us to dine at Ainhoa. It is an hour's drive – very beautiful – into the mountains. We go in two cars, his wife with us, reciting Verlaine and Shakespeare in the back seat, and one of their sons. He has asked me to book the table – he cannot remember the name of the restaurant (famous) but after detailed description of the ambience and the food, I have no trouble identifying it. In his car are two more guests and a daughter. I explain to the restaurateur that there will be eight but, being predominantly Spanish, we will also doubtless be late. Actually, we manage to arrive before the Duke, not too glaringly late: the patron is still presenting accounts to departing clients. We order drinks – peruse the menu – chat. After about three-quarters of an hour even his wife is concerned about the other car and the chill thought strikes me that they may have gone to the other *famous restaurant in Ainhoa. I telephone. They are there. It would make sense for us to make our profuse apologies to the patron, from whom we have by now tentatively ordered dinner, and rush the intervening mile or so to join our host, but he insists that he come personally to fetch us. The reason for this becomes apparent when he arrives. In the back of his car, starched chef's cap brushing the roof, sits, immobilised, the cook. The Duke has kidnapped him to ensure that he will still be available to cook our meal when we return to his restaurant, and will not have departed at an hour long past his bedtime.*

Drinks at the A's. This is very formal and civilised and Dodin goodies come as fast as the drinks. After stuffing ourselves for two hours we are asked to stay for a 'snack'. The snack, served by two waiters, is in the dining room – the table vast and the three courses delicious. The Duchess, however, as soon as we get in the car, announces her puzzlement at the veal. Was it, she wonders, meant to be hot or cold? If meant to be hot, it was 'icy'. If meant to be cold, why did we have hot gravy with it? Perhaps, she giggles, that is the meaning of a 'chaud-froid'.

Aimée de Heeren is the undisputed 'Queen' of Biarritz. This evening I go, without Bill, to a gathering at Aimée's. A gathering is the only way to describe it – one is asked for tea – or drinks – at 7 or 7.30 – and it is impossible to confirm whether or not one is going because there is no meeting point in the French of the Spanish servants and myself. I arrive, naturally first not being Spanish, even though at 7.10. The doors are open, the lights on – I walk softly in. A tea table is set in the small drawing room. The door to the dining room is ajar and I hear the murmur of male voices. I decide to leave on the pretext of a forgotten umbrella in the car, returning later – rain is just beginning. In the road I encounter two more cars arriving: Dr and Mme Vidal, in whose honour we have been told, sans *explanation, that the gathering is being gathered. The Vidals are characters escaped from a Jacques Tati cast list. We go in again – with Carmen Villaverde, who seems somehow in charge.*

If Aimée is the Queen, then Carmen, the Marquesa Villaverde, well into her eighties, is the Queen Mother – universally loved; related, as the Spanish and South Americans tend to be, to almost everyone; teetering continually on the verge of selling her vast white elephant of an estate, now beleaguered by motorways, dry rot and dearth of servants. These last necessities Carmen endeavours to kidnap from amongst the unemployed but hopeful students or émigrés from various airports on her occasional forays to her country of birth, Peru, or Málaga where she has a daughter. The incumbent is trained for a season: the Villa Pardo (named after Carmen's father, an ex-President of Peru) resembles Fawlty Towers for one glorious, hilarious training session and then they move on. Carmen goes back to the airports. She is, of course, related to Aimée by marriage – whose marriage I am never able to clarify.

Mme Vidal, out of her normal surroundings, is dressed as

for a Royal garden party, indeed there is something of a presentation robe about her whole toilette *– black and white silk dress; a white fine wool cloak tied at the neck and with a double-frilled collar; and a whole* parure *of corals, gold and diamonds. In fact, there isn't an inch of her bare flesh which isn't sparkling.*

This time we boldly go in to the salon, and sit. No one comes. Carmen begins a sort of conducted mini-tour of those treasures of Aimée's which the burglars have left – explaining in hushed tones that there used to be much *more. The Helleu drawings are remarked upon but only as having been done by Paulette Howard-Johnson's father. The distinguished Helleu's name escapes everyone, except me, and no one is listening to me.*

A nurse rushes in because Aimée's husband is ill upstairs – Spanish words are exchanged – she leaves. Eventually a butler appears and we are asked if we would like tea or a drink. It is by now about 7.30. We settle for drinks. The Vidals are looking distinctly startled. Marita arrives, very chic in a simple cotton dress. Poor Mme Vidal's jewels seem blinding. Sarestigui arrives, kisses everyone's hand and also asks for a drink. Isabel d'Orizaba arrives – we giggle quietly. Finally, Aimée appears – the servants twitter – candles are lit and the tea table is brought in from the small drawing room. Tea appears, and delicious cakes: the Vidals look stunned. They are French – surely it is dinnertime; if not dinner, then le cocktail? *Aimée looks charming in a blouse, wool skirt and brogues. An old copy of* Interiors *is paraded by Carmen, and Dr Vidal is made to look at the much thumbed pages of Aimée's house in Palm Beach. Corinna arrives –* she *has on white jeans and a pretty T-shirt and finally, about 8.30, to complete the tea party, Pepé de Santa Cruz.*

The explanation, muttered to me behind a tea napkin by Isabel, is that Carmen wanted to do a favour to the Vidals, and the one thing Jeanne longed for was to be invited to Aimée's. Aimée is obviously as bewildered by what to do with them as they are to be there. It is like court being paid to exiled Royalty who have long since abdicated but may still graciously receive the occasional faithful subject.

The Duchess of Windsor wore a particularly bouffant and splendid dress (overdone) to dinner at Carmen's, and behaved in a particularly Royal manner until a spark from the fire sent her up in flames. Carmen's dinner party became famous for the spectacular feu d'artifice.

Carmen tells of her good friend who has a thirty-metre swimming pool right in the centre of Biarritz. The Duke asks her name. 'Ah,' says Carmen, 'the name is very difficult. I cannot possibly remember it: but it is the last name in the telephone directory.'

'But,' says the Duke, 'you say this woman is a good friend of yours?'

'Yes, yes,' says Carmen, 'but the name is impossible. However, it is quite easy to telephone her – just get me the directory and I will show you.'

We get the directory. It is a Basque name – beginning with Z and quite impossible to learn. Should one day she be left out of the Annuaire, *Carmen will never again find her friend.*

Fifi, an American resident for summer months of long standing, is selling her pretty, desirable house. The sale is given the status of a state secret – the only people to be taken into her confidence are the bank manager, the friend who introduced the buyer, and myself. Fifi is kind, generous and deeply limited by the parameters of the very rich Americans. On the morning the contract is finally signed she telephones to ask me to whom I think she should break the news first. Peggy and Carmen are her priorities for fear they would be shocked at hearing the news second-hand. Five minutes later Carmen telephones, 'Fifi has just rung to say she has sold her house. It seems it was a very important secret. Imagine – such a drama! I don't give a damn if Fifi has sold her house. It does not interest me one bit. What interests me is the price. *Tell me, Robin, have you any idea of the price?'*

Pancho was a stray dog whose two regular beats were outside the bar in Place Bellevue where the beau monde *met each day at 1.30 and later outside the front gate of the golf club at Chiberta when they met again for golf. One day he followed Tutti de Forrest, who adopted him, and thereafter Pancho entered, along with his new master, all the hallowed precincts he had hitherto viewed from the outside. Two or three of the members objected to the dog on the golf course and, in due course, the secretary was bitten. The committee were assembled and Tutti was informed that Pancho was banned. So Tutti de Forrest went home and in one telephone call bought the club. He then fired the secretary, who had upheld their objection – appointed himself secretary, asked all the complaining members to resign, and he and Pancho played their eighteen holes together daily.*

Dedé and Jon are giving a party. They greet their guests with embarrassed apology for the noise of violent thumping coming from the floor above. The lady in the flat above has recently gone quite mad and they don't know what to do about it. She commenced by throwing suitcases down the stairs – has attacked one of their guests – has stamped on the ceiling until the light fitting on the ceiling has loosened – and is now stamping furiously as guests arrive. It is as if a mad plumber has been let loose.

We go for tea and *drinks with X (also alive) at his château which he is restoring, taking our Duchess with us. As we enter*

Interviewing Fraga for the Spanish film, 1963 – camera crew having problems?

With Helen and John Osborne on our Biarritz terrace, 1980s.

With Arnold Wesker at the Osbornes' garden party, Kent, in the 1980s.

With Jeffrey Bernard and Deirdre Redgrave on our London terrace, 1970s.

Intrepid house guests at Biarritz, 1980s – Lord and Lady Strathcarron on 'our' beach, proud of their means of transport from the UK.

With Bill, 'lecturing' on the QEII, in the 1980s – nothing but caviar!

Summer garden party at Laurence and Mary Evans's with Laurence Olivier.

With James Fairfax, Lee Remick and her husband, Kip Gowans, during the making of *Emma's War,* Australia, 1985.

Discussing *Madame Sousatzka* with Shirley MacLaine and John Schlesinger during the shoot.

With Geoffrey Bayldon, Dame Peggy Ashcroft and John Schlesinger, on the eve of Peggy's eightieth birthday, farewelling us on the set of *Madame Sousatzka*, 1987.

My two directors – Michael Blakemore, about to start on *Country Life*, views John Schlesinger, just finished *Madame Sousatzka*, with deep misgiving.

On the set of *Country Life* with the broken hand and Kerry Fox: Greta Scacchi at make-up and Nurse Patsy in background awaiting the next casualty, 1994.

On location for *Oscar and Lucinda*, Portsmouth, 1996, with Ralph Fiennes.

Wedding to Bill, June 22 1994.

Bill and granddaughter, Lyndall, in Sydney, 1994: 'Australia – here we come!'

the drive, we all agree that it is a perfectly hideous château and the Duchess points out that the view is also 'horrible'. Inside we are given a tour. X's brother-in-law draws me ahead, pointing out that X is doing it all wrong and that he has no taste. The green paint should be white; the curtains should be thrown out; the modern Japanese paper lanterns are an abomination, which indeed they are. X is full of enthusiasm and we are shown every piece of furniture and every engraving and painting, of which there are hundreds, and which all appear to be ancestors. On the beach the next morning, the Duchess muses on the fact that X used to be perfectly content with one or two eighteenth-century ancestors but now he is discovering earlier and earlier ones, as earlier and earlier gravures *appear. He has very speedily got back as far as the thirteenth century. He is, however, very charming and his childlike enthusiasm for his rather ugly château is endearing. It is only ugly on the outside. Inside, although crumbling, it is rather splendid. He has a marvellous* gravure *of Napoleon – and points out that his eyes were blue. He does not claim him as an ancestor.*

Later, we take Helen and John Osborne to visit. John both unimpressed and rude – scathing re: 'foreign aristos' showing off their possessions. A form of inverted snobbery, perhaps? The point about X 'showing off' being that it is not in order to impress but simply to share his childlike delight in his restoration of his ugly château – an infectious delight.

In our own building, one of the Spanish Basque 'cellar' dwellers is also deranged. When I plan to let my garage to someone else for more money (he has had it on a pittance for three years) he threatens to slash the man's tyres. His blonde wife works as a manicurist by day; she wears night attire, slippers, or lies semi-nude in the sun outside their cellar door when not at work. By night, she plies her trade on the streets, not far enough from our building to protect us from the noise of the occasional squabbles with her 'clients'. Ribero is unemployed, probably unemployable. We suspect he is an incompetent or would-be terrorist, so that when his car caught spectacularly on fire one night in the drive it was the work of a rival. Two of the French residents take it upon themselves to water our meagre garden. If they leave the hose unattended, Ribero darts out, turns it off and locks it in the cleaning cupboard under the stairs. M. Sagaro therefore buys a chain and padlock with which he secures the hose en place *and to which he and Mme Cini have the key. A meeting is then called to consider Ribero's protest that he has no key: if none is forthcoming he now threatens to slash the hose to pieces. We vote to give him a key. The next day I meet him – wild-eyed – in the hall. Someone has removed both our name and his from the letterbox slot. I replace mine: he is waving a paintbrush and has painted his name in thick and vivid green paint across the face of our communal wooden letterbox.* 'C'est les Français,' *he yells at me, clutching my arm. 'Look – look – they have removed* your *name and* mine*! Now, they can't remove the paint! I lose many important letters – many cheques . . .' He burbles on. I wonder if one day he might set fire to the building full of French and – trapped on the top floor – ourselves.*

Discovery, after seventeen years, of a new Biarritz experience – a morning break at the Bar l'Amiral, a workmen's type café, bordering the market. To date, I have only ventured as far as a large black coffee and a croissant but all around me are native Biarrots dropping in for a pichet *of white wine and a plate of* bigorneaux *or half a dozen oysters. This at 11 a.m. and many of the clientele at least as old, solitary, and female as myself. I feel adventurously touristic in my croissant and coffee solitude: the best and cheapest coffee in town. The croissants, as are the oysters, procured as ordered from the market across the narrow street. A new set of familiar faces unfold, replacements welcomed to the few now missing from the Côte des Basques. No sign this year of the blond German ex-submariner and his wife, but at the Bar l'Amiral there is a hawk-nosed blonde who has her café crème each day and a grey-haired bag lady with her glass of wine and small platter of* bigorneaux *who will spend most of the day there.*

Most of our Biarritz friends are now either on sticks and crutches, or operating with deaf-aids – sometimes both. There is a younger group, led by the Singers, but I fear we are too old for it. I go to one dinner there, alone, for the Michaels of Kent – all French except for Balfours, Kents, Aimée and me. Beautifully done, but I suspect I blot my social copybook by not curtsying or 'Sir' or 'Ma'am'-ing them. Cannot bring myself to do so. She is dreadful.

Big excitement early on because the old Spanish Queen Mother, the Countess of Barcelona, was here and all the Spaniards gone bananas; we had to line up and curtsy at the Agilars' and try to mumble a few words in her ear – not easy as she's in a wheelchair and her head is permanently dropped forward and sideways onto her bosom, so that presumably all she can see is the ground. We are later told that the Duke has surreptitiously introduced Bill as the Earl of Fairchild.

Bill tells of conversation with Miguel d'Yturbe. When he and Charlotte were evacuated from Mexico during the war, in a convoy, they arrived in London knowing only two people: the hall porter at Claridge's and a Lieutenant-General commanding some obscure brigade. On these two flimsy acquaintances, they constructed their lives.

Five dull days of coping with a film producer and his wife, here to work on a script with Bill. Dull, because I have her every morning on the beach and she hates the water, and we have them three nights for dinner and they both hate food. Our food, anyway. On their last night, the husband also makes it plain he hates Biarritz – 'Brighton without the architecture,' he says, and wonders why Bill and I have no 'home' – no 'base', and only live in 'flats'.

Charitably, I presume he is slightly drunk.

Margot is inconsolable at the death of her husband and feels that fate has singled her out for widowhood. The fact that she had forty years of perfect marital happiness and four lovely and loving children are not seen as consolation. Mike has played a dirty trick on her by dying first and she determines to kill herself.

As we tramp briskly over the fields she tells me she has the exact amount of pills and knows exactly how to do it. The problem is where and when. It cannot be at home because she might be found and resuscitated. A hotel would be equally uncertain. But the main worry is who would feed the dogs if she is not to broadcast her incapacity in advance. We discuss this worry over the dogs and her iron determination to go ahead with her suicide endlessly, although I am fairly out of breath and out of condition compared to her. As we pass a stable she darts in and I am shown a magnificent hunter. She croons to the horse; she bargains with the farmer who owns him. His size, price and performance are discussed. We leave with her wondering to me whether she could possibly afford the £2000 asked for him – but she wants him so badly. A good hunter would make such a difference to her life.

One more mouth to feed in the event of her death!

I have now lived longer in my Biarritz home than anywhere else in my life.

chapter thirty-one

Changing landscapes: changing work patterns. I was never able to spend as much time as I wished in Biarritz – always hauled back to base by guilt and clients. It seemed time to move on in every area – which I imagined, foolishly, would give me whole chunks of free time. So, having gradually extricated myself from the agency, I was, equally gradually, becoming a film producer.

I first dipped toes in the water with two films on which I was, respectively, Co-Executive Producer (a title I was subsequently to decline when final screen credits came to be printed) and Executive Producer. I then went on to earn, with sweat, tears, exhaustion and some exhilaration, my title of Producer with the next three.

First dip in the water was in 1984, both the year and the film. I never wished it to be made but as literary agent for the dramatic rights of the George Orwell estate, and at Sonia Orwell's insistence, I agreed to be part of the production team. We knocked back all the contenders, but one, Marvin Rosenbloom, a Chicago lawyer, in particular wore me down. His letters were lengthy, persistent and, above all, frequent. I eventually took pity on him; or, as now appears more evident, took the bait, and a very detailed and drawn-out correspondence began. This blossomed into actual meetings.

Marvin chose a moment when I was in Los Angeles on other business to fly in to see me, take me out to a sumptuous dinner and convince me of his sincerity. I felt some disloyalty to a previous contender who had gone to similar lengths - in New York that time - further augmented by sending me 1,984 red roses. I did not count them and he no doubt counted on me not counting them. But Marvin's determination was such that I, in turn, convinced the literary caretaker of the estate, Mark Hamilton, and Sonia, that we should take him seriously. I advised him to prune his American literary verbosity before writing to Sonia. His pages of hyperbole did not mark him out as a hot contender for the interpretation of Orwell's concise style.

Before he came to London to interview Sonia, I instructed him to familiarise himself not only with *1984* but with all of Orwell's work, particularly the Essays. I didn't expect him to actually embark on a crash course on Orwell at Chicago University but he did. He also took my advice about how else to win Sonia over - food, of course - and this he accomplished by taking her out to an even more delicious meal. We signed a contract. I was to have Co-Executive Producer credit, a fee, and a percentage of the profits. I was also to have approval of actual producer, screenplay, director, and principal cast.

I cooked Marvin many dinners whilst we thrashed out these details on his frequent visits. I met his wife. Thirteen years later, I have not heard a word from Marvin since the film was completed. I have heard *of* him: his elevation in the US lecture circuit circles to the prime Orwell expert; from the eventual *1984* producer that the film must now be in profit. 'Profit', however, is a word one soon learns to associate in the film industry with jockeying and bargaining - a purely paper power. It sounds good but you seldom get to see it. I never even got a Christmas card from Marvin. Nor the fee.

When the credit titles for the film came to be printed, the producer telephoned me. We had accumulated a whole team of various 'producers' by now – Executives, Co-Executives, Associates, Presenters – and many other imaginative titles, each one being squeezed in as their financial contributions excused it, so that their listing looks particularly top-heavy given the brevity of the film's title. As I had done nothing but acquire the rights for Marvin through good advice, cast my vote of approval on all creative elements, and cook a lot of meals, I waived my Co-Executive Producer credit and suggested that our physical producer, Simon Perry, give me whatever title he thought appropriate. It loomed large on screen: I have never seen it before or since but apt it certainly was. So, although I had contractually earned my first producer credit, I rather fancied the more accurate one I finished up with on screen – PROJECT DEVELOPED BY ROBIN DALTON. One notch up on 'Research by' for our Spanish effort, on which my input had been vastly greater.

I did go on to earn my next Executive Producer credit on *Emma's War*, an Australian film, as I secured our star, Lee Remick, part of our finance, distribution, and brought together the two physical producers, Andrena Finlay and Clytie Jessop, the director. However, interspersed with what might appear seamless success, albeit of slow fruition, were several spectacular failures, a lot of them undertaken through my chronic inability to say 'no', to turn my back on any opportunity or any applicant for my help or attention. They were none of them my obsession – for none of them did I feel passion – only a wish to help. This meant a great deal of time wasted by me and usually a certain amount of someone else's money. There was *The Promise*. There was *Halfway to Shanghai* (but that one *was* my idea, and my passion, so perhaps I will still make it). There was *Bruno Rising*; there was *The Children*, *Burmese Days*, an abortive attempt to make *Mirage* with Paramount and *Homage to Catalonia*, *Down and Out in Paris and London* . . .

Most of these failures are marked in my mind by various journeys in search of finance - *The Promise*, the brainchild of one John Watkinson, depended on money promised to John by a Mr Lai in Hong Kong. So to Hong Kong I went, en route to Australia. Diary jottings are the only record of that particular drain down which slipped our hopes, but as the Gulf War broke out whilst I was in the air, the events are muddled up in my memory.

I flew Cathay Pacific - an empty plane. As I bent down to remove my shoes a small Asian stewardess bent across me to place a full glass of champagne on my arm rest. Naturally it went down my neck, pants, and seat as I sat up, necessitating a complete change of clothes for me; change of place by clairvoyant chap in the next seat, who got the message early in the flight, and retreated to the other end of the cabin. Glued to room service and CNN in superb hotel - no sleep - but finally a meeting with Andy Lai on 62nd floor of Bank of China building and then lunch in Chinese restaurant where I was asked to choose. I said spicy Chinese - a mistake as it was all *spicy. Lai only seemed faintly interested in our film - so John not really to be relied on and our 'backers' my Hong Kong trip the poorer. So the remaining time is devoted to 'social' life, as Mr Lai doesn't really want to meet again and this is provided by sweet couple, friends of John, who live there and who it transpires had come up with Lai idea in the first place. Very kind and helpful but wife exhausting - does everything from cook for the Mandarin Hotel to other nameless occupations. They live in a tiny but charming apartment on Lamma Island for which she never ceases apologising because of having lost vast house and fortune in South Africa. She tore all over Hong Kong with me literally running after her, knocking down small Chinese, falling over rotten fruit - cut my foot on a piece of glass - blood everywhere. My new friend paused only long enough to buy me a plaster and then we ran for the ferry. Bloodied and exhausted, we climbed 192 steps to their apartment and hardly time to finish superb meal before I rush down to ferry again, only just catching it, and back to hotel for reflexology massage, somewhat hampered by bloody foot: two toes out of action.*

Then a very long wait in horrid little roped-off bar-cum-restaurant, at airport, supposedly courtesy of Cathay Pacific who have failed to provide a proper first class lounge to which I have by now rapidly become accustomed in my upgraded state. Luxury and privilege blur and soften the terrors of air travel, and, in my case, panic-induced incompetence. I have checked both ticket and passport six times since leaving hotel in chauffeur/nanny driven limousine. I have an irrational suspicion that the two bags I have just checked and labelled are not in fact mine at all – but clones, magically spirited into the car with me. I want badly to pee, but laden down as I am with cabin baggage, ton-weight handbag, redundant overcoat, ridiculous and already damaged coolie hat bought in street market (for sun I no longer sit in), and my son's new camera, equal in weight to my own cabin baggage, I am tethered to the table by security regulations. I have one hour and forty minutes to wait. And then God knows how long before I can unfasten seat belt and dash to the loo. The locals are dazed by the sudden security instructions – armed police in dozens in the banks and no one at the airport but bewildered Chinese ladies opening the odd bag but much too polite to look inside it. I am scanning fellow passengers for Arab features – no one else seems to care.

Other promises – other journeys – much more money was to be poured into *The Promise*, an ironic title – to it I owe my one view of Hong Kong.

I became very briefly involved with one Roger Peters (of Hungarian origin, though a US citizen, so one can be forgiven for never remembering whether the Roger or the Peter comes first). John Whitney[20] had rung to ask if I could spare him ten minutes – he was looking for money to produce Noël Coward's *Hay Fever*, and the ill-informed word seems to be around in town that I can easily locate it; and John 'rather liked' him. Immediately Mr Roger Peters, or Mr Peter Rogers, rings to invite me to meet him, in his suite at the Savoy where, he tells me, I can see the bed Noël Coward slept in. As I've seen several beds in which Noël has slept, in his own houses as well as the Savoy, it doesn't seem sufficient reason to battle across London and incur a parking fine, so I bid Mr Interchangeable to visit me. He brings his 'assistant'. He suggests 'drinks' time, after I suggested 3 p.m. for the proposed visit to him. He is over half an hour late and I am due out to dine. We had altogether about four such meetings, all of very long, time-wasting duration, but at least I did not waste anyone else's money on him.

However, concurrent with this dabbling, I was grappling with a passion for a book I had long represented as an agent, *Madame Sousatzka*, and the total commitment desirable for the birth of a film was being channelled into this.

chapter thirty-two

Sixteen years earlier I had begun to represent, as her literary agent, the novelist, Bernice Rubens. She had just completed a screenplay of her novel *Madame Sousatzka*, and was brought to my office by another client, Peter Medak, who was set to direct the movie. Bernice became a friend; the novel became an obsession. The producer's option lapsed and I began trying to sell it elsewhere. The files on rejections for the film rights from film and TV companies around the world fill a filing cabinet. Every time a major studio or TV company changed its top personnel I started on the rounds again. The theme of the book did not date. The central character, Madame Sousatzka, is an émigré piano teacher of a certain age. Along with financiers, the book was sent, via their agents, to many now dead stars - Ingrid Bergman, Margaret Leighton, Simone Signoret, Bette Davis, Anna Magnani; and some living ones, like Elizabeth Taylor. Nothing happened, and so one of my first actions on ceasing to be an agent was to buy the book myself.

So here - such as I remember from disjointed and undated diary jottings - is a partial anatomy of my first film as sole producer: written in the heat, or sometimes dreadful chill, of the moment. (If the intricacies of film-making bore you, as well they may - skip the following chapters.)

I took it first to Colin Callender, who was working for Primetime, and who seemed bright, intelligent and destined for success. Colin loves the book; pledges Primetime's involvement and we sign a deal letter. One week later, Colin leaves Primetime and I am faced with the decision as to whether to go with him or remain with them. I throw in my lot with Colin.

The next year is relatively plain sailing. Early on, I approach Roger Wingate, of Curzon Film Distributors, who funds us for development; he buys the book, gives us the money to engage Ruth Prawer Jhabvala, another ex-client, to write the screenplay, and to involve John Schlesinger as director, to work on the script with Ruth. I didn't know John but admired him greatly and now realise that if I had sent him the book at any time during the previous eighteen years, he would probably have wanted to do it and his long-time (and wonderful) producer, Jo Janni, would probably have bought it for him. I would possibly never have produced it. But he immediately embraced it.

This, I now recognise, was the time of euphoria. A long cherished dream is on its way to realisation. I inject into the project people who have been in my mind for many years as participants. One is Lise Fayolle, a French *soi-disant* producer, who I know has long loved the book, and the other is Jeanne Moreau, perfect for the part. Both come to London. Lise meets Colin and we establish that there may be a way for her to be involved financially in return for French-speaking territories. Colin, however, urges that I meet Gilbert de Goldsmidt in Paris, so off to Paris I go on one of my many subsequent visits. It is Gilbert who gives the book to Jeanne. Back in London, an enthusiastic Jeanne has lunch with Colin, John and myself. She has put on a lot of weight, though still attractive, but John does not feel immediate empathy, and so we put the idea of Jeanne at the back of our minds whilst we concentrate on the script.

Having come up with the idea of Ruth, I realise that I have introduced an Indian connection. Our Jewish mother, long visualised by me as a Maureen Stapleton character, becomes a beautiful Indian. Our nine-year-old boy genius becomes not only Indian, but fifteen. We put the subsequent casting problems also at the back of our minds. John leaves for the US to start work on his next film. Ruth sticks to her normal routine, which is six months in New York and six months in Delhi. Colin and I are based in London. This means that a script which should take six months from commencement to delivery of final draft takes over two years. During this time, I make two trips to New York and Los Angeles to work with John. John meets with Ruth once or twice in New York. Ruth goes to India to work on another film.

By May 1986, we have a version on which I think we can, with difficulty, raise backing. I return to London, leaving John in New York, beginning pre-production on his film.

With hindsight, I realise that I have been much too tentative in voicing my opinions and my worries. These worries involved the difference in approach between myself on the one hand, and Colin and Bill Gavin, who has been appointed by Colin as our sales agent, on the other. Bill's background is basically that of the salesman of a finite product, and Colin's that of a television producer; mine of an ex-agent. I believe we have a strong enough package to find a financier. Bill, in particular, and Colin, in his spare time, pour cold water on my enthusiasm and reiterate, as to an exasperating and naïve amateur, that we must wait for a final script, budget, cast. All I am allowed to do by this cautious pair is to attempt to find our Madame Sousatzka. We have all cooled slightly on the idea of Jeanne Moreau, and I propose Vanessa Redgrave. John takes a little convincing, despite his admiration for her; but finally having seen her again agrees, and I send her the script. She wants to do it. John starts shooting in New York. Ruth returns to India. I fume in London, for months of inactivity.

Finally, John returns, discouraged to find that nothing has happened. He hints at 'other scripts' which have been given him. I have one of my periodic arguments with Colin and Bill about getting on seriously with the financing. We have had a few turn-downs but based on an earlier draft. Colin and Bill agree to a meeting to decide policy and a full attack on finance. This takes place over breakfast at John's house, and his UK agent, Duncan Heath, is present. It is decided that we will approach Cineplex-Odeon, suggested by Roger Wingate, as US distributors; Granada as a UK TV pre-sales outlet; and British Screen for UK theatrical funding. I am to approach British Screen and ask for a meeting between its head, Simon Relph, and John; Colin will contact Cineplex-Odeon in New York where he is spending more and more time; and Bill will talk to Granada.

Cineplex-Odeon, in the person of Joel Michaels, Head of Production, expresses interest after Colin's phone call in New York but as he is en route to London I go to see him at the Inn On the Park and give him the script. Colin has set the magic figure of £2 000 000 on the budget. I, in my innocence and inexperience, have doubts, and qualify my belief by intimating to Joel, 'Maybe 2.2 or 2.3 million'. I have left all financial, budget and legal matters to Colin, believing that I can happily concentrate on so-called 'creative' aspects, and that Colin has the production experience I lack. It is high time we prepare a budget, which to date has been guesswork and wishful thinking. Colin knows that two million is the magic break figure for British films, and also for Cineplex-Odeon financial limits, and assures me that the way to go about it is to set a budget and then cut the picture to it. This seems to me a bit like buying a suit and then cutting off your arms and legs if they are too long for it; but I bow to his superior knowledge. We do, however, have a budget prepared on the intermittently appearing scripts – the first one, prepared by a friend of John's, comes out at

£5 000 000. Colin says this is ridiculous, and produces a bright young woman who is said to be expert in preparing and making low-budget films, Penny Corke. Penny's budget is bang on £2 000 000 on an eight-week all-location schedule. No one discusses this with John, who is now deep in post-production with little time for us, and whom I doubt has ever shot a feature film, location or studio, for eight weeks in his life, and it isn't about to start doing so now.

Concurrently with this, I have made my approach to British Screen and Simon Relph meets with John and myself. We are given a guarded promise of their maximum investment – £500 000. Bill Gavin is strangely silent – at least to me. He has other business with Colin. Colin tells me it has been agreed that Bill will approach Denis Foreman at Granada. Granada appears to be divided into two camps, the Foreman camp and the David Plowright (joint-chairmen) camp – and, for reasons I do not query, it is deemed advisable to choose the Foreman camp. Colin suggests that John should also call Denis Foreman personally. John asks me to do this on his behalf and to set up a meeting as he is too busy to telephone.

The Granada week is murky. Denis Foreman and John are both too busy. I try to reach Bill to inquire how he is faring. He explodes with rage on the telephone. I fail to understand why. What has gone wrong? I soon find out. It seems that Bill, who has not told us, has given the project to the Plowright camp, and they have promptly turned it down. Colin is puzzled and displeased by this.

A day or so later, Colin receives a letter from Bill saying he is bowing out of *Madame Sousatzka* as he 'cannot work for two (or is it three?) masters'. I presume the 'three' refers to Colin, John and – because I telephoned him – myself. Very soon after this, I learn that Bill has taken on the task of preselling the 'other script' of John's dark hints, now out in the open: a Michael Frayn original, to be produced by Michael

Codron, with Alec Guinness and Peggy Ashcroft to star. This is particularly bad news as we had already earmarked Peggy for our production. John, who has proven himself to date to be thoroughly open, and honest, whilst occasionally protecting himself from his own paranoia by keeping too many options open, as most directors must do, now tells me in detail about the reality and progress of what becomes our main obstacle. Bill Gavin, who has met John through us, obviously sees it as a better bet, and we of the three masters have been swiftly demoted to the sinking ship category.

I am both shattered and relieved - shattered because I had been deluding myself into a sense of security in the belief that Bill and Colin between them would put our project together with no great effort from myself; and relieved because it means I can now follow my own instincts, as opposed to their experience, on the best way to proceed. However, the next four or five months become a race between the two films to obtain finance, with John sitting on the fence. For the first time in my life, I try 'positive thinking' - largely in my morning bath. This consists of repeating out loud: '*Madame Sousatzka is* going to happen', and thinking, very hard, very negative and destructive thoughts about poor Bill Gavin.

I also begin to learn how to stand on my own feet and read columns of figures, starting with the budget. It isn't nearly as difficult to understand as I had feared. Of course, I have no idea what some of the items actually are, but at the very end there is a column which says 'Bank charges'. It is blank. I have, in the ensuing months, learnt something about banks. At Roger Wingate's suggestion, I have contacted a bank in Amsterdam - Pierson Heldring - and Colin and I have flown for the day to meet them, discuss terms, eat a delicious lunch, and do much duty-free shopping at the airport. I have left all the financial discussions once more to Colin, not wishing to make a monumental fool of myself. But I have tried to absorb some of it, and it seems a child could absorb the fact that Pierson Heldring are willing - indeed eager - to lend us the £3 000 000 we are now asking to make the film, this being a negative pick-up, on behalf of Cineplex-Odeon, or anyone else now in the running. The original £2 000 000 has long ago escalated, each time involving an approach to Cineplex-Odeon explaining that eight weeks' location was an impossibility. Each time they have baulked, but have finally toyed with the idea of £3 000 000. The interest on this £3 000 000 is approximately eleven per cent. Should not the sum of £350 000 therefore be under the heading of bank charges?

I feel rather ill, and call Penny Corke, hoping she will put my mind at rest. However, she tells me that nobody has told her it was a negative pick-up; she had budgeted for straight financing, but she is not surprised as she says Colin did the same thing on his previous film. I telephone Colin in New York. He is slightly taken aback, surprised that the column in the budget he has had for some months, and presumably read, is blank, but assures me we can 'lose' it somehow.

This is the worst worry of the entire film, I realise, at the time and with hindsight. I lie awake for several nights, wondering how such a large amount of money can be 'lost' as it represents more than any one person - star, director and certainly producers - will be paid. Cineplex-Odeon are forging ahead on a false assumption. By now, the film Colin has first told them would be £2 000 000 has escalated in three jumps of one million pounds, and each time Joel Michaels has said they cannot accommodate it. I have yet to learn it is ever thus.

Winston Churchill to the Secretary of the Cabinet in 1946: 'in telling a tale the words written in the circumstances of the moment are of far greater significance than any paraphrase of them or subsequent composition'. Few of the following opinions or viewpoints of events are 'subsequently composed': only immediate recording of bare facts and my reaction to them, where appropriate, at the particular moment. Time can change one's view and blessedly obscure it. In some instances, time not only heals but paints a roseate hue over memory - seldom the reverse. Thereafter, events have become chronologically muddled in my memory. I have a fragmented - and frantic - series of diary notes, as follows:

Lunch with Johnny Hargreaves at Pinewood Studios. Richard Soames, of Film Finances (insurers), has turned us down for a Completion Guarantee, without which no bank would cover the picture. He does not believe that John will stick to the budget, or that I have sufficient strength to control it. Johnny, of the Completion Bond Company (another insurance company), is the only other avenue open to us. We have a helpful chat: I send him the script.

With much trepidation, I at last give Bernice the script. She is naturally aghast at her Jewish protagonists turning Indian.

Breakfast with Colin. He has taken a job in New York with HBO and bows out gracefully, somewhat too late - but I am sad for him and for myself. He had put much work and some of his own money into it, and any mistakes he may have made have been due to lack of time to concentrate. I realise that my training as an agent has been an appropriate one, but I am still not tough enough to cut ties with him entirely. This is a lost opportunity: he is still, marginally, involved.

Finally, I call Joel and confess the omission of the bank charges. He is suitably shocked.

It is round about this time that we lose our 'star'. Jeanne Moreau has long since been forgotten and I have concluded a deal with Vanessa's agent. We have rescheduled the film to accommodate four free days for her to perform at the National Theatre, and she has accepted the money - the maximum we can afford. Everyone is delighted. Jimmy Sharkey, her agent, asks me for a deal letter, as she is going to Rome and may possibly receive other offers. I write the letter but as my own deal with Cineplex-Odeon is not finalised, I must add the obligatory phrase 'subject to contract' and point out that I sincerely hope this will be forthcoming within the week. Vanessa goes to Rome and telephones John that night to say she has just signed a contract to do a film with Franco Nero, and could we postpone our film by six weeks? Ours is partly a location film and we would thereby be in both winter light and Christmas - both out of the question. John is once more off to New York, so a frantic list of possible American replacements is made for him to see, whilst I plan to fly to Paris to give the script to Jeanne, who is unaware that we have ever wavered from our original plan to star her. It takes me two weeks to locate her as I first telephone her London agents to know her availability. They had ceased to represent her a year previously but, smelling a deal, do not confess this, whilst trying to find her and simultaneously telling me they are 'in touch'. Meanwhile I send a script to Anne Bancroft in New York. Miss Bancroft's secretary calls to say Miss Bancroft is 'interested'; would love to work with John; and would like to see the next draft, as she has certain reservations. I point out that as John is also in New York she could meet him and discuss these reservations. This, apparently, is not Miss Bancroft's method. She just wants to see the next draft. No one has time, at this point, to write a 'next' draft. I call John and suggest Geraldine Page, with whom he has worked, and whom he loves. He makes plans to see her for afternoon tea; she drops dead that morning.

At the same time, in Los Angeles, John's agent asks if he should give the script to Shirley MacLaine, also a client of his office, and a name on our list but low down because we see her as quintessentially American. John and I agree on her warmth and humour, however, and say she may be given a script but on no account as a 'firm offer'.

I have found Jeanne Moreau myself, and am flying to Paris to see her. We meet in her apartment, with her agent, Georges Baume. She has read the script overnight, loves it, is desperate to do it but in the two weeks in which the London agent has been busily lying to me she has signed to do a stage tour. She could perhaps break the contract as the producer is a good friend, but she must have a firm offer in writing before so doing.

I return to London and the telephone. Cineplex-Odeon are just as happy with Jeanne Moreau as they were with Vanessa Redgrave, but they are still not signing any contract. We are arguing about what is known in the industry as the small print. This, in fact, usually means large issues.

John telephones from New York. Shirley, too, loves the script and is desperate to do it. She has spoken to him for four hours on the telephone, doing a Russian accent. She also rings me and does a Russian accent. She will do it for Vanessa's money. She will do it for nothing if John and I will do likewise. She will stay with a friend instead of at a hotel. The Russian accent is terrible. John asks me what we should do. I advise we think about it - but on no account lose her - whilst I investigate a deal with Jeanne's agent, Georges Baume. This necessitates a telephone call to Joel in Los Angeles every time I talk to Georges in Paris, for, although Cineplex-Odeon haven't agreed to my demands or I to theirs, I must have their approval on the deal for our star if the putative budget is not to escalate still further. Shirley's agent has, as an aside, asked for twenty per cent of one hundred per cent of the profits. Shirley does not need money; nor, seemingly, does she care much about the money. Twenty per cent of the profits means that I had better practise this same nonchalance myself - not so easy as I do need the money, rather badly.

Georges Baume asks double the money we were to pay Vanessa and to which Shirley has agreed; Jeanne's secretary to accompany her and 'comfortable' rooms in a hotel such as the Connaught. I come clean about Shirley's interest and her terms only as a bargaining point where the fee is concerned. He does not believe me, which is why Jeanne Moreau never became Madame Sousatzka. It is also probably true that by this time she would have had to buy herself out of her stage contract for more money than we were paying her. The London agent has a lot to answer for, and we have lost so much time arguing about the small print.

Shirley is now our sole hope. She flies to New York to try out the Russian accent in person. We decide to deflect her from this kamikaze course by writing two lines into the script giving the character an American upbringing. Ruth, currently in New York, is called upon to do this. It transpires that she lives below Shirley in the same apartment block and they have never met.

Ruth is tiny, like a sharp little bird, with a lilting, tentative voice. There is absolutely nothing tentative about Ruth herself. The meeting takes place in Shirley's apartment. Her accent is now American, but with hints of Russian steppes in the lower regions. She wants, however, to get to grips with Madame Sousatzka's inner self, through Ruth.

'Tell me,' she implores Ruth, 'has she had love affairs?'

Ruth: 'Well . . . maybe . . . I'm not sure.'

Shirley: 'But does she fuck?'

Ruth: 'Ah, no: I don't think so . . .' in ruminative tones.

Shirley: 'Well, then, does she masturbate?'

Ruth, John tells me (for I am not witness to this delicious scene), rolls her eyes in a surprised effort at rethinking this intriguing facet of Sousatzka's character.

'Well, I don't know – I've never thought about that.'

But, at last, we have our star.

We do not, however, have a deal; a proper schedule or budget, along with an Associate/Line Producer; or our Indian cast. We have cast Twiggy, our first firm member of the cast, and in so doing I discover that I possess what can only be a heaven-sent instinct for casting: it certainly does not come from knowledge.

At 3 a.m. one morning, I awoke and like a light flashing in my brain I saw the face of Twiggy. John had been trying out other names on me, some of them more or less unknown to me. I telephoned him with my idea.

'Too thin,' he said, 'and too old.'

'How long since you've seen her?' I said, having actually only seen her myself in my nocturnal reverie.

And so John agreed to ask her to tea.

At tea, we talked about everything, gossip interspersed with discussion about the script. After Twiggy's first two sentences and whilst she was still in full flight, John turned to me on the sofa and whispered with delight, 'She's adorable - she's perfect!'

He had, however, to put her fears at rest about the sex scene required in the film.

'I won't take my knickers off,' says Twigs. 'I'm sorry but I can't do that. I don't mind so much about my tits but if you want me to take my knickers off, you'd better get –.'

A towel was called for. Twiggy lay on the floor. John draped it across her hips. 'There,' he gestured, 'we'll have screens all round you - a closed set - and we'll have a small cloth draped here,' flicking the cloth.

This wouldn't do. Finally, he agreed that somehow Twigs could hang onto her knickers and he would shoot around them. They both got up off the floor and we went on with tea.

After three delightful hours, Twigs looked at her watch and scrambled her belongings together.

'Well,' said John, 'Robin will get in touch with your agent.'

'Oooh,' said Twigs, 'do you *want* me then?'

John: 'What did you think you were doing here?'

Twigs: 'I thought I was coming for a cup of tea.'

We are discussing a deal with Peggy Ashcroft. I address myself to the remaining problems. Simultaneously, I become ill. Back to the diary.

Sunday: *This is called by some a day of rest. It is 8 p.m. and I am in bed, full of Strepsils, vitamin C, Disprin and a horrid gargle which smells of hospital corridors. The day started in the middle of last night with a rasping throat. This morning Lise Fayolle came to breakfast. Lise is once again prepared to finance the film, or, as she puts it, produce it. I trust she only means produce in the sense that she will produce the money, with the control that entails. With Lise, it is difficult to tell. I love her but am never sure she is entirely reliable. She will call me from Paris tomorrow and let me know, and if it looks promising, I should go to Paris - again - on Thursday to meet her new Swiss boss. I go back to bed.*

Shortly after, I am seriously stricken. Not, however, out of reach of the telephone. Mort Viner, Shirley's agent, rings about 11 p.m. about Shirley's deal, having failed to reach agreement with Joel. They never ring from Los Angeles until cheap rates, their time. It is blazingly evident that there are too many lines of communication and, like the London Underground or the Inland Revenue, not enough of them communicating with each other. Colin has half his mind, at most, concentrated on our film. He has another full-time job. He is, I suspect and sympathise with, most interested in recouping his expenditure to date. Much more than mine, but then I do not drive a new Mercedes convertible nor give huge media parties, nor employ a public relations firm. I simply worry about my telephone bill, my airline expenses, and - increasingly - my health.

Next day, my health has become my main concern. I have, somewhat thankfully, collapsed. Everything is done over the telephone and, because of my sore throat, that hurts.

Colin does not return calls. Colin's lawyer returns them too late. John's agent seldom returns them. Only John does, but as his worries are more demanding and paranoiac than mine, reassuring him hurts both my throat and my head. I croak to Los Angeles – first to Joel and then to Mort Viner. Joel asks if there is anything he can do to help. I tell him he can give us more money and he says, sadly, that it impossible. Mort talks about Shirley's dates.

Joel again: it has been pointed out by our lawyer that in England a completion guarantor will demand a nine-month delivery date from commencement of principal photography. We still haven't got a guarantor although Johnny Hargreaves is full of enthusiasm and I've once more approached Film Finances. Joel's opening remark is to send me the regards of one Robert Mintz, with whom in my agenting days I once had pleasant dealings. I now learn that he heads the Completion Bond Co in Los Angeles. He is prepared to deal with us on a six-month basis and on terms as favourable as I believe I can obtain from Film Finances. I know full well that John will *not* be prepared to promise delivery in six months, so I hesitate and say that I have grave doubts, as Shirley cannot start rehearsals until 28 September. Joel is in shock. He says he was never told this. It is once more obvious that there are too many producers. I attempt to reassure him but Joel sounds nervous – of his job, possibly.

It is crucial, he tells me, to have the picture ready for the Cannes Festival. I am relatively sure that this is not possible. I am increasingly fearful that we may be in the hands of a company of wankers, who have not even signed a deal. Making a beautiful film is not so important to them as making a splash at Cannes. I see, once more, the disintegration of the film.

Next day's worries are to go through the list of possible financiers whom we might now approach. Shirley has been to Columbia and they have turned us down. I telephone Gabe Katzka in New York who once liked it but whose partner turned it down because he said neither Vanessa nor Anne Bancroft would sell a ticket. Now we have Shirley, Gabe asks for a new script and says he'll let me know on Wednesday. I beg him to be discreet and not let Cineplex know.

'Listen,' says Gabe, 'why would I talk to that shit-arse Dobrinsky?'

I think I can count on his discretion. (Some years later I learn to like Garth Dobrinsky, the head of Cineplex-Odeon, very much, but these were early days.)

John is on holiday in the south of France. I telephone, and get him out of the pool. I sit in London's pouring rain, but it is he who sounds depressed. We talk about Shirley's dates. It is, indeed, looking very difficult, particularly in view of the capricious weather. If this were to continue throughout the year, we are in deep trouble.

John says in a sad, low voice, 'I think perhaps you had better find another director for this picture.' Far from throwing me, this opens a chink of light in the darkness of my horizon. Maybe I can withdraw honourably from the entire production? However, when I ask him if this is final or if he would like twenty-four hours to think over his decision, he perks up, and we are on course again. We discuss how we can cut costs – that is, the script. I spend the rest of the day surrounded by loose-leafed scripts, comparing, cutting, rewriting, putting in order. I have no secretary.

John is back. This morning I have arranged for Michael Owens from the *Evening Standard* to interview him regarding our search for the boy. He has to be fifteen, beautiful, a pianist, an ice-skater, and a good actor. The snag is he also has to be Indian. I telephone John to remind him.

John's agent, Duncan Heath, did not return my calls all day yesterday and makes me wonder what is going on. The 'other' film is still active. Insecurity is a treacherous condition: John's insecurity is deflecting him from what I sense is his natural inclination to honesty. He is allowing me to run myself into the ground whilst not committing himself one hundred per cent through fear of falling between two stools. Thank God I did not become a film producer until it is too late for me to encounter these emotions. I still feel I can walk away from it all, and I remember back to my aspirations when my husband died. I could *still*, perhaps, become someone's housekeeper. Or jump out a window.

In the afternoon, Gabe Katzka rings to say he will have an answer for me tonight or tomorrow and to remind me that they charge a ten per cent overhead fee. I stall. Because I have already rung Lise, Joel, everybody, and am trying to keep all balls in the air. I can hardly speak, can't eat, can't sleep, swallowing antibiotics. Late afternoon, Lise calls, it having been suggested that I might fly to Paris on Friday morning and meet her financiers. They decide, thank God and a Paris air strike, to come here instead, in their private Lear jet. They want a suite and a room in the 'best' hotel. London is full. I ring Claridge's late at night and pretend to the Duty Manager that he knows me well. He is far too good at his job to admit that he does not remember me. He has, of course, never heard of me in his life. But he finds me a suite and a room. I ring John to tell him to cancel his evening at the theatre and be prepared to dine with our potential backers instead. He says, somewhat gloomily, that at least we will get a good meal at Claridge's. Lise rings to ask me to book a table in the best Indian restaurant. I loathe Indian food. John is delighted.

We meet at Claridge's. The financiers turn out to be a young couple of infinite charm and seemingly transparent honesty. He is from Uruguay; she is from San Salvador. They are intelligent, polite, and immensely rich. We spend a happy evening and the following morning I go to a breakfast meeting, taking Colin as he is in London. We discuss a broadly acceptable deal, an immediate cash flow to my bank, and Michel leaps to his feet and shakes my hand. We leave in a daze. It is a fairytale. John says he found them 'adorable'. Colin, and all other advisers, are sceptical. I decide to trust my instincts.

My instincts are bolstered, next day, in the form of a bank draft for the urgently needed £20 000 - needed if we are not to lose essential cast and crew we have put 'on hold' - from Michel Vieyte. No deal has been signed or, apart from our breakfast meeting, even discussed. Colin flies back to New York.

I am now morally and financially committed to Michel Vieyte. He turns over all legal points - big *and* small print - to an English lawyer, having first asked my advice as to whom it should be.

At vast expense to Michel, a team of Swiss lawyers and advisers are flown to London where the English lawyer I have recommended spends a morning both proposing a deal devised by him in what I can only surmise to be paranoia of the small hours of the morning when he cannot sleep, and amuses himself with fantasies of running Universal, Paramount and Columbia and insulting my lawyer, Lise Fayolle and myself.

The next days are spent trying to reach Michel and explain that his lawyer is speedily unravelling our relationship and our rapport. Michel is charming, but adamant that the problems are minor ones and that I must deal with his lawyer. Lise telephones from Paris - hysterical. She says I will ruin her life if I do not go ahead with the deal with Michel.

John's agent, Duncan Heath, enters the arena and learns of the conditions now emerging. They are, of course, totally unacceptable to John, and as Cineplex-Odeon are still holding out on some points, I can feel both deals and my director slipping away from under me. Gabe calls, offering me any deal I want, but John is now anxious about the boy. He realises we have made a mistake having an Indian boy – will never find one – they don't play the piano – who can rewrite him Jewish? What happens if we don't find anyone? Has only just realised the difficulty with playbacks etc. Michel, despite his lawyer, has faxed him a 'pay or play'[21] *deal so now he no longer has to worry about whether he has a deal, he has all the more time to worry about how he makes the picture.* That *now becomes the impossibility.*

Call from Joel. He has been trying to reach me since Sunday. They – Cineplex-Odeon – will meet all our demands, even to sharing some of Shirley's percentage. I am both genuinely surprised and horrified. I tell him I think it is too late. He is, he says, shocked. He is, I think, a very nice man and is, I suspect, a victim of his job. Words like 'morality', 'conscience' and 'ethics' are thrown at me: words not often heard in the film industry.

Joel calls John. John calls me. He is scared that Cineplex-Odeon will refuse to exhibit our film in their cinemas if we do not do a deal with them. I pay little attention to this until the following day. When Joel calls twice. As far as it is possible for a nice man to become nasty, the tone of his conversation indicates this. It contains some very ugly threats. One of them is, indeed, regarding exhibition of the film.

Two days of frantic telephone calls ensue – to everyone. On the third day, ominous silence. On the fourth day, Joel suddenly gives way. All is forgiven: a deal is quickly signed. I return Michel's cheque and to his credit and after a short period of puzzled silence, he continues to speak kindly to me.

Apart from Shirley, Twiggy remains our only firm piece of casting. Noel Davis has been brought in as our casting director and hundreds of boys have been advertised for, interviewed, John more gloomy by the day, but we rush to complete the rest of our casting. Tremendous fun. It all takes place in John's study. All the actors are treated with the utmost courtesy by John. They are put at their ease by a preliminary cosy chat and we have the added enjoyment of watching Noel reading their parts with them, sitting side by side on sofa, and switching sex, accent and age. Lots of laughs. We all three then cast our vote when they leave the room and John requires that very few of them are to be put on tape.

We interview five equally beautiful young men for the part of 'Edward'. Exhausted and exhilarated we relax at six-thirty in readiness for an art department meeting. Noel then announces that an actor called Giles Daubeny has turned up - that he is obviously no good - all wrong - but that we had better see him out of *politesse*. He's a nice young man but, compared to the previous five, hopeless. John, however, polite as ever, goes into yet another explanatory interview. It turns out that the young man is Nick Daubeny, our Location Manager, totally bewildered by his 'audition'.

Peggy Ashcroft leaves the cast of the other putative film and joins us. Twiggy is put at ease with regard to her 'sex' scenes when we cast Leigh Lawson, her boyfriend, as her film lover, and we are all thrilled when they marry as our film ends.

Simon Bosanquet is now on board as our Associate Producer. Everything falls happily into place. Simon Kaye is our sound recordist, Peter Honess our editor, Luciana Arrighi our production designer, everyone working for less money than their norm, mostly for the joy of working with John again and due in very small measure to the fact that I find I can do very good deals. As an ex-agent, other agents do not try to be cunning or clever with me. Dog doesn't eat dog. Simon ensconces us cosily at Twickenham Studios.

We have, however, still not found our boy: two weeks before rehearsals. John thinks we had better quickly rewrite him Jewish. Ruth is in New York and we have already cast Shabana Asmi as his Indian mother, which would certainly look odd.

Finding Shabana was another small instance of our miraculous luck. We have tried the more obvious Indian film stars, tested all the possible Indian actresses in London, when Ruth suggests Shabana, one of India's greatest stars but unknown to us. She gives me Shabana's Delhi telephone number. Shabana, like most Indian stars, works almost every day of the year, often starring in two or three films simultaneously and changing her make-up in the car en route between locations; and in those periods when she actually takes a holiday, she does not take it in Delhi. She also never answers her own telephone. On the day I telephoned, due to a series of unprecedented mishaps, personal and professional, Shabana was briefly at home and picked up the telephone. She flew to England the next day and I drove her down to John's house in the country. She read the script that night, read for John the following day and I put her on the night plane back to Delhi. Heathrow airport came to a standstill at her appearance. Lavatory attendants rushed out, cleaning ladies dropped their brooms, porters their baggage. One of their very own superstars was amongst them and an Indian chant of 'Shabana! Shabana!' cheered her on her way to the plane.

The next day we get a call from an Indian businessman in Bradford who had seen our advertisement in his local newsheet. His schoolboy nephew wants to act. Navin is fifteen, beautiful, a natural actor, has never touched a piano, or donned roller skates. In two weeks he learns both sufficiently to start shooting; he continues with three hundred hours of piano lessons throughout and never strikes a wrong note. (He also continues with his school work and passes all exams with flying colours. I try to persuade him not to become a professional actor, but to stick to his ambition to study law and act at the bar instead, but I don't think I succeeded. He is still acting.)

Shirley has not yet arrived but I call her. She calls me 'Dalton' and John, 'Schlesinger'. Her abrupt manner is because she is worried about the cloak which she wears on her first entrance. What can she billow in, in winter? I, bored and tired, suggest nun's veiling. Also suggest that October isn't exactly winter. She, enraged, snaps: 'It's cold, Dalton.' This was the last cross word I was ever to hear from Shirley. She, like many actors, needs to clothe her character before she can feel secure and when she eventually arrives, she reduces our costume designer to tears on the first day. By the second day, when she has inhabited her character, she becomes the trouper she remains throughout.

The actual shoot of *Madame Sousatzka* was, I now realise, a uniquely enjoyable experience, as I believe is every film directed by John. His manners are faultless; his concern for his crew and cast legendary; and his humour reason enough to work with him, if there were no others. Even our rows were enjoyable. He would go purple in the face should I make a suggestion, scream at me that I had no idea what I was talking about, and that I was trying to ruin the fucking film and off he would trot. That night, at the end of a long day's work, he would sometimes telephone me - 'Darling, I've been thinking about what you said. Maybe it would work' (if a story point) or 'They could do it' (if a casting suggestion). Any of the crew could approach him with a suggestion or a complaint, to be greeted with courtesy.

Shirley, too, was terrific. As we had little money, she stayed with a friend; she demanded no limousine at her disposal outside filming hours; she was generous with her time, her jokes, her good humour to all; she mucked in. Her farewell presents were imaginative and bountiful and whenever we were worried, largely about the schedule and the weather, she had a chat with her 'people upstairs'. 'Robin,' she said, 'this film is blessed. I've had a word with them and it won't rain.' It didn't. Her 'people' never let us down. The 1987 hurricane which decimated the ancient parks, gardens and forests of

England struck six hours after we 'struck' our largest, most expensive and important location scene in the film. Six hours earlier we would have lost marquees, scenery, background giant trees, and possibly a few members of the cast and crew. To say nothing of time, schedule and budget.

Joel Michaels, too, put in different words what I was to recognise only later - two films later: 'You should never produce another film. This is the happiest production I've ever known and you'll never know another one like it.'

However, they will not forget me in a hurry at Twickenham Studios. Not since I drove Bill's car straight through the louvred glass front entrance, missing fax machine and young man just finished his faxing tasks for the morning by inches, demolishing small objects, but coming to rest just before the main reception desk and the three startled ladies behind it. Guido Coen, who ran the studio, on the third floor thought it was a bomb. As for me, I had thought I was driving my own car - not an automatic - and had muddled brake for nonexistent clutch. Bill has been anxious about me driving his cars ever since; the studio has never since given me that parking spot. A wide berth for me.

We have a rough cut. We are heroes. John for having made such a lovely film - I for having coerced him into making it for so little money. In this last instance, I am aware of the sacrifices made by almost everyone involved - cast and crew, to say nothing of Shirley and John - in reducing their demands. My own contributions have been small, but constant. I have been capable of frantically writing some additional dialogue the night before shooting when Ruth is absent in Delhi and the two bright young men I had brought in to write some additional scenes were unavailable; and I have happily joined John in providing our electrics team with crumpets to be toasted daily on their equipment: John accuses me of pulling up my skirts and literally kicking up my heels at our transport drivers to entice them to give us a free trip here and there. But it has worked. I find that even elderly flirtatiousness can wear down the toughest of negotiators.

The fact that Shirley said in her subsequent book that only about eleven people saw the film doesn't detract from the fond memories. All those eleven adored it; it is slowly gaining in retrospective acclaim and I am immensely proud of my association with it. I also recognise that the generosity shown me by John is rare indeed. At the Venice Film Festival where John, Shirley and I sat in the front row of the dress circle facing a cheering, clapping, standing audience below us, they remained firmly in their seats but I had a tremendous jab in the ribs from John. 'Stand up!' he commanded. 'Stand up and bow - you're the producer.'

Venice was the culmination of a magical experience. My old friend Giovanni Volpi invited me to stay for the duration of the Festival - at which he presented the Volpi Cup to Shirley for Best Actress - at his heavenly summer palazzo on Guidecca, and threw glorious parties for us. I woke up each morning surrounded by luxury, beauty and friends - to the gentle lapping of water under my window, the pealing of bells and memories of my Venetian youth.

We were chosen as the Royal Command film performance that year - publicity money can't buy. Queen Mother's turn, not the Queen. John, Shirley, Peggy, Twiggy and other members of the cast were interviewed on television. I stayed firmly in the background, and heard John say to his interviewers when asked some question about the making of the film: 'Robin Dalton is the architect of this film.'

If it was a building, I would dearly love to revisit it.

I am too ignorant - too new at the game - to know that producers do not give back money saved, so I proudly present Cineplex with a fairly hefty cheque from production money saved. I had no idea what an unprecedented shock this was. Joel Michaels comes to London and takes me to lunch. *He* takes the unprecedented step of handing back to me a tiny proportion of my gesture, as a bonus. I have the pleasure of being able to share this with Simon, without whom we might well have fallen apart, and Maggie, our accountant. Everyone loves everyone. I was naïve enough (and lazy enough) to always tell the truth. A reputation for the latter seems to unseat more seasoned veterans, but I had never lied to Cineplex and Joel appreciated it.

At this lunch, Joel makes a further rare gesture. 'We'll back your next film,' he tells me. 'Anything you want to make.' So started *Oscar and Lucinda*. It was not to be the next film: nine long years were to elapse, but whilst struggling to make it, I became involved in *Country Life*.

chapter thirty-three

Film Number Two was not blessed - not by Shirley nor by her 'people' who presumably control the elements. We were to have bushfires, record heatwaves, capricious light and, above all, accidents. The daily call sheets record the accidents, the newspaper the national disasters, chiefly the Australian bushfires of 1994, in the middle of which we film.

The film, too, had had a lengthy gestation period - nearly ten years. Raising the finance was my only significant contribution. If I was the 'architect' of *Madame Sousatzka*, with *Country Life* I was only its obstetrician. Its mother, father and only begetter was Michael Blakemore. Mike had written and given the screenplay to me to read, and had already enlisted the interest of his main cast, two of whom stuck with us for those ten years - John Hargreaves and Sam Neill.

One day I had the idea of casting Greta Scacchi as our female star when I, remembering she counted as an Australian national, introduced her to Mike over morning coffee in my apartment; this, in turn, leading to his casting her in his London stage production of *Uncle Vanya*, on which her role in the film was to be based. She remained as a faithful member of our team for the next few years.

Raising the money was not easy. Promises were made; small

amounts of cash advanced; promises were broken and cash refunded. Television companies were approached and every classics division of every US distribution company wooed.

Michael and I were both busy with other things - I with *Madame Sousatzka*, the very protracted pregnancy of *Oscar and Lucinda*, and a clutch of embryonic productions which were either to come crashing around me or simply subside into oblivion. Mike was busy with his very successful theatrical career; this, too, proved an obstacle to finance as whenever one of our cast looked like being available and I felt a glimmer of financial hope it was necessary for Mike to hold himself available until the glimmer brightened. Six months' total commitment was what I needed and Mike understandably could not afford to give it. So for it to happen, it had to happen fast. And, eventually, it did, with astonishing speed.

The Australian Film Finance Corporation began to fund a few films a year entirely. No fussing with UK and US distributors needed, but simply an acceptable Australian cast and an acceptable Australian distributor. Kind friends rallied in Sydney whilst I was in London and gave unstintingly of time and help with paperwork. I slammed in my application and three months later we were in pre-production. I needed a Line Producer.[22]

Catriona Hughes of the Film Finance Corporation suggested, among others, Adrienne Read. It was via telephone from Sydney and my first conversation with Adrienne was not propitious. I had not yet become accustomed to the Australian way of speech and Adrienne sounded businesslike and, above all, cool. Could I possibly warm to this rather stern-sounding woman? Catriona thought that a meeting between us was essential, and the FFC allocated enough money to enable Adrienne to come to Europe to meet Mike and myself by the cheapest, most uncomfortable method available. Mike was in Biarritz; I about to go there. Adrienne arrived in London one dawn after a 24-hour nonstop economy class flight from

Sydney. The following morning she was to present herself on my doorstep for a similarly cheap trip to Biarritz, lugging with her, in addition to her clothes, a ton weight in equipment - her strip board, and her computer.

Bill opened the door to her, flanked by her baggage. We had time to exchange just a few words before leaving for Victoria Station but time enough for Bill to whisper in my ear: 'You've got a good one there'. As a director of three films of his own, producer of one, and writer of some thirty, the voice of experience spoke and was proven right. In my gritty little oyster, I had found a pearl.

Our 'bonding', as Adrienne was to call it, began on that horrendous journey. Bill drove us to Victoria where we caught a train to Gatwick. Porters no longer exist. At Gatwick there was the little train from main station to terminal. From terminal the plane to Bordeaux. At Bordeaux the bus to the railway station, where we were stuck at a café for some hours before the train to Biarritz. We rushed to board the wrong end of our train - I burdened only with my own cases, Adrienne with hers and with the tools of our film. I didn't know then that Adrienne suffered from asthma and must have sorely missed her 'puffer' as we hauled luggage, knees banging, through overcrowded compartments, to find the right end of our train. I get train sick. We 'bonded'.

She was not to know that the first of our physical accidents was to strike that night at dinner in the local restaurant after a hard day's work. I swallowed a fishbone. The next days were spent by Mike and Adrienne hunched over the schedule and by me pinned down by X-ray machines, throat specialists, visits first to Casualty and finally in desperation to acupuncturist. The bone went down, neither its scar nor its scratching journey down my throat and the accompanying pain diminished. After five days we put Adrienne back on her train and prepared to leave for Australia ourselves. And so began our accidents.

In the first week I fall down a hole in the street and break my right hand. I cannot sign cheques. On Day 1 of the shoot, John Hargreaves cuts his hand crutching a sheep - tetanus shot (not sure about the sheep). On Day 2 our production accountant is run over - she cannot issue cheques. On Day 3 Kerry Fox falls off a horse - a trip to Sydney, X-rays, physiotherapy, and so on. On Day 4, our first night to view rushes, the entire district for a hundred-mile radius is blacked out by an electrical storm. On Day 5 our period steam train being brought hundreds of miles to our location is derailed. On Day 6 we discover that all of Day 5 (said train having been got back on rails) is a blank: the shutter had not been shut on the camera.

Day 6 - Bathurst: *We are in snake country and have been warned to wear long boots. We had planned to move after the morning's shoot had finished - wrapping*[23] *and travelling at midday. The crew call is at 7.30; the cast and crew pack their bags, check out of their hotels and leave bags to be collected from reception on our way out of town. On arrival at the production office we receive a laboratory report (*not marked URGENT*) informing us that the previous day's rushes are unusable. It had been our most expensive scene of the entire film (period steam train brought some hundreds of miles up the track, hundreds of extras in period dress summoned in the searing heat from miles around) and now has to be reshot. The current morning's shoot is up a rutted, dusty country track in an area which proves impervious to mobile phones and so incommunicado to the production office. Whilst the girls frantically man telephones in order to rebook period train, accommodation, extra equipment and catering, whilst cancelling our ongoing accommodation in Maitland, I leap into the breach and my car and tear off to the inaccessible, snake-infested front line to alert the troops. They are finishing breakfast. Mike, Sam Neill and a couple of the crew are* *sitting at the table as I plonk myself down to announce the change of plans and the fact that I am there as an extra 'runner' in lieu of telephonic communication.*

Mike's main concern is his laundry, packed and dirty and ready to be delivered, he had hoped, that afternoon to hotel laundry in Maitland. I offer to race back, unpack his bag, retrieve garments and have them sent to laundry in Bathurst. As Sam is sitting beside us and beside him on a bench is a cardboard box out of which is spilling seemingly dirty laundry, I ask if I can do anything for him.

'Yes,' he says, 'you could ask Barbara to ring me.' (Barbara in the production office seems to be besotted by Sam to the exclusion of more mundane tasks. A large photograph of him is pinned by her desk.) I explain that the reason I am there is because no one can ring anyone, so I offer once more my own services. Very reluctantly he pushes the cardboard box in my direction. 'Well, could you ask Barbara to leave this at the hotel reception desk for me?' And I tear off with what I assume is his *laundry and with no intention of bothering Barbara with it. Sam is in the next room to mine – Barbara is in the production office a couple of miles away.*

The laundry has already been collected from the hotel. I grab Mike's shirts, socks, pyjamas, underpants and, with Sam's box under my arm, I run to the desk in order to call a taxi to take them to the laundry to get back by that night. The girl at reception is helpful and gives me two laundry lists and two laundry bags. I write: 'Blakemore – 5 shirts, 1 pair pyjamas, 3 pairs socks, 3 pairs underpants', tie it up and turn to Sam's box. 'Four T-shirts', I write, '1 striped waistcoat' and – pausing at the last item – '1 short blue satin' – what? No way to describe it other than 'nightdress'.

The girl and I are equally bemused. But, nevertheless, a tiny ray of warmth penetrates my hitherto chilly perception of Sam. He is, after all, human – perhaps all too human – and I see why Barbara, and not me, was to share this secret. 'One nightie', I write. I also notice that he has written his own name, with three kisses, across the pocket. More and more fallible. We tie it all up. The taxidriver arrives. In the bottom of the cardboard box I notice a folded-up piece of paper – perhaps important? 'Dear Sam Neill,' it says, 'we are fans. Could you autograph the enclosed garments for us and leave them at Reception?' I just manage to intercept the departing taxi and retrieve them. For the rest of the day, I am intermittently smitten with the vision of Sam, returning after a day's work, opening his cupboard and finding pressed and clean a short blue satin nightdress on one of his hangers. Sadly, I could not tell Sam this story. I doubt he would have laughed.

We settle into our new location but mishaps follow us. Our make-up man swallows a fly. Two weeks later he sneezes and the fly emerges from his nose. Our best boy[24] is severely electrocuted – lucky to be alive. Our boom operator sprains his ankle. Next day another sprained ankle, a runner has his shoulder severely gashed by a falling piece of equipment, and the wardrobe supervisor traps her finger in a door.

The animals play their part. A horse in a van gets trapped by bushfires on the freeway. A rosella, supposedly shot by John and retrieved dead by Sam from the ground, necessitates both a bird stand-in and a vet standing by. Someone tells the vet he need not hang around all day, filming being what it is; the vet goes off to deliver a calf from a seedy cow and the cast are called immediately. Four hours' delay whilst we wait for the birth and the vet to return and dope the bird. Nobody thinks to sedate the stand-in, waiting nearby in their shared cage. When the unconscious star performer, tenderly wrapped in tissues, is returned to base, his companion seeing him, has a heart attack.

The cockatoo, a major player who has to say 'Merry Christmas', is a hired and seasoned performer, no doubt a member of Bird Equity. He eats through one antique birdcage (hired) and pecks away at the cane arm of an antique chaise longue (also hired). As Googie Withers approaches with a friendly 'Hello' for their scene together he gives her a jaundiced eye and screeches, 'Want a root?'

Heat takes over, briefly, from hospitalisation. Daily sheet for Day 30 reads: 'The generator broke down in the heat today. When restarted it created a power surge which damaged the DAT machine and videosplit. The Production Office has now been relocated to the Toll Bar Motel, due to the heat.' The heat has finally erupted into the worst bushfires in recent memory. We are encircled and lose two days' filming. Half of us trapped in Sydney.

Accidents are joined now by minor ailments. The sound recordist gets flu and passes it around the entire crew. Three days' rain - unheard of in December. Not constant rain, however, either a freezing downpour or a faint drizzle, so that we dash from wet to dry cover like demented sheep. John Hargreaves can't do his therapeutic walk so he *has* gone slightly crazy. When it is not freezing cold it is boiling hot. I remove the plaster from my broken hand and rest it on the dashboard of my car; it melts and becomes a pancake.

Our wonderful nurse, Patsy Buchan, becomes the pivot around which our production revolves. Our daily reports over a random ten-day period read:

13 Jan: 1. Unit Manager ill: sent home for bed rest.
2. Sam Neill flicked in eye by focus tape.
Suffering from hay fever - Nurse Patsy attends.

17 Jan: 1. Leslie Rouvray (make-up) sent home with migraine headache.
2. Greydon le Breton not well enough to work: he has

a stomach virus.
3. Andy Anderson cut his finger on a penknife.
4. John Hargreaves given gastrolyte for recurring bouts of diarrhoea.

18 Jan: 1. Gary Hill unable to work - diarrhoea, nausea and vomiting.
2. Greydon le Breton unable to work - diarrhoea, nausea and vomiting.
3. Stephen Taltz has headache: goes home ill.

21 Jan: 1. Nurse Patsy had an accident travelling to work. She treated herself and then went to set, saying she was OK. Patsy later became quite upset with shock and bruising started to appear on her chest . . . Patsy's car is a write-off.
2. Robin Dalton ate a whole packet of chocolate-coated coffee beans - has not slept for two nights.
3. Michael Blakemore tripped on a fir cone and bumped his left knee and twisted his left ankle. Arnica cream applied to his knee and an ice bag to his ankle.

22 Jan: 1. Michael Blakemore alarmed at minute wart suddenly appearing on his chest. Surgeon called to set - wart removed and is now in Pathology Dept of local hospital.
2. Nurse Patsy having therapy . . .

I am buoyed up by support from my 'team'. Despite what Adrienne and I came to call Mike's 'flashing eyes' when his ever erect antennae detected what he fears may be the slightest hint of disagreement, like John Schlesinger, he is above all a gentleman. His good manners and concern for others never waver. I am seldom consulted. No one is, except for his camera team.

Mike knows exactly what he wants and, as he is right at least ninety per cent of the time, I decline to risk the flashing eyes for the sake of the other ten per cent when he might have benefited from some outside input. For this is Mike's film. It is his concept, his execution, his words and his vision. His casting is perfection but I am invited to all read-throughs and casting sessions and fortunately we are always in accord. Looking back, through the scars of the intervening years, I see that my contribution to *Country Life* was as a financial midwife, a production 'nanny'. I raised the money; put together all the deals. I saw to it that Mike had food in his larder at our main location hotel; that a doctor was called when he showed signs of exhaustion or his always rampant hypochondria; that birthdays of various crew members were remembered; that Greta's house was suitably stocked and cared for on location; that John Hargreaves was allowed to move as often as he wanted - usually once a week; and, above all and to which we all owed much, that I had made the correct choice in our Line Producer.

My only unease was in my relationship with Sam. I was never sure whether it was shyness on his part, resentment over the struggles I had had with his agent over his deal, or simple dislike of me, which made him as distant as he remained from start to finish. Professionally, and on set, he was not to be faulted in performance or in behaviour. Jolly to the crew, of help to Michael, generous to his fellow actors and rather less jolly to me.

John gave us the most headaches, but worthwhile headaches. He was a great natural, instinctive actor. Direction was something threatening, coming to him from outside. His motor came churning out from within, driven by anger, fear and energy. This combustible package was happily tied together with strings of humour, and wrapped in charm so that one loves the look of it and only in use do the sharp edges hurt. The mischief and mayhem he caused were never premeditated. It was part of the game, but the game for John was not in the winning but in the playing. The end result, when the scars have healed, is worth every jab. He will have given a great performance and you will remember him with affection. His motives, you will realise, have had the good of the work at heart.

The film had notices in England such as one dreams about: 'a joy'; 'a summer delight'; 'a small masterpiece'; voted one of the top ten films of the decade. A 'work of genius' in Italy. Sadly, we had opened in Australia first to a correspondingly lukewarm reception, which I think might have been warmer had we arrived trailing clouds of international acclaim.

It wasn't all enjoyment and it wasn't all fun, but there was a fair share of both. *The Promise* got me to Hong Kong, *Madame Sousatzka* to Venice, and now *Country Life* to Moscow. If reviews in England were superb - in Australia muted - in Russia, the home of Chekhov, they were amazingly ecstatic. And I had never been to Russia.

chapter thirty-four

MOSCOW, *July 1995*

Flight fine but the queue to get through passport control (except they don't queue – they push) took as long as the flight. Dingy, dark hall, glum faces, chaos. Sweet girl, Alice, holding aloft a board to meet me. She calls two young men on her intercom and we scuttle to an office – actually a sort of cubicle which was either a Government entity, the Russian equivalent of Hertz or even Thomas Cook, or Interfest (the Festival concern). Whichever of the three, they appeared to know nothing about me, viewed my faxed 'invitation' with deep suspicion (they said it was forged), had long Russian arguments with Alice, were in some doubt as to whether I was to stay at the Metropole – or anywhere *– and in the midst of all this a driver suddenly appeared and we were whisked off in a Mercedes to the Metropole. Which seemed straight out of a 1950s Third World film (in fact,* Zhivago *was filmed in its dining room) – but, so far, I've seen nothing but the glittering (in the worst sense) lobby, huge and barn-like with many chandeliers, and the very bad-tempered and suspicious girl at Reception who took my forged invitation twice and has now confiscated my passport.*

Another (very) young man, Igor, appears. He smiles – reluctantly – but is also deeply suspicious and does not appear to think I should be here. It is now about 11 p.m. and I have had a four-hour flight. I am told by Alice to sit down and she *then disappears. My luggage has long ago been whisked away at the entrance – God knows where, as I am not yet a 'guest'. Finally, Alice and Igor reappear and Igor asks what sort of room do I require. Whereupon I made my first* huge *mistake. 'Just a single room,' I say, 'as long as I have a bathroom.' This causes the only mirth I am to see in Russia – but with some speed I am whisked up and into* miles *of empty, sinister corridors and deposited in a cell. Or so it looked in the 25-watt lightbulbed gloom. I collapse with depression into an over-stuffed armchair. The bed is small. There are many magazines on the table – all about Aeroflot and all in Russian. I tell Alice I cannot stay in what looks to me like a servant's room. Alice agrees. I have since discovered that I must pay for everything except actual room as I am not on VIP list and therefore do not receive the $90 per diem which I have been promised. Alice argues with Igor about this. Igor says he can do nothing until his boss arrives in the morning but to come and see him at 10 a.m. I offer Alice food and drink but she says it is far too expensive for me and goes. Igor tells me I have a lovely bathroom, which is what I asked for. I tell him I cannot sleep in the bath. He smiles. He thinks I am mad. Encouraged by the smile, I tell him I may cut my throat (with gestures) if I must remain in this room. This is too much puzzlement for him.*

There is one pillow. But there is also CNN on TV. I watch a terrifying one-hour film on crime in Moscow and splash out on a mineral water and delicious smoked salmon sandwich. And a pill. More or less sleep. In daylight, room not quite so bad. Breakfast fine – grapefruit, muesli, and lukewarm tea. Also, lukewarm bath water. Alice says she will appear at 10. I *then discover I could have had a complimentary tour of everything – Kremlin, cathedrals, Pushkin Museum, the lot, with guide, at 10; but due to appointments with Igor and Alice (my second mistake) I sit and watch CNN. Alice turns up at 10.40. Igor is not there. Alice looks awful. She has been mugged at knife-point en route home. She says she has been crying all night. I ask what he took and she says the $30 her grandmother had given her for her birthday. I pump $30 into her hand from my precious hoard (as I am not sure how to get more cash in Moscow if there is to be no per diem), which she takes with amazing speed for one so traumatised, and says, not 'Thank you' but 'You didn't have to do that'. However, now I know Alice better I think it could have been a sort of pride, although I have had fleeting moments of nostalgic regret for my $30. Alice tells me all about her family during the day. Her parents are divorced. Her mother is a theatre director, her grandmother an opera singer (she died* yesterday *– the one who gave her the $30?), her father is rich. She goes to university in Nebraska. She is very, very nervous since being mugged and begged her mother not to go to their country house this weekend. In talking of the mugging she says it is not the money – the money was not important. I mourn my $30. Alice blushes quite often when she talks about it or when I mention it to the others. I am ashamed of my suspicions.*

But, to 'My Day'. It seems to have been spent going from one Festival office to another. Kerry Fox has joined us. My driver – or a surly substitute – is always there, but never at the exact right time. Nobody smiles in Moscow. Except Igor, who now breaks into a nervous giggle whenever he sees me. Alice interprets as I argue my way around. The first fight is to change rooms. With Alice, Igor, and the two Gauleiter ladies, I am shown a suite – very splendid. I say 'fine'. Igor asks if I would not like to see other rooms. My third mistake: I say 'yes'. Room No. 2 is not a suite but large and comfortable and close to the elevator, instead of a mile walk, and they all say it has a better 'view'. It seems fine too, so plumping for the near elevator, I choose this one. I find that it is difficult to appreciate the 'view' as the curtains don't open completely and the one window is quite small. I also see why Igor thought Bathroom No. 1 was so good. It was twice the size of this one. Ditto cupboard space. So, I start the day-long battle for something stronger than 40-watt bulbs in my four lamps. It took four phone calls – one young boy holding a tiny lamp at door – two personal visits to the Guest Relations Desk (Svetlana, the lady there, loathes me) and, finally, I have four 60-watt bulbs, having been told by Svetlana that the hotel electrical system would not support them. I am waiting for the hotel (vastly chandeliered) to explode.

Other fights won by Alice – I am now a VIP, which I should have been in the first place. This means I can eat *$90 worth of food (excluding drink) per day in the hotel: no cash. I have just had a supper of very inferior and frugal caviar and blinis in my room – and a rather disgusting and expensive solo lunch in the restaurant. And much vodka with Kerry in the bar. Everyone whom I might conceivably wish to know or see is on the two-day river trip. I should have been on it. They had put me on a plane which guaranteed I would miss it by one hour.*

So, after wasting more than half a day on chaotic visits to officials, Alice and I set off on foot, in heat, to Red Square and the Kremlin. Alice says Russian ice-cream is the best in the world so I buy two rather revolting cones. Everything is half-covered in scaffolding. My feet hurt dreadfully. We trudge through the Cathedral of St Basil (the famous one on all the postcards) and into Kremlin and into Cathedral Square and I choose just one *of the six cathedrals to visit – and am rather pleased with my choice. It is the Cathedral of the Archangel Michael and burial chamber of the Czars, so I am surrounded* by David's ancestors. It is tiny but very beautiful and my feet are now blistered so I miss the famous Assumption one and we trudge home, limping, and are caught in a thunderstorm. I soak feet, have tea in room, change and meet Kerry to set off to get tickets for Jefferson in Paris (fancy going to Moscow to catch something on at the Curzon). One hour in a squabbling queue (except they don't queue) later we learn that all tickets are sold and that Vanya on 42nd Street which I really wanted to see was showing at 3 p.m. It is now 8 p.m. No one had given me a programme. Decide I shall spend time eating my $90 and watching CNN. And so, as Pepys would say, to bed. Ten p.m. on second night. Not a film seen nor a proper person met.

No pill, so, although waking several times, a proper night's sleep, until Mary Colbert, the journalist who had been instrumental in our inclusion in the Festival, woke me at 8 a.m. The Ambassador may not have the promised party for me with which I have been enticed to Moscow. Phil Noyce sends apologies but is going to Croatia. Mary is set for a long chat – I feel as if I've been hit on the head. Car coming at 1 p.m. to take me to press conference and film, together with Kerry, where we have to give speeches, so I decide on huge breakfast in bed in my $90 target attempt. Eat a quarter of it.

Get ready for Mary at 11. Still waiting at 11.50, fully dressed and reading about the Moscow I thought I could have seen, but now can't be bothered. Trace Graeme Clifford who says the river trip was fabulous. Furious I missed it. He knew nothing about Country Life – it is impossible to tell which films are on and who is in them; in fact, nothing except nationality or director is listed. No word re: ambassadorial junket. Have exhausted CNN – have seen Bianca Jagger rattling on about Nicaragua three times. I expect Kerry has by now seen all Moscow. She has been terrifically resourceful and goes to the gym every morning and the Sunday market via metro.

Back in room, 9.30 p.m. Feels like 2 a.m. Waiting once more for room service – caviar and a chicken sandwich this time. Amnesia has taken over. Everyone finally turned up at 12 – Mary, Alice and room service to make bed at the same time. We all meet with Kerry, in lobby. The priorities are: 1. coffee which Mary wants all the time; 2. transport, a dicey affair; 3. tickets to our own film and invitation to Embassy party (now pizzas instead of the promised oysters) and – discovered far too late – many, many glasses too late – Russian champagne; 4. Mary scribbling frantically in car my and Kerry's CVs in order to introduce us; 5. trying to leave messages for Graeme, and also Harvey Weinstein who the hotel and Festival people insist is here (he certainly has a room booked), but who obviously is not as he was in New York with Greta two days ago. Mary keeps going away whilst Alice finds and then loses car – eventually one arrives (no longer a Mercedes, something off the scrap heap) and we career at high speed to our press conference. Mary, I and Kerry, a couple of interpreters and a couple of Festival directors on a dais with microphones and warm Coca-Cola (all the water is salt *water). Press all Russian and adorable. Enormous enthusiasm. Chekhov is the* star: *and Kerry behaves like one (intelligently but determined). I hold my own. I am kissed and hugged by innumerable journalists and told over and over that* Country Life *is by far the best rendition of Chekhov ever to be made, including all Russian versions. Mary says she will tape all interviews for Mike but forgets to tape the questions – only gets the answers.*

After the conference, several journalists rush up to question us and make appointments for individual interviews the following morning. Kerry is determined to make the most of this. I am desperate to pee. But Mary says there is plenty of time for that (a palpable lie) and we are whisked off to a TV interview in a vast, echoing underground hall. The interviewer is one whom I have kissed many times and we go on beaming at each other. Alice is, of course, indispensable. Kerry masterminds the lighting and notices that the battery on camera has expired. More questions about Chekhov. Finally I call a halt as we are late for our own film. Insist on loo. This time it is another mile walk to a grim tiled horror house, and the race to the cinema feels more like an ambulance on the way to the hospital. At cinema, the Ambassador and wife and various officials in anteroom full of food and drink (salt water and tinned orange juice) which no one offers us. Richard Gere appears – everyone very intimidated. He seems a nice chap. We troop onto stage – presented with three huge bouquets – Mary, me and Kerry – and we all speak. I try to mention Mike and the FFC as well as Chekhov. Kerry never mentions anyone. We sit through the film in Ambassador's box. Hardly a titter from audience and hardly a clap at the end. About half a dozen walkouts – a good ratio I am told. Mr and Mrs Ambassador, Kerry, Mary and I leave by back door for his car but Mary rushes back to exit by main entrance where she tells us later there was a horde of fans *awaiting us. I invite one of the more persistent Festival officials to the Embassy (Ambassador is now Geoff, sweet and bemused) and we are just about to pull away when Gere's female partner comes running up to the car and calls to Kerry through the window that Richard and she really admire her work and that he wants to invite her – now – for a bowl of pasta. Kerry is half out of the car when I point out that we are co-hosts with Ambassador at our own party and that would perhaps be a little rude. Gere's lady and I indulge in undignified verbal tussle over Kerry's person – I loudly proclaim our regrets.*

This is ignored but it becomes obvious that Geoff is dying to be with Gere, so poor wife goes on ahead. I give her my bouquet. We all go and accept Gere's hospitality. He is, of course, only expecting Kerry. We take little Russian with us – to nice restaurant on terrace. Richard Gere very polite but we are offered nothing *as he is a Buddhist and disapproves of drink. He loved* Sousatzka *and loves John with whom he made* Yanks. *He and I talk so much poor Kerry doesn't get many words in. After twenty minutes of chat I say we must go to Embassy, but as Gere is President of Jury it hasn't been a bad thing. Embassy is a bleak and terrifying edifice – modern Russian – used to be Chinese Embassy. Many hidden torture chambers, one feels. About fifty assorted Russians await us, plus horrid Festival Director who is a Russian Producer-Director. I ask him what he does – not popular, I expect. And mad Kenneth Griffiths with the young Welshman who wrote and directed Hugh Grant film* The Man Who Went Up a Hill but Came Down a Mountain *also in competition. Trapped by Ken to discuss Michael Collins as he died in my father-in-law's arms. Pizzas and champagne filthy. Lots more photos, speeches, kisses. Finally collapse back at hotel at 10 p.m., declining dinner with Mary and more Russian journalists and settle for fourth run of Bianca, red caviar (better) in room. Take pill.* Horrendous *nightmare about losing clothes on top of mountain/roundabout/beach and clinging on by fingers. Message?*

Set alarm for 7 because have breakfast date with Mary and Graeme Clifford in fabulous dining room. Warm welcome from Klaus Maria Brandauer (who seems to remember Homage to Catalonia *and me, or maybe he's just a very good actor). Find out place full of Georgians I should have met – dozens of people I should have met but there has been no* list. *The three journalists with whom I have interviews don't turn up. Alice dispatched to get my visa money – £154 in roubles. Mary says I am a VIP (neither she nor Kerry are) because she told them I was elderly, having been sent my passport details, and she and they expected a tottering old lady on a stick. May just end up tottering. Keep going out to leave messages for journalists but after third attempt discover lady at desk had not the faintest idea of my name and never asked me.*

So three journalists think I'm very rude – if they ever did turn up.

Four furious hours later, when I could have seen a bit of Moscow. Alice left me stranded in room when she went to fetch my roubles – lying through her teeth about how long it took – in order to go to Gere's press conference. She thinks he is 'cute'. She has told the Interfest office that I had said I wanted two hours' rest. In that two hours I panic, alone, over roubles, transport, unrecovered passport, which the desk can't find, and ticket confirmation. When Alice finally appears it is a rush to the airport. I could have eaten buckets of caviar. Instead I have eaten horrid BA meal on aircraft. Alice deposited me in VIP lounge, but thank God they wouldn't accept me. It resembled an interrogation chamber from 1984. *At ordinary check-in desk I made a* friend *– an Englishman from Manchester emigrating to Moscow because of the crime in England (he had obviously not seen the 'Crime in Moscow' TV documentary), takes me under his wing. Alice leaves. Mary has instructed her to return my $30 but this is not mentioned. I give my new friend my remaining roubles – about £3 worth and he buys me a filthy cup of coffee. But he gets me on board full of Valium: and gobble lots of proper champagne. Regret now I didn't shout, stamp feet, demand and spend a fortune at hotel – apparently all expected – I made fatal mistake of smiling, thanking and frugality. Could have invited everyone in sight to dine with me instead of saving crusts of bread from breakfast tray.*

Regret I saw so little of Moscow. Lesson learnt: do not smile in Russia – instantly suspect.

chapter thirty-five

During the filming of *Country Life* I was forced to learn more of the technical details involved in production, having rather thankfully left them all to Simon on *Madame Sousatzka*. More good friends were made, among cast and crew; and support from our financiers, the Australian Film Finance Corporation, was firm and unflinching. But all through its production I was juggling with my next obsession - *Oscar and Lucinda*.

This obsession took up nearly ten years of my life. Family and friends all urged, 'Give it up, for God's sake, that book will be etched on your tombstone' (as well it may be), but the fact that I didn't was not so much the same urge which drove me to make *Madame Sousatzka*, but the feeling of responsibility towards Peter Carey who had entrusted me with his book; the NSW Film and Television Office who had given me the money for Laura Jones's screenplay; to Laura herself; to the AFC who had given me marketing money - I simply could not let them all down, and I could not free myself of the profound emotions the book unleashed.

After Joel's blank cheque it had all seemed relatively simple. John Schlesinger had remembered a book he had long wanted to make - William Boyd's *The Ice Cream War*. I rang Boyd's agent, Stephen Durbridge. It was not available - but he had a manuscript of a new book by Peter Carey, shortly to be published, which he thought I should read. The manuscript was biked round to me: I read through the night. Even before I finished the book I rang Joel: 'I've found the story I want to make - it's called *Oscar and Lucinda* - it's a huge film - the book will win the Booker Prize and we have to move fast.' Stephen sent another manuscript to John and I sent a copy to Joel.

John is going to a health farm for a week and takes it with him; the first tiny nail in our edifice of production, for John reads very slowly, is always busy, and would undoubtedly not have had the time to read if he had not been bored and hungry. Two days later he rang me - 'You have to get this book'. I ring Joel and tell him John is as crazy about the book as I am. I am told to bid for it: no ceiling on the price is mentioned.

I first optioned it officially on 17 May 1988.

Happy, happy days. The deal is done - the book is ours. The problem is finding the right writer. Eventually we agree upon Charles Wood. John has worked with him before and I have admired some, if not all, of his writing for years.

In our few early script meetings, I feel instinctively that this complicated story should be told in a linear mode - a straight line from beginning to end, but Charles doesn't agree and delivers a script to us full of brilliant passages but because of flashbacks almost unintelligible in storytelling on the page. He generously rewrites it, but it is still a first draft. John does not work closely on a script until second draft - believing in giving a writer more freedom until then.

Dramatically and sadly, at this point Cineplex-Odeon closed their production arm. We were left high and dry. No money to pay for a second draft; no money to keep John from going on to a more definite production; no distribution company. The option lapsed. I waited for a suitable interval - praying that no one else would buy it - and started all over again, with my own money this time funding the option payments. Peter Carey showed faith and trust, and allowed me to continue. I still hoped that John would remain available but I could not afford to pay for both option and second draft.

Luciana Arrighi, who had been our production designer on *Madame Sousatzka*, and who had been involved with us on *Oscar and Lucinda* from the outset, rang me one day. Gillian Armstrong in Australia had asked her if she would ask me if I would consider her as director. I realised that, with an Australian director, my own Australian production company, and an Australian writer I had a very good chance of raising development finance from one of the Australian Government bodies for a new draft. John was characteristically generous and gave me his blessing. Peter Carey, who had been thrilled with the idea of John directing, was happy to accept Gill, an old friend. Gill's US agent suggested three writers, sending me scripts to read, and, miraculously, one of them was *An Angel at My Table* by Laura Jones, a writer with whom I had wanted to work since seeing the film. (I had, as an agent, represented the dramatic rights of Janet Frame, the author of the book, so I knew what a superb job it had been.) A quick trip to Australia, a meeting with Gill and Laura, funding from the NSW Film and TV Office swiftly arranged, and I was on course again. Laura and Gill officially engaged August 1991: over three years into my obsession.

Laura was never to read Charles Wood's screenplay, and I never looked at it again - pushed it to the back of my mind, as a legal precaution against plagiarism. We all three started out with the impossible ideal of making it a three-hour film, as had John and I - possibly even to cut into three one-hour segments for TV - as in *An Angel at My Table*, if necessary. But as we progressed commercial reality took over and so started our cuts.

(After completion of the film I was to read interviews and to hear that John Schlesinger had never been able to reduce the script beyond four hours whereas Gill had done so. Poor John had never had the chance to try. I hope he does not read Australian newspapers, nor listen to recorded interviews.)

The five long years during which Gill, Laura and I worked on the script and the casting are uniquely recorded thanks to the invention of the fax. The files fill a cabinet drawer and in great detail show the genesis of a film. We were to be in the same country perhaps three or four times only. The faxes are also a valuable help to memory.

During those years we were all three taking time out to work on other films but coming back continually to the *Oscar and Lucinda* task in hand. The ending was to prove our stumbling block with all possible financiers. One day, Gill sent me a message saying we simply had to come up with a brilliant idea which would convince them. Here is my reply:

1 December 1992

Dear Gill,

A progress report.

I met with David Aukin at Channel 4 yesterday and he is 'pondering' finance . . .

But – we discussed script problems at length, with Jack Leschner, mostly to do with that bloody ending and in the discussions I had an idea – radical and perhaps over the top – but they both pounced on it as providing a proper end contained within a romantic story and leaving the audience with some satisfaction. I telephoned Laura last night to try it out on her and she did not explode so now I am trying it out on you – not thought out in any detail and in broad outline.

Lucinda goes on the journey with Wardley Fish, playing cards by campfire – betting or whatever. Perhaps she has taken the deeds of her factory with her to hand over to Oscar anyway, as proof of her trust/love? Meanwhile, we have a longer gap between Oscar's commitment to Miriam (entailing the actual wedding?) so that we see Miriam's pregnancy. Lucinda arrives just too late – i.e. after Oscar's death (or even in time to see him, talk to him, and realise that he has married Miriam?). He dies as in script. Miriam gives birth, but dies in childbirth. (Are you still with me?) Lucinda brings up baby. A much more fulfilling life, in terms of our 'romantic' story than running a factory, etc. It is then Lucinda who rebuilds the Church. After all, there is no reason to transport it to Glenifer: she can simply donate it to Hassett. That was only in the book and it only involves a small dialogue change. Oscar's baby inherits the bet, and Lucinda is his surrogate mother. The Narrator therefore has every reason to know the full story as his grandfather was brought up by Lucinda – this was always a hole in the narrative. It also gives up a chance to play the scene between Miriam and Lucinda, as is, instead of by letter. I would also like to see some bet, involving all of this – perhaps with Wardley Fish before it all happens – in which Lucinda vows never to gamble again if Oscar is safe, but transfers this vow to the child . . . there you are. Will I qualify for the Betty Trask award? This is given every year to the best piece of bodice-ripping romance fiction. Please talk to Laura . . .

Love,

Robin

I had been rather pleased with my idea. Gill's response was a dose of cold water. She was 'overwhelmed' and thought it might be too radical for people and critics who loved the book. Before replying, I quickly try it out on some potential investors, like Channel 4, as well as those already in place such as the NSW

Film and TV Office from whom I hoped to raise more money for a further draft. I also took the precaution of speaking once more to John Morris of the FFC. So I come clean about my burrowing behind the financial curtain and reply later that day:

1 December 1992

Dear Gill,

I appreciate I have thrown a large pebble in the pond but to date reactions have been positive – particularly from Channel 4, and now just received fax from Greg, enclosed, from whom I might get more money. Laura was somewhat intrigued, and now I need you to have a good think when you are finished the current job. I have had even more thoughts along the same line.

The one person I will not talk to about it is Peter, although he has been surprisingly receptive on new ideas so far. Better to see if Laura and you agree, and we can get finance, and then tell him. Contractually, I have no need to tell him, but obviously I want him to be happy. As for your worries about critics who loved the book, those are somewhat outnumbered by people who loved the book right up to the ending and then threw it across the room in a fury!

I spoke to John Morris, who will put aside $5 000 000 in 'risk' money and perhaps double that if guaranteed. But he said it all depends on the deal, and Phaedon was supposed to ring me this morning to discuss what that might be – to date has not done so . . .

Looking forward to hearing from you when you have had time to think,

Love,

Robin

This, however, still does not convince Gill. She replies that she is sorry but neither she nor Laura are won over by the new ending - they find it too neat, too much, too sweet - almost another story. They have thought long and hard about my new ideas but are adamant that they feel wrong. They *do*, however, quite like the idea of a baby.

She ends her fax - endearingly - 'Sorry - don't be too cross.' It is difficult to be cross with Gill for long; her methods those of the spoilt child aware of its power; an undeniable flirtatious charm summoned at will, producing in her victims a craven wish to please. And, as with a spoilt child who has gone too far, she produced in me a maternal instinctive wish to protect her from herself.

By now we have discovered that we are both Sagittarians - mutual tact not our strong points, although we both make a conscious effort and our faxes are thick with self-aware apologies.

However, Laura has already agreed that we must know Lucinda's future - death? marriage? emigration? - and now she agrees to try my ideas, and, with some adjustments, writing the ending more or less as suggested. We drop the wedding, but see the pregnancy. We very reluctantly drop Wardley Fish's arrival in Australia for reasons of budget and schedule. Much later, Laura was to add a brilliant touch when Hassett burns the bet, thereby tying up ends and keeping him a catalyst in the story until the end. Later, I also suggest that we finish the film with Lucinda teaching Oscar's son to swim: this is now the ending of the film.

Gill is now, reluctantly and warily, satisfied, but worried that some people, including Judy Davis whom we have been thinking of as Lucinda, liked the old one. I suddenly have an unlikely ally, however, in Gill's LA agent, Beth Swofford, to whom Gill turns for advice on every aspect of what I had once merrily assumed was 'my' film. Gill reports on 4 February that Beth *loves* the new ending and immediately wants to start sending it to production companies. She is neither my agent, nor the producer, so I endeavour to dampen her ardour.

The remainder of our faxes regarding the script are too specialised, too detailed for the lay reader. Perhaps one day, as Gill suggested, they may form part of a film archive. Their only significance in this memoir lies in the contrast between the fact and collective memories of it.

At the same time as we worried about the script and the finance we were investigating the cast. Gill had very definite ideas from the outset, few of which I agreed with, but I bowed to her judgement whilst also reflecting on those actors whom she wanted (and I most emphatically did not want) and those whom she did and whom I thought might get us the finance. She has a splendid instinct for casting, so it is compromise time: sad but tempting if one cannot substitute a passionate belief of one's own.

In London one night I dined with the director Anthony Page. He had just tested and decided to cast in the lead in *Middlemarch* for the BBC one Ralph Fiennes. He told me he had never known an actor give a better reading. Suddenly my passion found a target. I had never seen any of Ralph's screen or TV performances but had been thrilled by his stage performances at the RSC. Why had I never thought of him - he *was* Oscar.

I rang his agent, Larry Dalzell. He sent tapes, photographs, anything I might send to Gill. Gill was cautious. Her agent's reply was more succinct: 'I know, Robin, you have your heart set on Ralph Fiennes but no one in Hollywood has ever heard of him.' She, and Gill, continue to chase Gill's other choices but not before, with Gill's permission, I have sent the script to Ralph. His gut reaction was immediate and he was delighted to test for us. Meanwhile, Steven Spielberg has offered him the role in *Schindler's List* (which eventually caused Hollywood to hear of him – and for the agency who had never heard of him to sign him up). Anthony and the BBC are understanding. Gill is in LA and I pay for her (out of the money given to us by the AFC because of the new ending) to go on to New York to meet Ralph and discuss the proposed test subsequently directed for us in London by Noel Davis. He is superb: I want no other Oscar; I don't really want to make the film without him.

Gill goes to LA again and returns in great excitement to announce to Laura, 'You'll never guess who is hot – Ralph Fiennes!' I no longer have to battle so hard.

chapter thirty-six

What began with a passion for a story, an uplift to the spirit, took so long to realise that the spirit was almost extinguished by the end, but to have given way to that would have been to negate the message of faith in Oscar and Lucinda's story and it was that faith which sustained me throughout. They were characters who inhabited my dreams and shared my days. For me, the book is a classic example of what a film based on a book should contain - a theme as well as a plot, a meaning over and above the words. To choose one as difficult to contain in two hours as *Oscar and Lucinda* was perhaps simple masochism, but supremely satisfying.

Another three years or so were to pass before we were in actual production, during which, and on until completion, I kept a daily diary, but this is not the place for it. By the time we were in pre-production Shirley's 'people' had deserted me entirely. Joel's dire warning was beginning to bite. I began to feel as Alice must have felt in Wonderland, and as we progressed I entered a surreal world - curiouser and curiouser. Alice fell down the Rabbit Hole through the Looking Glass and there met Kafka. I didn't laugh much during the production of *Oscar and Lucinda*; few people did. Not many mishaps, either: Ralph was nearly bitten by a snake; I was nearly washed away by floods; Nurse Patsy, back with me again, was mainly needed for treating heat exhaustion. The crew were wonderful, working their guts out in forty degree heat with astounding good humour, and little thanks. The cast and heads of departments were all terrific. Laura's continuing dedication to the script was a joy. Janet Patterson's costumes were an inspiration. The glass church designed by Luci was a miracle. It all looked beautiful. As with the peacocks and the peace in Italy, I think with affection of the cast and crew and if I look back searching for pleasure I shall think of a week on location by the sea in my beloved Cornwall again, feeling strangely at home.

In time, I hope I shall only remember all this and will have forgotten the thrust of ambitions, the hurt of disloyalties, the shock of betrayals, the cuckoo in my nest. Far better to relegate them, as in our Italian tower, to the past, along with the mice in the beds, the slippery winding staircase, the unreliable Principessa, the lethal stove, the poisonous frogs.

I fear I had been spoilt by my first two ventures into production, and it has been a salutary experience: salutary inasmuch as I am tempted (until the next passion?) to close the doors on film production and look for the next EXIT sign. Perhaps, simply, into life? Back up through the Rabbit Hole into sunlight?

chapter thirty-seven

Getting married for the third time, apart from fulfilling the prophecy of the Sydney fortune-teller in my teens, surprised both Bill and myself. Neither of us had given it much thought in our 29-year relationship. Friends no longer urged nor wondered. Children had their own lives and marriages to occupy them.

It was also surprisingly difficult to achieve. Bill refused to have anything to do with the actual arrangements and so it was left to me to find out how it is done. I had forgotten.

First, I rang my daughter.

'What do I do?' I asked her. Patiently she explained that one goes to one's local council and gets a licence. That rang a bell.

'Ah! Caxton Hall. I remember that. It's where I married your father.'

'Mum' - patience wearing thin - 'it doesn't exist any more. You'd better go to Marylebone Town Hall.'

So the imposing building I passed most days as I turned into Regent's Park on my way home was where they married you! Parking was a problem; once inside embarrassment prevailed. I felt my age, and distinctly silly, asking a uniformed chap in the entrance where to go to get married but once up the stairs it was as simple as filling in a medical form at the new doctor's office and I was treated with the same solicitude. A sweet-faced matronly lady interviewed me.

'Have either of you ever been married before?' she asked, not quite reaching out to pat my hand. The air of hospitalisation thickened. Had to confess, 'Twice before - both of us', but her smile didn't flicker. We wanted to do it quickly as I was due to go to Australia to produce *Oscar and Lucinda*. This entailed a special fee of £60, but my new lady friend and I set the date and I went home to tell Bill.

'Marylebone Town Hall!' he exclaimed in horror. 'I can't possibly get married there. It's where I got married the first time.' He refused to listen to my protests that the interior would certainly have changed; that it was most unlikely it would be the same room and certainly not the same, presumably long dead, official. Different wife seemed not to be relevant. Eventually, I persuaded him to at least try a dry run; come and have a look; reassure himself that once inside all would be so different that his first wedding would not be remotely conjured up.

It took us some time to find a parking spot, several blocks away. As we got nearer his footsteps began to falter. He started to complain about his operated-on hip. Dragging by the hand was necessary by the time we reached the front steps. Once inside I propelled him up the curving staircase past a large arrow pointing upwards to a sinister sign with one word: MARRIAGES.

But on the first landing, defeat was final.

'My God!' he shrieked as the first clumps of confetti appeared on the steps ahead. He ran out of the building, hip forgotten. I never got my £60 back.

So a registry office was out of the question as we lived in Marylebone. A church? Well, a Presbyterian minister would probably do it. My own first Presbyterian wedding had been consigned to obscurity by respectable subsequent widowhood, so perhaps we need only mention Bill's second - church - wedding. Once more it was left to me.

I went off to St Columba's in Pont Street, advised by all friends who had been married there, after a divorce, by a particularly liberal-minded minister. This, too, was remarkably easy to arrange. I told Bill.

'*Pont* Street! Are you mad? I can't possibly be married there. It's where I got married last time, and by the Moderator, what's more.'

We had exhausted the possibilities of London. Our friends Caroline and Ken Hyman lived in the Thames Valley. I rang and asked them if Bill could be presumed as living with them for the requisite three weeks needed to establish residency; if they would be our witnesses; and if they knew where we could be married in their area. Ken was delighted. 'You'll love our vicar,' he said. 'He'll marry you', and later that evening the vicar and Bill were in deep telephone conversation. It went on for ages. Christian names were exchanged. I waited until the end of a very long call.

'He can't do it,' says Bill. 'He would if we actually lived in his parish and perhaps if we didn't have quite so many divorces between us, but it's really pushing it. He said to try the Presbyterians - says they'll marry anyone. Very nice chap. Would love to come to our wedding.'

However, after a telephone conference with Kenny, we decided on their local registry office. Unfortunately, this turned out to be High Wycombe. High Wycombe is one of the worst examples of modern transport planning in a spectacularly ruined rural and provincial England. What was once a small country town has become another spaghetti junction. I certainly could not navigate it alone so this time Bill drove whilst I attempted directions. Any married couple could duplicate the dialogue.

'Turn left!'

'How can I when you only tell me at the last moment?'

'Well, how can I tell you earlier when you're going so bloody fast and I haven't got my glasses on?'

'Can't you see there's a fucking car right behind? How can I go slower?'

'Well, we should have turned left. Now we're stuck on this motorway' . . . and so on, until some time later one is released from a speed deathtrap and is forced into a maze of one-way streets all ending up where one has begun. Unspeaking. Expletives exhausted.

High Wycombe Registry Office, when eventually reached, proved welcoming. An enchanting chap relieved us of another £60 and set the day. We felt much encouraged; previous marriages brushed aside.

We went back to London and set about organising a jolly wedding party. Bill wrote witty invitations. He took the plunge and informed his ex-wife and his adult daughters. The date for my film was put forward, and so was my proposed trip to Australia. It seemed easier to postpone wedding party until my return but pretend we had nevertheless got married on the chosen day as Bill could not face explaining change of plan to said ex-spouse and children. Another £60 down the drain.

Two months later we started again. Sadly, the new date meant that our enchanting chap had retired but we asked him to the wedding, too, and an equally enchanting lady took his place. We re-organised the wedding party to take place in the evening: wedding in the morning and a celebratory country luncheon with Kenny and Caroline.

Another trip to High Wycombe. Bride and groom arrived, unspeaking, at the registry office and had it not been for the lunch and the party, both subsequently wonderfully enjoyable, we would probably have turned back at the first available exit to that unspeakable motorway, never to return.

Full circle. It would be nice to have one's life end as it began – enriched with laughter. My life with Bill has echoes of life with my father – indeed, of my mother's life with my father. He makes me laugh.

Last Christmas we went to stay in Rutland with our friends the Galitzines. We left for London the day after Boxing Day in deep snow. Twenty miles down the motorway, Bill remembered he had not taken his 'heart' pills with his breakfast. Bill views his body with some trepidation. This was, to him, a major cause for alarm.

'Darling,' I tried, 'you won't die if you don't take your pills for one meal.'

'You don't understand,' he snapped. 'It's not your heart.'

I rather regretfully agreed. I had a fairly battered old heart. He had a better than new one – four lovely, clean, bypassed arteries. But I tried to pacify him. At our feet was a bottle of water which I grabbed triumphantly. 'Here's some water! Take them now.'

Clenched teeth now. 'I have to have something to *eat* when I take them.'

I tried pointing out that we were a bare, fairly speedy, twenty miles from his substantial breakfast. It didn't work.

'I'm going to stop for a biscuit,' he announced.

We both now proceeded with clenched teeth. Through the frosted windshield no warmly lit Happy Eater nor Little Chef appeared; only a forlorn one-pump petrol station with small attached shop loomed at us.

I sat, frozen and tight-lipped in the car, whilst he went in to get his biscuit. He seemed gone a long time when a tap on my window alerted me to a concerned face.

'Excuse me,' said the face, 'but your husband has just had rather a nasty fall – I think he's twisted his knee.'

Bill was perched on a stool, happily clutching his biscuit and a coffee, surrounded by solicitous attendants – the garage owner, his biscuit-supplying wife and the man who had tapped on the window.

'Nasty fall,' they all said. 'Can't put his foot to the ground.'

'I only slipped on the ice,' said Bill, grabbing another biscuit and swallowing his pills. 'Just twisted my knee.'

No, he would not let me call a doctor, an ambulance, and no, he would not go back to the Galitzines. He was perfectly all right now that he was not about to have a heart attack, and he would proceed the seventy-five remaining miles to London. I held out my hand for the car keys. He looked at me with shock and horror.

'You're not driving my new Mercedes.'

Two of the men helped him, hopping, into the car. Three of us inched, shoved and wrestled his six-foot-three frame behind the wheel, pushing the offending leg, as best we could, under the panel; and off we set, on automatic drive.

London, by six o'clock, was dark and feebly snowing. Bill refused to go to his doctor – insisted on going home – would go backwards up our stairs on his bottom. There was only me to manoeuvre him out of the car. He fell over immediately, saving himself on the car door. This time, with no helpers, it took longer for me to push his bent leg in again. He refused to go to Casualty. We sat gloomily side by side in the dark.

'I'm *only* going to Edward VII [the King Edward VII Hospital for Officers, or sometimes just Sister Agnes', or Edward VII to the cognoscenti] and that's it,' he said. 'I am *not* going to Casualty at some bloody hospital.'

I locked him in; turned on heater and radio and went up to telephone – first to his doctor – no answer; the surgeon who had operated on both his hips and who had admitted him to Edward VII on both occasions – no answer; finally, to my own doctor, at home for Christmas, who does not particularly warm to Bill. 'Sounds to me as if he's fractured his patella. Your only course is to take him to Casualty.'

I telephoned Edward VII and also the Wellington, where he had been given his quadruple bypass. They were both sympathetic, but both explained what I already knew - that without a consultant to admit him, they could do nothing. Both promised to try the dim chance of finding a suitable consultant on the premises - being 7 p.m. on the twenty-seventh of December, not likely. Five minutes later, when I was considering taking down blankets, pillow and hot-water bottle for the night, the Wellington rang. A young consultant had been located, on his way out the door, and if I brought my husband round at once, he would admit him.

Five more minutes and a porter and I yanked him out of the car again and wheelchaired him up to a large comfortable room. He was quickly surrounded by nurses, whisky and soda in hand, luggage from our Christmas weekend brought up, young surgeon on tap. Within minutes, and satisfied at last, he was wheeled down to X-ray.

'Nasty break,' announced the young surgeon on return. 'We'll operate in the morning.' Bill was perfectly happy. He had another whisky, ordered his dinner, and took his evening pills. I sat patiently until he was settled and rose at last to go home.

'How are you getting home, darling?'

'I'll drive the car, of course!'

'You're not driving *my* car!'

'What do you propose we do with it?'

'Leave it here.'

I explained that it was in a doctor's bay and that the Wellington forecourt was not a parking lot. He, very grudgingly, handed me the keys and explained how one inserted them into a lock, how one released a brake, how I must drive at twenty miles per hour, hugging the kerb, the two blocks to our house, how I must be sure to park exactly outside the house, as close to the kerb as possible. I thankfully went home.

The following morning I left our front gate en route to the hospital at the same time as the woman next door left hers. 'Oh,' she said, 'I am *so* sorry about Bill's car.' I looked. It was there, exactly as he had instructed me to park it. On the kerb side, shining and pristine. The driver's side, at the mercy of oncoming traffic, lacked a wing, a bumper and a serviceable door. All for a biscuit.

The operation seemed inordinately lengthy, so I thought that perhaps the four and a half hour anaesthetic explained Bill's alarming disorientation and slurred vowels, lasting through not one but two nights.

'Get me out of here – you know I hate Dublin' first alerted me to the problem. 'They've put a skull and crossbones on my door', and 'I don't like the way they've placed your bed in that corner' finally alerted the young surgeon. 'Would you object if I had a psychiatrist see him?' he asked, at the same time admitting that the operation had not even been a technical success, and that a further operation was necessary. The second one took place the following morning.

When I telephoned to inquire, the sister assured me he was alive and had been discovered trying to get out of bed. To go to the Harrods sale. The sister and I had a giggle; I made plans to visit him later in the day, and arrived on the heels of the psychiatrist.

Bill's voice was still slurred – worse, in fact – after another two and a half hour anaesthetic. My daughter, gloomy as always, prophesied, 'You've not only got a cripple on your hands, Mum, but a gaga one at that.' He managed, however, to give me a detailed account of the visit of the psychiatrist, speech barely intelligible.

'Such a funny little man came to see me. Said, "Do you mind if I ask you a silly question, old chap?" So I said, "No." So he said, "Do you know what day it is?" I said, "Wednesday." He looked a bit surprised. "Well, do you know what *date* it is?" So I said, "Yes, it's January the third." He looked even more surprised, so to help the poor chap, I said, "Would you like to know *how* I know it's Wednesday January the third?" "All right," he said. "'Cos it's the first day of Harrods' sale, and everyone in the fucking world knows that except you people in here."'

It was, of course. 'Didn't see him again.'

We did, eventually, receive his bill - £90. Diagnosis: 'Confusion'.

epilogue

Age has to intrude at some point in one's consciousness. I suppose I have never thought about mine, perhaps because death has always dramatically intervened in the lives of the majority of those close to me. They have been fortunate enough to experience one before the boredom of the other. Reminders of my own age have only come to me from other people.

Once on return to Australia I was interviewed on television. Three women friends telephoned with compliments.

'You were terrific. But - darling - the teeth!'

'You were wonderful, darling. You showed up all those women who have their faces lifted. You've got all your living in *your* face!'

'You gave me confidence. I thought, there's a really sexy lady and *she* doesn't worry about her weight!'

Teeth less than gleaming, wrinkles abundant, waistline abandoned, I soldiered on. Then last year I was on Margaret Throsby's show, choosing five pieces of favourite music. Thoroughly enjoyable. Ms Throsby was a most sympathetic and flattering host. I was feeling rather smug. Towards the end, she leant closer across the microphone towards me. 'Do you mind if I say something?' 'No, no,' I said, grinning foolishly. 'You are an amazing woman [more grins]. No, I don't want to sound inappropriate here, but you really are – you look amazing, you are amazing, and you're just about to celebrate your eightieth birthday in a couple of years' (grin fades). I protest: 'A little bit more than a couple . . .' Ms Throsby relents, 'Well, a little bit more. But you haven't had anything done to your face, have you?'

I had just burnt my hand very badly. I tottered out of the studio to my doctor son's house for him to dress it. 'Now, Mum, be very careful not to knock it.' 'Yes, of course, Seamus.' 'No, Mum, I'm serious. Listen to me – old people's skin is very *friable*.' What a perfectly beastly word! 'You know when old people knock their shins, the bruise doesn't heal', and so on. I left in some dudgeon. My telephone was ringing when I got home – my daughter in London. 'Mum, I'm very worried about your hand. You should see a specialist. Babies and old people don't heal well.'

This old person heal very well. I think of Cary Grant's famed reply to a fan's telegram: 'How old Cary Grant?' 'Old Cary Grant fine, how you?' This old person fine, too.

After I had produced *Madame Sousatzka* I was inundated with letters from musicians and their agents enclosing CVs, tapes from film scores, tapes from hopeful composers who wished they were film scores. I seldom played them. One came in an envelope from the US with no covering note. This intrigued me more, but it took some days before I popped it into my bedside cassette player one night, and settled back to listen. Over the misty span of half a lifetime came the Southern drawl of wartime fiancé, Josh. 'Robin, I've been looking for you for forty-seven and a half years . . .' He was not dead. Alive and well and married to Alice, and now part of a telephonic foursome – Josh and Alice, Bill and I, exchange birthday and Christmas greetings, and health reports. When the past becomes more enticing than the future, it is a gradual process – known as getting old. My past seems a safe, yet glowing, country of fulfilled wishes.

It's been a good life. If I had had more patience - or foresight - or ambition - it might have been a much better organised life, a more successful life. I fear recurrent threads emerge - food, sex, work, and love - but I hope that it is love which has been the purpose and the anchor. The other three have swum on the surface, allowing me to dart up through the waters, take an occasional gulp, and swim back down to the solid foundation. As for the multitudinous marriage proposals, these are a true picture of the period - far more enticing than the present invitation to sex alone. They were sometimes fuelled, I expect, by just such a motive, but, as I grow older, I'm inclined to think it may simply be that I became a very good cook.

The journey is not yet over, but I can see, looking back, that if I had stopped to think, many times along the way, I would possibly have chosen other paths; perhaps pulled over and taken my bearings. But it always seemed, on those occasions, that there was no hard shoulder on which to catch a breath.

e n d n o t e s

1 (page 1) Michel de Montaigne, *Selected Essays of Montaigne*, Essay 26 'On Educating Children'. Penguin Classics.

2 (page 11) Elinor Glyn was the author of many bad best-sellers, most notably *Three Weeks* (1907). The high priestess of romantic rubbish.

3 (page 26) Harry Roy was a famous American bandleader of the 1930s and 1940s; also famous for having married the Princess of Sarawak for whom he wrote the song 'Sarawaki'.

4 (page 28) Sir Stafford Cripps was the Chancellor of the Exchequer in Prime Minister Clement Atlee's post-war Cabinet, guiding Britain through the years of austerity - no more than five shillings was allowed for a restaurant meal.

5 (page 30) A famed, very genteel *salon de thé* of the period.

6 (page 30) Margaret Vyner was a legendary Australian beauty, actress, famed model in Paris and London, collaborator - with her husband Hugh - on a clutch of successful plays, mostly light comedies of the 1950s and 1960s. She was immortalised in the Cole Porter song 'You're the Tops', one line being 'You're Margaret Vyner'.

7 (page 30) Hugh Williams was the star and leading actor in innumerable West End plays and films and later a playwright. One of the wittiest men I have known.

8 (page 35) Prince Mario Ruspoli was a painter. He was not so well known as his playboy cousin Dado Ruspoli, but possibly more serious - and nicer.

9 (page 36) Jimmy Donohue was an immensely rich Woolworths heir and playboy - as far as I can remember, fun - but ended up later as the supposed lover (unlikely, as he was homosexual) and certainly the 'walker' of the Duchess of Windsor. The Duke was fiendishly jealous of him.

10 (page 45) The Hon. Sir Steven Runciman, C.H., was the younger son of the first Baron Runciman; an historian, academic, and world authority on Byzantine civilisation.

11 (page 46) 'But I - I am a friend of the Royal family!'

12 (page 49) Bea Lillie, Lady Robert Peel, was the Canadian-born international actress and entertainer, star of music hall, revues, many Noël Coward plays and solo performances of *An Evening with Bea Lillie*. Hilarious off stage and on.

13 (page 104) Arthur Jeffris was a millionaire expatriate American collector and art dealer who began the first of the primitive painters' galleries in London. Well known in artistic circles in Venice, he was driven to suicide in the Hôtel de France et Choiseul in Paris following the Italian homosexual witch-hunt in the 1970s. Apart from bequests to a few friends, he left the bulk of his considerable fortune (British Tobacco) to the King George V Home for Sailors, in memory of much pleasure given him in life by the sailing fraternity.

14 (page 153) Robert Ruark was an American novelist, the Wilbur Smith of his day. His most famous book was *Uhuru*. He fancied himself as *the* big White Hunter.

15 (page 160) As well as being an agent, film producer, restaurateur (most notably at the White Elephant Club, the show business hang-out, now overtaken by the Groucho Club, the Caprice, the Ivy et al.), Leslie is still opening restaurants and still producing films.

16 (page 163) John Heyman is now a hugely successful international film financier. It all happened! His prime company is World Film Services.

17 (page 173) David Brown is now one of America's most successful and distinguished producers, both as one half of the Zanuck-Brown partnership (*The Sting*, *Jaws*, *Driving Miss Daisy*) and on his own account.

18 (page 174) Mel Frank and Norman Panama were the American writer/director team responsible for some of the top hits of their day, such as the Bob Hope *Road to* films and *A Touch of Class*.

19 (page 208) The French film-maker Jacques Tati's best-known film was *Monsieur Hulot's Holiday*. M. Hulot was decidedly accident-prone - hence my appellation.

20 (page 290) John Whitney, ex-producer, then head of the Independent Broadcasting Authority.

21 (page 308) Pay or play: a commitment to pay a full fee whether or not a film is subsequently made.

22 (page 316) A line producer is the person who performs the hard technical tasks involved in shooting a film: hiring crew, overseeing budget, watching the clock - generally, if they are good, bullying them all with tact.

23 (page 318) To wrap: to finish filming - for the day, the location, or the film.

24 (page 320) Best boy: chief electrician.

index

Endpapers

1st row (left to right): greeting guests at the Thai Government dinner – with Lieutenant Thana and General Phao; two dear, dead friends on Sydney Harbour – Lee Remick and Ann Cobden – during the making of *Emma's War*; my bodyguard and train about to leave for Chiengmai; *Strictly Ballroom* – at the Trocadero – but not with 'Aub' Smart nor, alas, with Don Lucas

2nd row (left to right): brochure for Contactus; with Fleischman bust; Arthur Jeffris, Venice – in his gondola (there were only three private ones in Venice in those days); best man and bridesmaid – Bill McMahon and Shirley Arnott – and the daisies

3rd row (left to right): Madame Sousatzka – cast and crew; with (from left) Eric Ambler, Nina Lerner (the *fourth* Mrs Alan Jay Lerner), Anthony Page, Mrs Jack Hawkins – in our garden at Elm Tree Road; letter from Noël Coward

4th row (left to right): Googie Withers wearing *Country Life* apron; FBI Report in which I am listed simply as 'Australian woman': everything interesting deleted; with Margaret Williams on Biarritz terrace; later Mediterranean holidays with Bill and Maureen Dufferin at her villa in Sardinia; on location for *Oscar and Lucinda* – with (from left) Bille Brown and Ciaran Hinds

Aunts Up the Cross *Robin Dalton*

My great-aunt Juliet was knocked over and killed by a bus when she was eighty-five. The bus was travelling very slowly in the right direction and could hardly have been missed by anyone except Aunt Juliet, who must have been travelling fairly fast in the wrong direction.

So begins Robin Dalton's story of her childhood, a secure and magic place surrounded by eccentric aunts and uncles and an army of guests and hangers-on sharing a sprawling, disorderly house in the bohemian heart of Sydney's Kings Cross.

This small and perfect memoir of a solitary child loose in a house full of outrageous, theatrical, and utterly unpredictable adults has become a classic.

Glass After Glass *Barbara Blackman*

Barbara Blackman's gift for the feel and weight and place of words, the music of words, draws us into her life as daughter, lover, friend, wife, mother, grandmother. She writes of the wonderful ordinariness of 'household things, children above all, dirty, earthy and high to Heaven things'. Her portraits of family and friends, many to become among Australia's finest artists, reveal both a delightful sense of the absurd and a great capacity to love.

'Brightness and sunshine pour from every page of this book . . . when you have finished reading it, you will be a happier person than you were before you began.'
CANBERRA TIMES

More, Please *Barry Humphries*

The details of Barry Humphries' life are still amongst the best kept secrets of our time. Recent volumes devoted to his work and career shed very little, if any, light on this most private and circumspect of artistes. Hitherto, he has deliberately furnished his hardworking biographers with blatant mystifications and whimsical fictions.

In consequence the revelations and confessions contained in this book will astonish his growing international public with their novelty and in no way echo the amiable, but wildly inaccurate, narratives of his recent memorialists. Here, at last, and in his own lapidary prose, is his account of his life up to the present.

More, Please was his first utterance and they are the two words that will inevitably spring to the lips of all those who read this book.

Coming to
EUROPE
Charles Street
Sincerely yours,
Let us be your....
Entertainment Planners
Personal Service
Shopping Aids
Accommodation Fixers
Travel
UNITED STATES GOVERNMENT
Memorandum
TO W. C. Sullivan
DATE
FROM W. A. Branigan
SUBJECT CHRISTINE KEELER; JOHN PROFUMO
INTERNAL SECURITY - RUSSIA - GREAT BRITA
and that he procured girls for wealthy clients.
Mr. Wells stated he had been to a luncheon on 2/13/
Corbally, Dr. Ward, Mrs. Robin Dalton, an Australia
Madame Sousatzka
750
1